Other Books by Michael Wood

Stendhal

America in the Movies

García Márquez: One Hundred Years of Solitude

The Magician's Doubts: Nabokov and the Risks of Fiction

Children of Silence: On Contemporary Fiction

Belle de Jour

The Road to Delphi

The Road to Delphi

The Life and Afterlife of Oracles

———————

Michael Wood

For Denis
these wanderings in alien lands
with all best wishes
Michael

29 . v . 2004

FARRAR, STRAUS AND GIROUX • NEW YORK

Farrar, Straus and Giroux
19 Union Square West, New York 10003

Library of Congress Cataloging-in-Publication Data
Wood, Michael, 1936–
    The road to Delphi : the life and afterlife of oracles / Michael Wood.— 1st ed.
      p. cm.
    Includes bibliographical references and index.
    ISBN 0-374-52610-9 (alk. paper)
    1. Oracles in literature.   2. Divination in literature.   3. Oracles.
4. Divination—History.   I. Title.

PN56.O63W66 2003
809'.9337—dc21

                                                           2003048060

Designed by Barbara Grzeslo

www.fsgbooks.com

for Elena, Gaby, Chris, Patrick, and Tony
companions on the road

CONTENTS

The Road to Delphi

ON THE ROAD

This book has its beginnings in an image and some scraps of dialogue that presented themselves to my mind rather abruptly one day. There were two figures on a road. Men, women? Age, nationality? Hard to tell. The light was poor, their cloaks were wrapped around them, they were hurrying along. What language were they speaking? I don't know, but I seemed to understand them perfectly, the way we understand talk in dreams. I also knew, without being told, that they were traveling to consult an oracle.

One of the figures said, "What if it doesn't say anything?" The other said, "It won't say anything; it won't just give us simple instructions." The wind rose; clouds scuttled across the moon. The first figure said, "What if it says just what we want to hear?" The other said, "What do we want to hear?"

Much later, when the night was almost completely dark, and only shifting shadows were to be seen, a voice said, "What if it's closed when we get there?" Another voice said, "Closed? You mean like a museum or a library or a shop?" The first voice said, "Yes. Or like a ruin or an abandoned house." The second voice said, "Well, I suppose we would have to tell the story of our journey, what we saw on the way there and the way back, and why we came."

ONE: THE CLEVER ANIMALS

What are such things, that even the gods can't repair?
What are the gods, who can't repair such things?
                    Gjertrud Schnackenberg, *The Throne of Labdacus*

Words of promise

What do we make of the extended metaphorical afterlife of oracles, an institution that in the West ended ages ago, in the first centuries after the birth of Christ? How many long-dead practices are
still instantly recognizable, their name a part of everyone's ordinary
language? How many features of an ancient religion have turned
into computer software, for example? If you go into almost any
bookshop in North America, you will find whole sections devoted
to something called Oracle, and I remember the ripple of pleasure
and surprise I felt—along with a certain sense of historical mockery—when, a year or so ago, I heard the announcement at Gatwick
Airport, "Would the Oracle representative please go to the information desk." The information desk. Where else? There is also a
sign on a motorway in England that says "For the Oracle take
Junction 7."

But the West is not the only place in the world, and even in the
West there are still plenty of literal oracles, even if they are not always called that. Toward the end of this book I look at what I find
oracular in some of the practices of modern medicine, and I glance

at the role of oracles in contemporary economics. I would do more than glance if I were not so baffled by the subject, but I hope I shall have said enough to suggest certain long continuities in the patterns of oracle consultation. Fears and hopes change as history changes, and so do the relations between fears and hopes. But the balancing of fears and hopes is a human constant, and oracles are an important part of that balancing act. As you will quickly see, the words of Macbeth about the prophecies of the three weird sisters run like a half-heard refrain through this book. He says rather cryptically that the sisters "keep the word of promise to our ear/And break it to our hope." This is a way of suggesting that we hear what we hope for and get what we fear. There are kinder oracles, but hope and fear are always their business. Macbeth calls the sisters "juggling fiends," but that's when he feels he has been tricked by them. Oracles don't have to be fiends, but they do, mostly, have to juggle.

Time does play a role in this story, and oracles can die. Even if our contemporary oracles have a power that is far from being just figurative, we don't have anything like the ancient institution, with its wealth and stability, its many temples and gods and their far-reaching influence. There were oracles in ancient Greece as early as the eighth century B.C.—the high point of their activity seems to have been between the seventh century and the mid fourth. Greek peace treaties regularly included free access to the oracles as one of their first clauses. In their later life, Mediterranean oracles were chiefly consulted by individuals rather than cities or states, and their authority waned. But they were still lively enough in A.D. 391 for the Emperor Theodosius to issue an edict against them.

Twelve centuries are quite a while, and we measure the duration of our modern oracles in months and years, maybe the length of a government or an administration. But we are not entirely lacking in structures of authority, and we do string together rickety remnants of the old apparatus. It's very amateurish, compared with the old professional discipline, but it's not random. To indulge our appetite for signs and omens, as I shall suggest later, we need only superstition of the loosest and vaguest kind. For the consultation of oracles, we need a god, or an agency we are willing to treat as a god, and we need organized practices of inquiry.

So although I don't want to confuse the life and afterlife of oracles—the first five chapters of this book deal with oracles that are still fully in business, the sixth with the oracles' most famous cousins, the seventh with the death of oracles, and the rest with their ghostly ongoing presence—I do want to show how the two forms interact with each other. "The past is another country," L. P. Hartley famously wrote. "They do things differently there." They do, and the difference is crucial. But if there were no similarities we wouldn't be able to see the difference.

Dictionaries, in their sober way, get into a terrible stew about the words *oracle* and *oracular*. They all agree that the source is the Latin *oraculum*, derived from *orare*, to speak. It may seem odd to have a Latin term as our chief name for a practice that in the ancient world belonged to the Greeks rather than the Romans, but the Greeks, scholars tell us, didn't have a single word for oracle. The dictionaries further agree that an oracle can be a place or a person or a message, but beyond that they start to waver. The terms obviously suggest both infallibility and ambiguity, and have done for a long time. But how can this have happened? The *Oxford English Dictionary* lists infallibility among the words' meanings, but since it is a very sensible book, and doesn't believe in infallibility of any kind, it nervously keeps shifting to a second, mediated sense: the oracle is "supposed to," "believed to," "reputed to" be infallible; it is "regarded as" infallible. You can't blame a dictionary for what people think. And if dictionaries can get anxious, there is surely true lexical anxiety in the wonderful "reputed or affecting to be" infallible.

The implication is that either people believe you're oracular or you have to put on the show yourself, but surely there's quite a difference, and couldn't one follow from the other? Larousse doesn't believe in infallibility either but gives "*souvent ironiq*," "often ironic," for three out of its several uses. In French, it seems, the claim to infallibility and a knowing doubt about that claim usually do not represent two meanings of the word, just its single, rather complicated meaning. Webster's gives us a clear but not unproblematic run: "a divine revelation"; "a typically ambiguous or enigmatic revelation or utterance believed to issue from a divinity"; "an answer delivered with an aspect of oracular certainty." The first meaning suggests genuine truth, the last something completely bogus. Webster's also has its moment of nervousness, speaking of an oracle (the person) as "one who is considered or professes to be infallible." This is precisely the same as the *OED*'s "reputed or affecting to be": plenty of room for maneuver.

Of course the word *oracle* and its relatives can be used in an unequivocal way, emphasizing only one of their polar meanings. "I do believe it, against an oracle," a character says in *The Tempest*. That oracle is an epitome of certainty and nothing else. And when a character in *Ulysses* is said to "oracle" out of the shadows, the suggestion is of pompous emptiness, not any kind of wisdom or knowledge. But most of the time, the opposing meanings of the words tend to chase and haunt each other. Assertions of certainty are flecked with hints of uncertainty; acknowledgments of uncertainty invoke the certainty we wish we had. The very notion of an oracle is itself like an oracle: it sounds smarter than we are, but it may tell us only what we want to know—or what we knew all the time but refused to believe.

"All things are full of gods," the Greek philosopher Thales said. At first hearing, it seems as if the sentence must mean pretty much the same as "God is everywhere." But a little reflection shows that it

means almost entirely the opposite, and the reversal is deeply instructive. Even if we interpret the word *God* in the broadest and
most ecumenical way, "God is everywhere" means that a single intelligence or agency is behind all observable creatures and phenomena, that although God may disperse himself into every corner of
the universe, he is always everywhere himself. The secret truth of
what looks like an immense diversity is that it is a unity after all,
held together by the undivided mind of God. "All things are full of
gods" means there is nowhere a god can't be, no feature or aspect of
nature that can't reveal a god to us; but it doesn't tell us which gods
or goddesses will reveal themselves when, or how many gods and
goddesses there are. The secret truth of this second, equally immense diversity is that it is immensely diverse, and doubly popu-
lated: by the many creatures and phenomena that seem to be there,
and by the gods who are there too all the time, but not always visible.

David Hume thought the abstract idea of God was civilized,
while the concrete idea of gods was primitive. Friedrich Nietzsche
thought the reverse. But the point of Thales' phrase is not to argue
for polytheism, or to get us to argue against it. The point is to ask
us to think of the world as haunted by the divine, and to see how
the divinity can talk to us through the world. If the divinity is the
single Jewish or Christian or Islamic God, he can and will talk to us
through the world, but he also talks in other ways: through direct
revelation, for example. The Greek gods revealed themselves directly too, but so selectively and so anarchically that their appearances often looked like tricks. To remember that they are in all
things is a form of piety, because the thought protects the gods
against their own mischief. We don't have to see them to know they
are there. This idea is as abstract as Hume could wish.

And what if we don't believe in God or the gods? Well, to know
in any detail what we don't believe in would be a form of belief.

Let's say we believe the world is full of signs, and the signs form a system. We could refuse to believe even this, of course, but then the world would be a very dull place, and we would, most of us, be lying about our actual experience of it. Beyond this, believers in the gods know who left the signs for us to see, and they have elaborate, institutionalized methods of reading the signs. Unbelievers don't know where the signs came from, and are unpersuaded by any of the claims of authorship on offer. But they can't stop reading the signs, and in their inspired or frightened moments even they may believe that they are seeing more than isolated marks or clues, that they are picking up pieces of a broken but extensive language.

Schools of doubt

Skepticism about oracles is very ancient. It is worth a quick glance at its history, old and new, because the language of skepticism itself—its grammar, as Wittgenstein would say—already contains shreds and announcements of other views, and helps to give a picture of the complexity of the subject.

This skepticism wears different faces over time, of course. But there is a remarkable consistency over time, too. The voice of Thucydides in the fifth century B.C. is not so different from the voice of Montaigne in the sixteenth century A.D. or of Milton in the seventeenth, and all three resemble any number of twentieth-century voices. Thucydides characteristically bundles oracles together with other forms of superstition, the kind of thing people reach for when they are in trouble, but not otherwise. "Everywhere predictions were being recited and oracles being chanted by such persons as collect them," by "reciters of oracles and soothsayers, and all other omenmongers of the time." The Athenians, in an imagined or reconstructed dialogue, say they do not wish to be "like the vulgar, who . . . when visible hopes fail them in extremity, turn to the invisible, to prophecies and oracles, and other such inventions that delude men with hopes to their destruction." When Thucydides finally speaks of "faith in oracles being for once justified by the event," the weight of the sentence clearly falls on all the other, nonjustifying instances, and this particular case (the oracle concerns the length of the Peloponnesian War) looks more like luck than destiny, an interesting mathematical coincidence rather than a confirmation of a prophecy.

At other points Thucydides neutrally reports the consultation of oracles as a cultural fact, one of the things that cities and people do: "The same winter the Athenians purified Delos in compliance, it appears, with a certain oracle." The Epidamnians ask the Delphic god's advice about whether they should hand over their city to Corinth, and they take the advice they get. The Spartans found a colony "after first consulting the god at Delphi"; earlier, they inquire of the same god whether they should go to war. These are not riddling questions and they don't provoke riddling responses. What Thucydides is describing here—as a number of other authors also do—is the accomplishment of what we might call a political rite, although this would be a form of politics from which religion could not be divorced. The *Oxford Companion to Classical Civilization* tells us that "a decision, to go to war for instance or dispatch a colony, had normally been made by the state before approaching the oracle. What was sought was a divine sanction."

The phrase Thucydides uses on several occasions, "inquired of the god," seems amazingly silent on the form the inquiry takes, and on the complicated mediations known to be in play, the train of question and answer that goes (at Delphi) from inquirer to priest to pythia—the woman inspired by Apollo—to god, and then from god to pythia to priest to inquirer. Plenty of room for error and distortion here, even without a jot of ambiguity in the god's response. Is Thucydides' silence an indication of a lack of interest, or just the effect of an assumption that everyone knows the procedures already? Or is such a silence perhaps a more general characteristic of oracle-stories at the moment of inquiry, a quasi suppression of the known indirection of the process? We are seeking certainty—why would we insist on the uncertainty of the approach and the message? In any event, when inquiries are made of oracles, even in quite different cultures, they are indeed often very bluntly described. "I acted at once," Oedipus says in response to the priest's plea for his help. "I sent Creon, my wife's own brother, to Delphi." Robert Alter tells us that in ancient Israel "to inquire of God" or "to inquire of the Lord" were idioms for consulting an oracle, and in 2 Samuel the phrase "inquired of an oracle of God" makes a complicated process sound simple, just a matter of asking a question and getting an answer. In Shakespeare's *Winter's Tale* Leontes at first refuses to believe the oracle that clears his wife's name, but he doesn't think there is anything oblique or uncertain about asking for the oracle's advice and getting it. "I have dispatch'd in post," Leontes says, "To sacred Delphos, to Apollo's temple/Cleomenes and Dion, whom you know/Of stuff'd sufficiency . . ." Shakespeare's Apollo dispenses with priest, pythia, and all apparatus, speaking directly to the messengers with an "ear-deafening voice," although it's possible they hear it only as thunder, since the message is then written down for them and sealed by the priest, "Apollo's great divine."

I shall return to these denied and half-denied complications, but for the moment I want only to underline the fact that in the fifth century B.C., as in the twentieth century A.D., one can report on the widespread practice of consulting oracles without believing

they mean anything or being drawn to a consultation oneself.
Montaigne cites Cicero on the decline of oracles and mutters
against "the obscure, ambiguous and fantastic speech of prophetic
jargon," deliberately left vague so that posterity can make of it
what it will. This is pretty much what Milton means by "oracling,"
when in *Paradise Regained* he has Christ put Satan in his non-
prophetic place:

> But what have been thy answers, what but dark,
> Ambiguous, and with double sense deluding,
> Which they who asked have seldom understood . . .
> No more shalt thou by oracling abuse
> The Gentiles; henceforth oracles are ceased,
> And thou no more with pomp and sacrifice
> Shalt be inquired at Delphos or elsewhere,
> At least in vain, for they shall find thee mute.

In a later chapter I explore the theological argument involved here,
and the elaborate mythology behind it, the notion that all oracles
ceased with the birth of Christ. But the central emphasis at this
point remains on the elements of obscurity and deceit. The religious thought doesn't seem at all remote from the secular suggestion of the following dialogue, which appears in Leonardo
Sciascia's novel *One Way or Another*. The person being discussed is the
Italian equivalent of a district attorney.

> "When I ask him something he replies by playing the oracle."
> "All the same, these legal people; oracles, yes, oracles. But be-
> lieve me: they don't play the oracle because they know something
> and don't want to say anything; they're just doing what has al-
> ways been done in the oracle trade."

Primo Levi uses the same image in *The Periodic Table* when he distinguishes between being a practicing scientist and being a consultant: "All you have to do is take off your smock, put on your tie, listen in attentive silence to the problem, and then you'll feel like the Delphic oracle." And when the literary critics W. K. Wimsatt and Monroe Beardsley, in 1946, wish to dismiss what they call the intentional fallacy—the notion that an author's intentions are in any way relevant to the understanding or assessment of a work of literature—they close their case with a crisp metaphor that seems both very ancient and entirely up to date: "Critical inquiries are not settled by consulting the oracle."

It's worth pausing over what is suggested here, not because we don't know what Wimsatt and Beardsley (or Sciascia or Levi or Milton or Montaigne or Thucydides) mean, but because we do know, and may therefore assent too rapidly to the move that is being made. The oracle—the suggestion goes—is supposed to possess certain and privileged knowledge; but this is sheer superstition either because the oracle knows only what ordinary mortals know or because what the oracle claims to know—the future, for instance—just cannot be known. The idea that a god is really speaking through the oracle is not a reflection of a religious faith, but merely the mark of a desperate need for more than human certainty—or in Milton's case, the sign of a failure to grasp the nature of the true God. The ambiguous speech of the oracle, this argument implies, does not deliver a dark or as yet unrevealed truth; it conceals, often very ably, the fact that nothing is being revealed. In Wimsatt and Beardsley's image there is, I think, the further implication that there is something rather base about consulting an authority on an issue you ought to be able to work out for yourself. It would be base to consult even a real authority; what could possibly be said for consulting a bogus one?

This is eminently reasonable, and a good antidote to much

hocus-pocus. But confident doubt is always a little shortsighted, and liable to collapse into negative dogma. All things are full of gods, even if they are often figurative, and those gods talk all the time.

Cold star

What follows is a set of stories and commentaries, with instances from literature, history, theater, and film, but I should also like to believe that this book has something of an anthropological feel about it. In an autobiographical work Roland Barthes suggests that the ethnographic text has "all the powers of the book we love." He writes of his pleasure in the historian Jules Michelet's ethnological project, the "desire and the art of questioning the supposedly most natural objects historically, that is, relatively." Barthes's examples of such objects are faces, food, clothes, complexion. This would make his own book *Mythologies*, as he says, an anthropology of everyday life in France.

What are the powers of the loved book? "It is an encyclopedia, registering and classifying all realities, even the most futile, the most physical" ("*même la plus futile, la plus sensuelle*"). "Of all scholarly disciplines," Barthes says, speaking of himself in the third person, "ethnology seems to him the closest to the work of fiction." I'm not sure about the passion for classification, but Barthes's examples are precisely what I think of as (figurative) anthropology, and the proximity to fiction is important. He is saying, I take it, that bits and pieces of human behavior—gestures, idioms, stories—are endlessly fascinating, and for their own sake. Once you give them another sake, you're lost, or they're lost. This is not real ethnography because it's not systematic, and scarcely a form of study. But it is a form of curiosity, and a curiosity that is not only literary. It embraces the diffuse particulars not so much of the world as of human behavior, whether fictional or factual.

To think anthropologically is to think about social practices, even if you're not an anthropologist, and especially, in recent years, if you are a classical scholar. There are plenty of instances available here, but "Ritual is a mirror of social action," a sentence we find in Catherine Morgan's book *Athletes & Oracles*, is a good one, and so are several phrases in Mary Beard's letter quoted in Keith Hopkins's *A World Full of Gods*. "Religious ceremony stands for and negotiates the political and social order." "These myths . . . make sense of and yet mystify the relations between humans and gods"—where the relations in question are religious relations, obviously, but also reflections of and variants on social relations. But to think anthropologically in the way Barthes is suggesting—that is, to enjoy the perspective but not to have the same interest in its usefulness or explanatory force—is to be interested in the social as a form of human behavior rather than the other way around, and it is to work in an area that keeps edging off into fiction, even and especially if it seems completely, incontrovertibly historical. The idea of fiction keeps in play the idea of speculation, of the world of possibilities, of options, other readings, other behaviors. The idea of anthropology keeps in play the social life of human beings, reminds us how social we are, how much we live in context, live with others, gather our meanings from them and for them. Contemporary anthropology, the scholar George Marcus says, offers us not "the marginal, the exotic, the extreme case" but "cultural accounts of spaces that have not had them."

The space I am interested in has had more historical accounts than cultural ones, and is a rather cloudy space anyway. It is a space of crisscrossing beliefs: that we can and cannot have access to more than daily, approximate levels of certainty. This is a huge field of human habit and longing, and just looking at it raises all kinds of issues of logic and time and chance. An oracle answers our question, and we interpret the answer. That is, we match the answer to events or places in the world, and we feel, when the match is good, that the oracle knew what was going to happen, or what was the right thing to do. Many would say that the oracle, if it knew anything, knew only the odds, although a game theorist might show us that those odds are surprising, not the odds our common sense said we had. But most people consulting oracles want something better than odds of any kind. They want the certainty we can have in reality only when the story is over, and one thing is clear in this complicated territory. By the time the desired knowledge becomes a story, it can't be separated from the story, it can't be anything other than the story, and we find ourselves living in double time: in immediate, action-driven time, the time of our options, and in the belated time of narrative, the time when the game is over. While the story is running, we long for the magical certainty of the end. Once it's over we try to get back into it to alter the coordinates.

"And the clever animals had to die." These are the last words of a little fable by Nietzsche that sounds like an early warning of a *Star Wars* movie:

> In a remote corner of the universe flickering with countless solar systems, there was once a star where clever animals invented knowledge. It was the proudest and most deceitful moment in world history; but it was only a moment. After Nature had taken a few breaths, the star froze, and the clever animals had to die.

Why did the animals have to die? We don't know. We know only that their whole existence was just a brief episode in a long history. And we know—although the word itself seems half ruined by the fable—that the animals invented knowledge. These animals are not identified by their ability to stand upright, think, laugh, or remember, to list a few of the more familiar definitions of the human. They are not identified by their love of knowledge, or their success in its pursuit. Their great achievement, their mark in history, is to have dreamed up the very idea of knowledge. Their further achievement, although Nietzsche doesn't say this immediately, is their capacity to forget what they have done, to conceal, even from themselves, the fictional status of what they call knowledge.

Many scholars and scientists would say the fable is either mischievous or pointless, the wrong news or no news. Of course we didn't invent knowledge. Knowledge concerns, precisely, the uninvented world, the world that can get along without us. This is what distinguishes knowledge from belief, or fantasy. Many others, perhaps more interestingly, would say it doesn't matter whether we invented knowledge—that is, it doesn't matter whether the question can be settled or not—because the knowledge we have does the job it is supposed to do. It explains the world to us, it is (mostly) verifiable, and when better knowledge comes along, we are able to recognize it and scrap the old model or the disproved facts. Knowledge is real enough for us, even if in God's (or Nietzsche's) mind it is only a fiction.

But there is a realm of knowledge, even of knowledge in this sensible, practical sense, where the possibility of invention comes back to haunt us. What Nietzsche says literally is that the clever animals invented knowing, *das Erkennen*. They decided, to paraphrase and interpret a little, that knowing things, as distinct, for instance, from loving them or using them or giving them up, was going to be their preferred mode of life. Animals like this are bound to get into trouble. They can't love life more than the meaning of life, as Dostoyevsky's Alyosha Karamazov recommends. They are going to want to know everything that can be known. And much of what can't be known too, much of what probably isn't knowledge at all. But since knowing is what they do, knowledge is what they look for, and they are likely to give the name of knowledge to anything they find. The result is that whatever the truth of Nietzsche's larger claim about our cooling star, invented knowledge abounds on it. Alongside knowledge that looks like (and probably is) the real thing, we have mountains of sorry mimicry. As Roberto Calasso points out in his brilliant discussion of this fable in *Literature and the Gods*, "If one doesn't discover knowledge, but invents it, the implication is that it involves a powerful element of simulation." But there is yet another realm, a place between these rival, relative certainties. In this place we don't know whether what is offered to us as knowledge is invented or not. That is, we don't know whether it is invented, and don't know whether *knowledge* is the right word for it. This is the realm this book seeks to explore.

TWO: WHAT GOD, WHICH GOD, WHERE?

A philosophy which does not include and cannot explain
the possibility of prophecy by means of coffee grounds
cannot be a true philosophy.

Walter Benjamin, *Letters*

The gods talk all the time

The gods talk all the time, to each other and to humans. They provide omens and portents; they send dreams; they speak through
sibyls and oracles. What distinguishes oracles from the other
modes of conversation is the direction of the traffic. The gods
don't instigate this form of talk, they respond. I'm not saying that
the gods can't be questioned in other ways, by means quite different
from what we may usually think of as oracles. Dreams can be
provoked; entrails can be consulted; books can be opened at random; dice can be cast. But I am saying we may want to rethink our
terms a little. What if we decide that whenever we believe the gods
allow themselves to be questioned, by whatever means, we are talking about oracles? That this is a working definition of what an oracle is?

An oracle, I am suggesting, allows a dialogue with a god, or
with the unknown, as distinct from a god's invasion of our lives or
the more general practice of divination, the reading of all the signs
and omens freely scattered in the world. An oracle gives signs, but

only because we ask it to, and the rare instances in which an oracle is said to have spoken without a prior inquiry look like fables that misunderstand the genre.

An oracle may foretell our future, and frequently will. But it may tell us other things as well or instead. Everything will depend on our question, and on the oracle's mood when it is asked. When Croesus, king of Lydia, wanted to test a whole set of oracles before putting a couple of crucial questions to them, he challenged their knowledge not of the future but of the physically removed present. He wanted the god's representatives—he sent messengers to the oracles at Delphi, Abae, and Dodona and the oracles of Amphiarius, Trophonius, Branchidae, and Ammon—to identify what he was doing in Sardis, his capital city, exactly one hundred days after his messengers had set out, and his goal was to discover, as Herodotus puts it, "what it was the oracles knew." As it happened, he was cooking a lamb and a tortoise in a bronze pot, no doubt his idea of an improbable thing for a curious king to be doing, but the pythia, the woman who was the voice of the god Apollo at Delphi, had no difficulty in getting this right. Neither did the oracle of Amphiarius, but we hear no more of this success. However, before the pythia proved the god's telepathic powers, she made an announcement that I think we must take as a figure for knowledge in general: for an all-encompassing knowledge of the details of the world, among which future events play a significant, even a dominant, but not an exclusive role. She said,

> I count the number of the grains of sand on the beach and
>   measure the sea;
> I understand the speech of the dumb and hear the voiceless.

We find the same figures of speech in Pindar's Ninth Pythian Ode, where the all-knowing Apollo at first pretends not to know

the history of a girl he admires. The centaur Chiron realizes the
god must be joking and asks him what has "stirred him to this
irony." After all, the centaur continues,

> You know the appointed end
> of each thing and the ways they are brought to pass;
> and the number of the spring leaves earth blossoms, the number
> of the sands in the sea and the rivers,
> shaken by the waves and the streaming winds; and things to be
> and whence they shall come to pass.

The god knows what things are for and how they come about;
what will happen and how; he can count whatever seems countless.
He knows the past and the present and the future, and holds in his
mind, unmuddled, the sheer profusion of the world. He knows,
and through his oracle will tell us, whatever we want to know—or
more precisely, whatever we can't know by ordinary, daily ways of
knowing. If we are skeptical, we say that this is just what the god is:
the sum of our missing knowledge. His oracles are precise mirrors
of our needs, marking all the places where our available knowledge
doesn't seem to be enough. Perhaps they are nothing more than
that; but that would be a lot.

But what do we need? What have we asked of oracles? Here is a
minuscule sample of questions asked over time:

> Will I have children?
> Will my mute son ever speak?
> Should I invade the territory of my enemy?
> Should we found a colony?
> What are the correct rites to accompany the building of a temple?
> Which god should I worship?
> Will my mortgage come through?

What prayers should we offer for the relief of famine?

How long will I reign?

Whom should I fear?

Should the government accept the loan on the terms proposed by
the IMF?

How shall we rid the city of the plague?

Who are my parents?

Is my wife unfaithful?

Is anyone wiser than Socrates?

Should I marry?

Shall I devote the rest of my life to the elucidation of the work of
the spirits?

Should we offer sanctuary to this man or give him up to his enemies?

Was the previous oracle telling the truth?

These instances, some real, some fictional, but all identifiable, come
from ancient Greece, medieval Scotland, Renaissance France, and
twentieth-century England, Ireland, Africa, and Brazil, but my
guess is that we could document very similar questions almost anywhere. It looks as if what we ask of oracles, at some stage or another, in some place or another, is nothing less than everything. But
although there are thousands of questions, certain patterns run
through the relation of inquiry to response, and those patterns can
be mapped and, with a little oracular help, understood.

The power of oracles, in their very different cultures, appears to
rest on three alternative pictures of what is happening. In the first
and most frequent, the god, a personal or personified agency,
speaks through whatever medium he chooses: priestess or sibyl,
dream, chance encounter, disposition of dice or lots. In the second
the universe itself, less personally, allows the shape or propitious-
ness of the moment to reveal itself, say by the way the stalks or

coins of the *I Ching* group themselves or fall. And in the third, chance itself becomes a kind of authority, since the paramount virtue of this kind of oracle is that it is removed from the tilts and biases of human desire. The ancient Greek oracle by lots at Dodona would be an example. Questions were written on lead slips and placed in an urn. The priestess took a question out of the urn at random, and then, equally at random, took a lead slip with an answer out of another urn. No room for maneuver or manipulation here, although of course there would still be plenty of room for interpretation.

In fact, I doubt whether any religious culture could fully acknowledge this third picture in its own right. The distinction between just being not-human and being divine smacks too much of skepticism, and believers would assume that what looked like chance was the working of the god or an expression of the secret harmonies of the universe. But the removal of choice from the realm of the human, the guaranteed impartiality of chance, are not trivial matters. They can be helpful and they can be very dangerous, and the mechanics of this third picture must have been in operation at many oracles, whatever the local theory of the practice.

Tossing a coin is the simplest form of oracle of this kind. Of course, usually it's not an oracle at all, just an evasion or a game, and we frequently ignore the results when we don't like them. But imagine this situation: You really don't wish to decide an issue yourself, or just can't decide, for all sorts of reasons. You don't wish to hand the matter over to a human authority, a judge or a parent or a friend, and you have no grounds for believing that your god will answer your prayers on this matter. You toss a coin and decide to abide rigorously by the result. This might not be smart but it wouldn't be irresponsible. And if your chief worry is the inevitable slant and self-interest of human perception, you could hardly do better.

Inquiring of the god

But how do oracles actually work? "They inquired of the god," as I have said, is the phrase we hear in many languages and many cultures, and sometimes we don't hear much more. But there is more. The consultation of oracles can be an intricate and detailed affair, and it has been reconstructed many times over.

Sometimes oracles are ancient books of wisdom, like the *I Ching*, associated with a particular method of divination, an elaborate system for getting forty-nine yarrow stalks or three coins to yield the hexagram of the moment. Many people all over the world still consult this oracle, and I cherish the story of my friend whose psychoanalyst, at a moment of significant decision, suggested they jointly turn to the *I Ching*. The book didn't tell them what to do, but the results were illuminating for them both. And there is of course a memorable literary representation of the book and the method in Philip K. Dick's novel *The Man in the High Castle*, where several characters read the swerves of their lives in the hexagrams:

A withered poplar puts forth flowers.
An older woman takes a husband.
No praise. No blame.

The small departs.
The great approaches.
Good fortune. Success.

If you walk in the middle
And report to the prince,
He will follow.

The Chaldean oracles were well known in classical antiquity
and in the first centuries of Christianity but have not come down
to us, except in fragments and quotations, in any collection earlier
than one made in Byzantium around A.D. 1360. It was called *Magical
Oracles of the Disciples of Zoroaster*. According to the French scholar
Edouard des Places, the existing oracles don't take the form of dialogues between the god and the faithful, "but some of them preserve some traces." Effectively, the work as we have it is a volume of
wise sayings, often all the wiser for being a little opaque. "All
things are born of a single fire"; "For the intellect does not subsist
independently of the intelligible, and the intelligible does not subsist apart from the intellect"; "On the back of the goddess an immense nature is lifted"; "And do not add to destiny"; "Do not
change the barbarous names"; "Seek paradise"; "The truth is in the
depths." Maynard Solomon's wonderful book on Mozart gives us
an account of a playful parody of this form of wisdom. Mozart
appeared at a carnival dressed as an "Oriental philosopher" and
handed out copies of a broadsheet containing eight riddles and
fourteen proverbs, entitled "Excerpts from the Fragments of
Zoroaster." In an elegant Freudian reading, Solomon suggests that
"Mozart, as the carnivalesque son, takes the place of the father by
donning the robes of a powerful, exotic lawgiver . . . He has seized
the trappings of divinity and wisdom, has fashioned himself as an
oracle, as one who can penetrate ultimate mysteries. He has transformed himself from the supplicant Oedipus into the all-knowing
Sphinx."

E. Evans-Pritchard, in a classic work of anthropology, describes
in detail the sophisticated use of an apparently primitive oracle by
the Azande in Africa. This is the so-called poison oracle. Poison is
given to a chicken, and a question is then posed to the poison.
"The questioner commences to address the poison inside the fowl"
and "continues to address the poison inside the fowl." There is no

point in putting the question "before the poison has had time to consider the matter placed before it or even to hear a full statement of the problem." Since the poison is not always fatal, the chicken either lives or dies, and provides an answer this way. The formal framing of the question is quite elaborate, and the procedure is sometimes repeated if the answer seems dubious. "The killing of a fowl does not give in itself a positive or negative answer," Evans-Pritchard says. "One must know how to observe not only whether the fowl lives or dies, but also the exact manner in which the poison affects it . . ." He also tells us that it is "seldom that the oracle is addressed without analogies and circumlocutions," a feature of the consultation that would allow us to relate this oracle to many others. Evans-Pritchard speaks of the "overwhelming faith" of the Azande. "The oracle is not to them a matter of chance, like the spinning of a coin, by which they are agreed to abide." But just as the poison is personified, spoken to as an individual agent and pictured as thinking, so chance itself might be the instrument of an oracle—no longer mere chance, we might say, or no longer our own rather impoverished notion of chance.

In modern Tibet there are still priestly oracles that closely resemble those of ancient Delphi, but in classical Greece alone the number of oracles and the range of oracular practices are extraordinary. At Dodona, now Tcharacovitsa, near Jannina, in Epirus, there was a sacred oak, as well as the already mentioned oracle by lots. The god in residence was Zeus, and there is mention of a consultation in the *Iliad*, although the oracle in that case appears to have worked by so-called incubation. In this method the consultant performs certain rites and then sleeps in the temple precincts. The answer to his question appears in a dream. In some cases priests dream the answer on the consultant's behalf.

It was the oracle at Dodona that told Odysseus, in a lost play by Sophocles, that the hero would be killed by his son. When

Odysseus dies at the hand of a stranger, and not Telemachus, the oracle appears to have been proved wrong, and the surviving fragments of the play include various bits of triumphant and irreligious abuse. "Now no one from Dodona nor from the clefts of Delphi would persuade me," a character says, and the god at Dodona is said to have been made "to lose his praises." But the appearance of error is itself an error, since the stranger turns out to be one Telegonus, a son Odysseus didn't know he had by Circe.

We don't know how the god made this prophecy to Odysseus, but it probably wasn't through a dream, since more frequently mentioned modes of communication for the god at Dodona are the rustling of the leaves of the great oak—this is the most famous method and the most widely attested in literature—and the moaning of the doves who lived in the tree, also well represented in literature, although Herodotus took the speech of the birds to be a metaphor for the language of the priestesses. "The story which the people of Dodona tell about the doves came, I should say, from the fact that the women were foreigners, whose language sounded to them like the twittering of birds." In their commentary on Herodotus, How and Wells tell us that " 'to speak like a bird' was a Greek expression for talking unintelligibly," and when the Trojan Cassandra, in Aeschylus' play *Agamemnon*, is accused of twittering "like a swallow," the reference is to the speech of barbarians as Greeks heard it. The doves, in this reading, would be a literalization of a figure of speech, and yet another, rather intricate instance of the proverbial obscurity of oracles: the bird sounds would be hard to interpret if there were any, but as it happens there is only a foreign language. The very notion of the birds is a misinterpretation, a metaphor gone awry. We do perhaps hear them again when the birds speak Greek in Virginia Woolf's *Mrs. Dalloway*.

It is also possible that the oak tree actually spoke, ambiguously or not—that is, used words rather than allowed its leaves or the birds to do the talking. Part of the tree was used to construct the *Argo*, the boat of Jason and the Argonauts, and that boat could certainly speak Greek, since at one point it vocally refuses to carry Jason and Medea. Stories are also told about a murmuring fountain at Dodona, and of bronze vessels that gave messages in some mysterious way. At some point the priests mentioned in Homer gave way to priestesses, who prophesied in ecstasy on the model of (or in anticipation of) the pythias at Delphi.

Meanwhile, at Delphi, even in ancient times a notorious center of ambiguous speech, the procedures were relatively undisputed. Complicated, and swathed in mystery, but at least nameable as procedures. Although even here, a good deal of detail is lacking because as the classical scholar H. W. Parke says, "The practice of consulting the oracle was so completely established in classical Greece that no author thought it necessary to give a plain straightforward account of what happened." At Delphi the god to be consulted was Apollo rather than Zeus, but he was there only nine months of the year. In the winter he traveled. Dionysus remained, but the oracle was closed. The assumption is that major consultations took place once a month, so that there would be nine in any given year. At other times, there would be consultation by lots, presumably conducted in a manner similar to the consultations at Dodona and elsewhere. *Cleromancy* is the technical term for this form of inquiry.

But Delphi's fame rested on the god-inspired women who prophesied on major occasions. The inquirer—individual or city or state—posed his question to the priests at Delphi, who, after appropriate rituals and sacrifices, communicated it to the pythia, the woman devoted to the service of the god. The term *pythia* first appears in Herodotus. Armed with the question, the pythia entered an inner sanctum, sat on a tripod, went into a trance, and was visited by the god, who answered the question. Although Priam's daughter Cassandra is not a pythia—indeed is a sort of anti-pythia, for reasons we shall see—her portrayal by Aeschylus in his *Agamemnon* is generally taken to be modeled on the performance of the ecstasies of the pythia at Delphi. We don't know how intelligibly the pythia communicated the god's answer, or how much she understood of it herself, and therefore don't know how large the role of the priests was in making sense of the god's message. As the great French scholar Bouché-Leclercq wryly says, "The job of secretary to the pythias wasn't the easiest of jobs." Unless of course the priests made it easy on themselves and reported what they themselves thought, or what they imagined the inquirer wanted to hear. There was plenty of suspicion of bribery of priests, and of the pythias, even in ancient times.

In all the well-known cases the priests—or the pythia herself—reported orally to the inquirer in Greek hexameters. In exceptional cases, where the inquirer couldn't be present himself, or a king or a city-state had sent envoys, the answer was written down and given to the inquirer's representative in a sealed packet. One of the most detailed accounts of a consultation at Delphi, but also one that is late and lurid and literary, is Lucan's. Appius, anxious about the coming civil war, consults the pythia, at that time a woman called Phemonoe. She struggles against her approaching possession by the god, and says that "all time is gathered up together," that the centuries crowd her breast and torture it. She also says, as a predecessor of hers did to the messengers of Croesus, king of Lydia, that she knows the number of the sands on the seashore. But now she is speaking as the god, not as herself, and she gives Appius his apparently consoling prophecy. He will "escape the awful threats of war," and "stay at peace" in Euboea. As indeed he does. He dies there before the civil war has really got started.

In *The Double Tongue*, William Golding's last, all-but-completed

novel—Golding died in 1993; the book was published in 1995—the
pythia at Delphi tells her story, from the time she was a young girl
with certain magical-seeming powers through the careers and
deaths of her predecessors to her own old age. The narrative is set
in the early years of the Christian Era, and the oracle has known
better days. The situation is intensely political, and the pythia,
whose name is Arieka, is guided by a skeptical Greek priest called
Ion who seeks, finally in vain, to use the oracle to maintain some
Athenian power in the face of rising Roman might. He doesn't believe in the voice of the god, and indeed doesn't believe in the god
at all, but he does believe in the usefulness of the idea of such a
voice. And yet Arieka is not simply his puppet, and if her trances
are not revelations, neither are they simple fakery. Against Ion's
cleverness and doubts and in the face of her own uncertainties she
asserts a belief in the god who speaks through her. "I believed, no,
I felt I knew there was something connected with the hidden center
of existence that lay there and sometimes spoke."

Only sometimes, even so. Here is how Arieka describes the ambiguous gifts of unattractive girls "whom a god has blighted"—
where the blight seems to be whatever makes them unmarriageable.

> They acquire, these unfortunates, strange abilities. Or perhaps
> abilities is the wrong word. The situation is not really describ-
> able, except that the girl becomes very clever in a useless way . . .
> It is a furtive power. They wish: and if they wish in the right
> way—wrong way?—sometimes, if the balance is ever so slightly
> on their side, then—just more often than not but only just—
> they get what they want or somebody does. The world is riddled
> with coincidences and the girl sees this. She uses this when it is
> available. Perhaps to somebody else who gets what he wants. Or,
> I mean, gets what he didn't want. You can never prove this . . . It

is no oracle, does not win battles. It cannot cure the plague but
only some headaches, cannot cure heartache but can supply the
necessary tears for it.

It is no oracle, but gifts of this kind are useful to a pythia, and to
the priest who translates her words. "Between us we were very
clever," she says of herself and Ion.

> And sometimes we were lucky. If you add the occasional luck to
> the information service which Ion's pigeon post shared with all
> the other oracles . . . we were occasionally very lucky indeed. But
> never as lucky as Croesus with his lamb and tortoise in a bronze
> pot!

Croesus, whose testing of the oracle we have already seen, and who
heaped treasures upon the temple at Delphi, belonged to the
golden days of the oracle some six centuries earlier. Arieka's mention of him is both a kind of joke and a fit of nostalgia. It wasn't
Croesus who was lucky, it was the oracle, and *luck* is hardly the word
for an age of faith.

The attraction of Golding's haunting and witty imagining of
this ancient institution is that it balances the skepticism that is as
old as the oracle itself with gripping accounts of the possession of
the pythia by the god. "The god. What god, which god, where?"
she cries. The possession is real, in other words, but even Arieka
can't name the possessor except in terms her culture gives her. It has
to be Apollo—who else could it be? What else could it be? The
centuries between Arieka and us have produced many answers, but
Golding does not go further than the woman's trance and the
woman's cries. "There is a void when the gods have been there,
then turned their backs and gone," Arieka says. What if the gods

were never there? Golding invites us to make of these questions what we can.

Death in a plane

The future, as I have suggested, is far from being the only concern of oracles. But it is the subject of some of the trickiest oracle answers we know, and it is an area where the finest minds may become muddled. At least some of this muddle can be cleared up with a little patience, and a willingness to make distinctions, and to listen to what our own use of language has to tell us.

Can we know the future? Mostly not, it seems. And often it takes us entirely by surprise. But we do regularly make two quite contradictory assumptions about it: that it is unknowable, and that once it's here we saw it coming. Who knows what tomorrow will bring, we say, and so do people in many quite different cultures around the world; and also, I knew it, I knew it all along. Both idioms are familiar, intelligible, current in all kinds of languages, and often persuasive.

We do know certain things about the future, of course. We know that night will fall, that the seasons will revolve, that fire will burn us if we give it a chance, that the laws of gravity are not likely to be suspended any time soon. But this is not what we mean when we ask about knowing the future. We don't mean the future in general, the simple prolongation of the rules and regularities of the past. We mean the future in detail, the one we would love to know about, whether we can or not; the one where the precise results are in, the races over, the jobs either got or missed.

Can we predict the future? This looks like the same question but turns out to be rather different. Of course we can predict the future, we do it all the time, but can we predict it correctly? Yes, on occasion. We also predict it incorrectly pretty often, but getting it right once or twice is all we need to make the question matter.

Here's a prediction. I'm a meteorologist, one who often gets things right. I consult every chart and instrument I have, and I say it will rain tomorrow afternoon all along the eastern seaboard of the United States. Tomorrow comes, the morning is fine. In the afternoon it rains all along the eastern seaboard of the United States. Or: I'm worried about a child or a parent. She is about to undergo a tricky medical procedure and I have no faith in her doctor or the hospital. I say it's not going to work, she should get another opinion. She doesn't get another opinion, goes ahead with the procedure, which is a complete mess, takes months, even years to correct.

We can all think of dozens of examples of this kind, and have all had dozens of experiences of this kind, either as predictor or the victim of prediction. We may see this class of experience as that of the informed estimate—sometimes highly informed, sometimes informed only by guesswork or prejudice, but in each case, for our present purposes, turning out to be right. Most oracles, we might think, don't *know* the details of the future but only have an astonishing and trusted record of correct guesses.

But let's tighten the screw a little. I'm not a meteorologist or a worried parent or child, I'm a magician. I say tomorrow at precisely 3:37 p.m. the first drops of rain will fall on Bleecker Street, and when tomorrow comes the rain starts to fall just there at precisely that moment. I say the proposed procedure will fail precisely in its forty-fifth minute because the surgeon will have become distracted by the thought of his gambling debts and because the hospital is trying to save money on the quantity of anesthetic it allows for this kind of case. The procedure fails at just this moment and for just these reasons, although we don't know about the surgeon's gambling debts until he appears in court on another negligence case. What has happened here?

The precision changes everything, converts an informed estimate into something quite different. There are, I think, only three ways of accounting for my success as a magician, if I have it. One is an extraordinary lucky break, or pair of lucky breaks. This is a possible explanation but not really a plausible one, since most people would say that such a degree of precision in the completed prediction would rule out chance. In plagiarism cases, for instance, the crucial thing is to prove that the resemblance between two texts or two tunes cannot be accidental, and this is usually established by the detail, the sheer local specificity of the resemblance.

Second, my magic may just be a trick of some kind, an engineered appearance of successful prediction. I could have used a hidden rain machine to simulate rain; I could have looked at the hospital's accounts over several months, and known the surgeon personally. Even then I would need a bit of luck with the timing.

And finally, I could just have known the future—I really did know, and the event proves it. That is, I not only successfully predicted a particular future, as I would have, or could have, on the basis of an informed or even uninformed estimate, I actually knew all along. There are two corollaries of this possibility, one taking us further into magic and one pulling us back out of it. If I really know the future, then the future must already exist in the present. Time will need to be not only linear but also symmetrical; it will have to be a temporal form of space. The future will stretch out before us as the past stretches out behind us, and although harder to know, it is knowable for the same sort of reasons: it is finite and fixed, all dice are thrown. We often picture this condition as the already-composed book of destiny, and the philosopher Gilbert Ryle describes our plight with admirable English nonchalance: "A thing's actually taking place is, so to speak, merely the turning up of a passage that has for all time been written." Things just turn up, like a lost quotation or unexpected (but foreordained) visitors. The other corollary of my successful foreknowledge, if I have it, is that although I as a magician may know the future in this way, most people are not magicians, and no one else will know that I was right until the event has occurred, the rain has fallen or the procedure has failed.

With this thought we find ourselves quite suddenly in new territory: no longer that of magic or prediction but that of story-telling. Or to be exact, we find ourselves, as I have already suggested, in a place where predictions have to become stories, where the prediction depends on its place in a plot, acquires its final meaning only because of that placing. Whether we think of Macbeth or Oedipus or the dark stranger the gypsy had in mind for us or the horse we just knew was going to win the Derby, these events are confirmed by the time we talk about them—that is to say, they have entered into stories, they are stories. This is not to prejudge the actual validity or authenticity of the prediction itself. It could be god-given or cooked up after the event; in either case, it is only after the event that ordinary mortals will know that it is true. Actually, in human time, even the gods will know that it is true only at that moment; until then they will have known merely that it was going to be true. A man in England is said to have dreamed, well before September 11, 2001, that a plane crashed into the twin towers of Manhattan. We don't have to doubt the truthfulness of the dreamer or the reality of the prediction. But slightly better security at Logan airport in Boston, or better coordination among American intelligence services, would have turned this eerie forecast into just one more dream, a prediction with no relevant outcome.

The whole language of truth is strange in this connection. We say generally that prophecies come true or don't come true: we say more specifically that interpretations of oracles are right or wrong. We are not going to change these usages, since we know perfectly well what we mean by them, but we could be a little stricter now and then. Prophecies are neither true nor false at the time of their utterance. They are awaiting confirmation; they are checks that still have to clear. Prophecies are fulfilled or not—or more precisely, are deemed to have been fulfilled or not. Someone, priest, judge, layperson, a whole culture, has to declare the result, or to use a different metaphor, to say whether the ball was in or out and when the game is over. And the prophecies oracles deal in, as I shall suggest more fully later, are always fulfilled, unless they are refused altogether. The question is not which interpretation is right, since many interpretations could be that. The question is which interpretation *counts* once the results are in.

There is a deep and persuasive appearance of necessity in all cases where an achieved outcome is seen as matching a prediction. The event really does seem inevitable. That is because, given sufficient agreement on the interpretation, it is inevitable—now. Not because it had to happen, but because it already has happened.

Things get a little dizzying here, and we have to ask our first question again. Can we know the future? Another way of answering this question would be to imagine we can, and then see what it feels like. In a haunting poem the great Brazilian writer Carlos Drummond de Andrade pictures a plane crash strangely suffered in both ignorance and knowledge of the event. "I awaken for death," the poem begins.

I shave, dress, put on my shoes.
It is my last day: a day
not broken by one premonition.
Everything happens as usual.
I head for the street. I am going to die.

The speaker describes his day: a visit to the bank, lunch, phone calls, letters, appointments, a headache, packing, the car to the airport. The plane takes off. There are no hints of death here, for the speaker or anyone else, but the poem is full of the awareness of what is going to happen.

> What good
> is the money, if a few hours later
> the police come and take it
> from the hole that was my chest?

"I walk toward death," the speaker says, "I do not say goodbye, I know nothing, I am not afraid." And later:

> I make dates
> that I shall never keep, I utter words in vain
> I lie, saying: "Until tomorrow."

In the plane "death arranges seats to make the wait/more comfortable," and all twenty passengers are going to be killed "right now." "Or almost now." And then lightning hits the plane, bringing "death without previous notice":

> a shattering blast of air, splinter of wind
> on the neck, lightning
> flash burst crack
> broken we tumble
> straight down I fall and am turned into news.

This death is both always known about and "without previous notice," and the last word of the poem helps us to see just what is happening. The speaker is the person who lives through the unmarked day and also the reporter who tells the story. There is plenty of sadness in both roles but nothing surprising or, alas, unusual in either of them. What is not only surprising but impossible is the combination of the two roles into one. The result is more than a paradox or a contradiction. Knowing and not knowing are not logical opposites here, to be resolved perhaps into an ambiguous or even magical state of mind: I know and I do not know. Knowing and not knowing are time frames. The later time has invaded the first without changing it; it shows up as knowledge but helpless knowledge, knowledge that can't get into the story but can only doggedly insert itself into the telling. The narrator, we might say, can't reach the character, and Drummond de Andrade makes the point painful by turning them into the same person. Still, we do now know where we are. We are like the spectators of Orson Welles's *Citizen Kane*, possessing the answer to the riddle of the sled called Rosebud, which no one in the movie has, and which we can't share except with other viewers. The effect is repeated again and again in film and literature, one of narrative's major moves, although it doesn't ordinarily creep into the story itself as it does in this poem. We are looking not at eerie prophecy but at mischievous reporting, not at firm foreknowledge but at displaced hindsight—more precisely, hindsight uncannily dressed as foreknowledge.

So one answer to our question about knowing the future is: sure. We can always know it when it's happened. In this sense our idiom about knowing things all along may be correct, and not just a mystification. Quite often, of course, such a phrase is self-deceiving, an attempt to hide, even from ourselves, how surprised we are by what has happened. But sometimes it represents a simple truth. We foresaw the future. At the time, before the event, our foresight probably felt more like fear or hope or a wager. But now it feels like knowledge. It is knowledge, although perhaps not quite the knowledge it pretends to be. We know the prediction—that is, we know that we or someone else made it—and we know the result, and we know that they match. What else is there to know? Or: What room is left for whatever is not knowledge?

These questions are very familiar to gamblers, in both their upbeat and their downbeat forms. You bet on a number because you know, with the intimate conviction of a visitation from a god, that it will come up. The number comes up. You knew it would. Or you don't bet; you're playing a guessing game. You're sure a certain number will come up, and it does. But would it have come up if you had bet on it? Conversely, you are quite sure a number will come up and it doesn't. This doesn't alter your conviction, or your memory of your conviction, only turns it into an irresistible error.

We can say that those who get things right in great detail must know the future by magical means, but we can also imagine them as knowing it in the same way and for the same reasons as we know it once it has arrived. We have heard the story, and so have they—or they can be pictured as having access to the completion of a story that is still in the making. This is not quite the same thing as the image of symmetrical time or the already written book. These people have just got ahead of the script still under construction, and there is nothing in such a fiction that requires any real-life belief in precognition. We can invent creatures who know the future as if they had read the book in which the future is already the present or the past, we can even invent gods who know the future in this way, not because we know the future, but because we have read books or heard stories. The fiction is a transposition of a familiar fact, a familiar fact made magical.

THREE: SO MUCH FOR NERO

The clearest oracle is the least understood.

Pierre Corneille, *Oedipus*

Equivocation

The interview wasn't going badly but the candidate wasn't comfortable. He had on a smart, mildly fashionable new suit, with the cuffless trousers and short boxy jacket of the kind the Beatles were wearing about that time. But this wasn't a place for fashion. It was a place for tradition, a quite different animal. It was a place in Whitehall, London, the occasion one of the last stages of the candidate's soon-to-be failed quest to enter the British Foreign Service.

The room was high ceilinged, rather dark, and seemed to stretch off into infinity behind the candidate as he faced his questioners. There were fifteen of them, and they sat behind a horseshoe-shaped table. The chairman, an elderly man with a beak of a nose and much dandruff on his pin-striped suit, said, "Mr. Wood, it has been remarked that General de Gaulle governs by a policy of high-sounding equivocation. What do you think of that?" The candidate didn't think anything, because he couldn't place the word *equivocation*. It was as if he had never heard it before, as if it were a nonsense word designed to illustrate the possibility of meaninglessness—a word like *brofthrugpindak*, for example. The silence stretched out, but the word didn't get any more familiar. It was simply opaque, five unintelligible syllables. Finally the candidate murmured his lame, delaying reply. "I suppose you could say that," he said.

The interest of this story, if it has an interest, is that the candidate not only knew perfectly well what *equivocation* meant, it was one of his favorite words, indeed one of his favorite subjects. He had many reasons for loving literature and writing, but if he had been pushed to name one, he would have said the chance of equivocation, of equivocating himself and of seeing equivocation endlessly at work. He would have said equivocation is a form of riches, and not only because he had been reading William Empson. He would have agreed that equivocation is not always a good thing, but he would have added that riches are not always a good thing either. So the implied criticism in the question wouldn't have bothered him. Then why couldn't he recognize the word at the interview?

I don't know. He was very nervous, and fear takes many things away from us. Perhaps fear took away this word just because it mattered to him. In any event, the result was that he just couldn't see his old friend in this daunting new location, or less metaphorically, just couldn't connect the interpretable world of literature with the (he imagined) much more solid and stable and serious world of politics and international affairs. Many things have changed since, although not unequivocally.

Events and stories

Are oracles always ambiguous? No. Classical scholars have been insisting for some time that Greek oracles could and did give clear and unequivocal answers, and there is no reason to believe that other oracles couldn't do the same. The god's instructions, one French scholar says of Apollo, were "always direct and perfectly clear"; "of a perfect clarity," says another. Plutarch, who was Apollo's priest at Delphi, said the god liked to create riddles to test the powers of our minds, but was always ready to find "a remedy and a solution for the problems connected with our life by the oracular responses which he gives to those who consult him."

In the book I have already mentioned, Catherine Morgan offers a nicely shaded speculation. Perhaps the oracle's answers, at Delphi in any case, got more complicated as city-states grew and intercity relations became more complex. Morgan says "ambiguity is undoubtedly one of the most celebrated traits of the Delphic oracle . . . even though its extent and significance have been greatly exaggerated." "Undoubtedly," she continues, using that discreetly preemptive word for the second time on the same page, "the majority of responses were straightforward, and, as Joseph Fontenrose has stressed, the oracle's *reputation* for ambiguity was always overshadowed by its reputation for truth, and was anyway a late development." "Late" means early classical, sometime after 600 B.C., and the Delphic oracle certainly had its reputation for ambiguity by the time of Heraclitus, who famously said, "The Lord whose oracle is at Delphi neither speaks nor remains silent, but gives signs." The just-mentioned Joseph Fontenrose argues valiantly that even this splendid formulation doesn't amount to an attribution of ambiguity, and I will return to this formulation and this argument. For now I want only to make two points, or offer two distinctions. First, a straightforward response is not necessarily unambiguous; and second, a reputation for knowing the truth (and therefore being worth asking) is not the same as a reputation for telling the truth.

So there is a riddle here, and it concerns the very idea of equivocation. Even if Greek oracles can be clear, they can also be ambiguous, and if the reputation for obscurity is "late," it is inordinately powerful and usually eclipses, in most people's minds, whatever clarity or simplicity the oracles' responses had. We could grant that this reputation was an anachronism, an outsider's view, or just a blunt historical error, and still find it extremely interesting.

It helps to distinguish between oracle-events and oracle-stories—that is, between oracles given in historical time before the outcome of their advice is known, and oracles that figure in stories told after the event, after the advice and its outcome have met up in the pattern the story wants to show. Simplifying wildly, it looks as if the archeological evidence in Greece suggests that historical oracles were fairly clear, while the literary evidence reveals ambiguity all over the place: straightforward events, stories of equivocation. There are no stories, the French scholar Roland Crahay says, that are not later than the fulfillment of the promises they recount. This should, and does, make historians very suspicious. But the logical map must look something like this: an actual oracle can be clear or ambiguous, depending on its style; and so can an oracle in a story. But the clarity or ambiguity of an actual oracle is in suspense, so to speak. We don't know how the promise or the advice or the prediction will turn out. To put it crudely, we don't know whether the oracle's text can stand as it is or will need editing or reinterpreting to show that it will have been right all along. Oracle-stories could easily recount the success of an unambiguous oracle—a prediction of victory followed by a victory—but they scarcely ever do, and this allows us to displace and refine our question. Oracles in stories are not necessarily equivocal; they are merely equivocal when necessary. The question is not why an unambiguous practice should acquire a reputation for ambiguity but why so many cultures invest so deeply in ambiguity and associate that ambiguity with oracles. We can ask oracles about the past as well as about the future, and we have, it seems, a deep interest in stories that show we were right or wrong long before the actual occasions of our rightness or wrongness. These are stories of destiny, but of a destiny that could have been mistaken. It wasn't mistaken but it could have been, and the chance of error is written into the very terms of its success.

So it's not so much a matter of the equivocation of oracles as of our need for stories of equivocation, a genre where oracles often get to play starring roles. And indeed, in these stories, we seem to make two quite different investments in equivocation, although the two are almost invariably caught up in each other. The first investment is obvious. There are times when only equivocation will preserve the oracle's credibility. Suppose an oracle says, as Apollo's oracle did to Croesus through the pythia at Delphi, that if the consultant attacks the Persians, a great empire will be destroyed. In all the many versions of this story, Croesus assumes the empire in question is that of the Persians, not his own, and he is disastrously wrong. But let's suppose the pythia was not being ambiguous, just flowery, and let's suppose Croesus was not wrong about the oracle, only about the war. The pythia did mean the Persian Empire, and perhaps even, in this imaginary reconstruction, named it as such— the more equivocal terms were inserted into the story later, when things had gone so badly for Croesus. In this mode of interpretation the oracle will always have been right, because the historical record will have been fixed the way it is in Orwell's *1984*: the past prediction is adjusted to meet the later result. The oracle is infallible because the story has an editor who knows how to make it look infallible.

And yet the mode of equivocation in oracle-stories is not quite that of the rigged history in Orwell. There the prediction is doctored until it is unequivocally correct, an elementary form of cheating, like betting on a horse when the race is over and we know who won. In oracle-stories the promise or the prediction needs only to have a chance of having been right, needs only not to have been unequivocally wrong. Faith, enthusiasm, and ingenious interpretation will do the rest.

And with this we arrive at the second investment in equivocation. Oracle-stories characteristically not only center on equivocation as part of their plot, the way they make the oracle come out right. They are *about* equivocation. They need the oracle to be both right and wrong; they need more than one outcome to lurk from the start in the oracle's utterance. It is because the oracle could have been wrong in these stories that we are fascinated by the way it came out right. In the equivocation we see the rightness and the wrongness all at once: the story disentangles them, but the tangle is what we remember, what we return to, the haunting point of so many stories.

Well, it is the haunting point if we feel at all close to the human subjects of these stories; maybe not if we take the side of the gods. When a king is told a great empire will be destroyed if he takes the offensive, or that he is safe on the throne of Scotland until Birnam Wood comes to Dunsinane, we may just chuckle at his naïveté, his failure to see the tricky double meaning, the ambiguity that is crying out to us, the readers or hearers of the story. But many of us won't chuckle. I don't chuckle in these instances, and I don't think either king is naive. They are both doubly disadvantaged: by the equivocation of the oracle and by the fact that everyone else, apart from these hampered players, knows the end of the story. What is haunting, I suggest, and what constitutes the recurring appeal of these stories, is the double meaning itself, and the sense that we, too, in such a situation, might have missed it. Our privileged position is a pleasure but also a little frightening, because we know we're not likely to have it except when we're listening to oracle-stories. We keep thinking of the misplaced destruction of an empire, and the stratagem with the moving trees, each soldier taking a branch as camouflage. But we also hold on to the unmistakable note of promise inhabiting these oracles, their air of reassurance. If a reliable authority said your pension funds were safe until Westminster Abbey moved to Wapping, you wouldn't think immediately of engineering feats and the snags of city politics, you would think you were being told "forever" in a forceful figure of speech.

Before and after

There is a famous poem by Cavafy, which begins, in Edmund Keeley's translation:

> Nero wasn't worried at all when he heard
> the utterance of the Delphic Oracle:
> "Beware of the age of seventy-three."
> Plenty of time to enjoy himself still.
> He's thirty.

Nero returns to Rome, ready to resume a long life of pleasure. "So much for Nero," the poem ends.

> So much for Nero. And in Spain Galba
> Secretly musters and drills his army—
> Galba, the old man in his seventy-third year.

"He felt so confident," Suetonius says, "not only of old age, but of unbroken and unusual good fortune, that when he lost some articles of great value by shipwreck, he did not hesitate to say among his intimate friends that the fish would [bring] them back to him." He heard the news of the Gallic uprising "with such calmness and indifference that he incurred the suspicion of actually rejoicing in it, because it gave him an excuse for pillaging those wealthy provinces according to the laws of war." Nero got the oracle wrong not casually but spectacularly—his style in most things—and like many figures in such stories he stumbled from irony into irony. The last musical piece he performed in public was called "Oedipus in Exile." One of his last phrases, apparently repeatedly uttered, was, "What an artist the world is losing."

The Delphic prophecy given to Nero was "no doubt fabricated post eventum," H. W. Parke says casually in his 1967 book. Earlier he and his colleague Wormell had been a little cagier. Nero, as most would, took the oracle's utterance to mean that he would die when he was around seventy-three—and more important, that he wouldn't die before then, whatever happened. Parke and Wormell comment, "But after [Nero] had committed suicide, the pious saw that Apollo had indicated the danger coming from Galba, who was in his seventy-third year when he rebelled and overthrew Nero. This story, of course, is not known from evidence before the date of its alleged fulfillment. So it might be a later invention. But the prophecy is so simple that there is no need to be skeptical. The choice of the number seventy-three may have been a mere chance shot, which was sure to find some coincidence to confirm it."

There are three interesting scenarios here. In the first, Apollo foresaw the death of Nero and its timing, and announced it in exactly the way the story tells it. It's just that we have no record of this announcement that is not later than the fulfillment of the prophecy. In the second, Apollo may or may not have foreseen the death of Nero and its timing, but in any case he didn't say anything about it. His knowledge is evoked afterward, in a kind of fable, and carefully placed before the event. This is the work of "the pious," who necessarily believe the god would have foreseen everything anyway. They are falsifying the record, but they are, in their eyes, faithful to the god's abilities. "Post eventum," of course, is a phrase that has its own little equivocation or excess of meaning and insistence. It doesn't just mean "after the event"; it means "really or se-

cretly after the event, in spite of appearances." We use the phrase
only when someone has made a claim of ante eventum wisdom,
passing off what we think is hindsight as foresight. So to the piety
of the pious corresponds the sturdy common sense of the skeptical—both groups capable of excessive (positive or negative) certainty.

In the third scenario Apollo is almost entirely absent, even as a
fantasy, although the prophecy is real—that is, historical. The
priests at Delphi, or the pythia, decided to give Nero a number in
answer to his question about his future, and settled on seventy-
three. They didn't mean anything much by this, they were just playing at fortune-telling. They knew nothing about Galba, but they
did know that in the next forty-three years plenty of prophecies
would come and go, right and wrong, dramatic and mundane. Who
would remember what they had said to Nero? And if anyone did
remember, there was still room for interpretation. They had said
"the seventy-third year"; they hadn't said the seventy-third year of
what or whom. You could always find a seventy-three somewhere if
you looked.

Why is it that the third scenario, ostensibly closest to modern
rationalism, seems the most unlikely even to a (moderately) reasonable person like myself, and I am sure to many others? Well, it
makes the oracle's activity trivial, and whatever Delphi was in the
ancient world it wasn't that; and above all it misses or tries to dis-
solve into banality the eerie mystery of the story itself. Because of
course the interest of the tale lies not in Apollo's foreknowledge,
which we can either take for granted or disbelieve in altogether, but
in the convergence of the prophecy and Galba's age. This would be
fascinating if it was sheer coincidence, indeed more fascinating
than if it was divine prediction. Divine prediction would just re-
quire the god to turn the pages of the future's book, look ahead in
the already scripted plot. Coincidence requires chance to behave

like an ironic designer, to produce out of the random events of empire and rebellion not a script but an irresistible *sense* of the scripted. It's true that out of all the numbers available in the Roman world, this story requires a concentration on seventy-three, and chance can't do that all alone. Only narrative can do that, a selective and forgetful gaze.

But if narrative gets the effects, history and religion provide the materials, and what we are doing now, surely, is combining scenarios one and two. The pre-placing of the post eventum prophecy is not simply a lie, or an easy pious fable. Nor is it an attempt to fake a feeling of destiny, to make the world look more predetermined than it is. It is a subtle suggestion that the future, undetermined until particular individuals or societies move toward it, but determined in all kinds of ways once they do, always hides in the past, and in theory could always be seen, by humans as well as by gods. This is a fantasy, perhaps, but it is a fantasy most of us are addicted to. Who has not tried to read the beginning of today's calamity in the memory of yesterday's error—as if it were already there, I mean? In the Nero story, the human consultant stares at the evidence and makes an obvious, plausible, and quite erroneous interpretation. But the error is a strange one, since the right interpretation is simultaneously unavailable and staring the consultant in the face. Or whispering to him, since this is partly what Macbeth means when he speaks of the witches keeping "the word of promise to the ear." He heard what he wanted, but he could also have heard the other meaning, since it turns out to have been lurking in what was spoken. What is most haunting about the many stories of this kind is not that the future is obliquely foretold and that the oracle was right all along, or even that the consultant goes so disastrously astray, but that he hears and misses—couldn't reasonably have been expected to get—a truth of the most precise kind, the exactly relevant number or name. Being in the literal presence of such a particular truth seems to matter more than missing it—or rather the missing it matters only because the truth was tantalizingly close, right at hand and yet totally invisible, like the purloined letter in Poe's story of that name, sitting on the mantelpiece but noticed by no one.

An oracle's answers are often actual and virtual versions of Schrödinger's cat, which, sealed in a box in a famous thought-experiment illustrating the uncertainty principle, was both dead and alive. This is a very special form of ambiguity, more like a dual setting than a double meaning—like a dual-voltage electrical appliance, for example, with a switch for its use in different locations or on different occasions. Apart from the tricky prophecy about the great empire, Croesus was also told by the Delphic oracle that he would reign until a mule became king of the Persians, a phrase he managed to take both literally and as a figure of speech. "For he did not suppose a mule would become king of the Persians," Herodotus says, but of course Croesus did suppose the idiom was a hyperbole, a way of saying forever, or for a very long time. It did not occur to him that Cyrus, a child of a Mede and a Persian, might be called a mule. The standard interpretation of this famous story, first found in Herodotus, but repeated many times since and in many places, is that Croesus misread the oracle, heard only what he wanted to hear. But what he misread was history, and when history turned out the way it did, the other meaning of the oracle kicked in, either because it was what the god had in mind all along, or because the god had hedged his bets and was waiting for the result. For our purposes we don't need to decide whether the god was prescient or merely crafty. The oracle works either way.

There is a technical term for this kind of double speech—amphibology—and of course oracle-stories are full of it. An oracle warned Hesiod to beware the grove of Nemean Zeus, and he did, staying away from it entirely, or at least staying away from Nemea.

But then he was killed at another shrine of Nemean Zeus, in Aeto-
lia. The Athenians asked the oracle if they should mount an expedition to Sicily and were given a favorable reply. The voyage was a
disaster, and when the Athenians asked what went wrong, they were
told another Sicily was meant, a small hill not far from their own
city. The Trojans were promised they would end their travels and
settle a new land successfully when they found their ancient
mother, "*antiqua mater.*" Anchises, Aeneas' father, explained that this
must mean Crete, and reconstructed a whole Trojan history to support this view. But an attempt to settle Crete was a fiasco. The god
later clarified that Italy was the *antiqua mater*, the motherland by another lineage. A group of Greek soldiers, in their warlike enthusiasm, cried out their word for victory. This word happened also to
be the name of their enemy, who were much encouraged by the cry
and won the battle.

Of course such double meanings are not confined to oracles;
they are the basis of all puns and of many common forms of misunderstanding. Oh, you mean *that* Jennifer Lopez, not the one who
does the weather reports on CNN. Keith Thomas reminds us that
"Henry IV was told that he would die in Jerusalem, but 'Jerusalem'
turned out to be the name of a room in a house belonging to the
Abbot of Westminster." And we can of course extend amphibologies beyond an identity of names and into the realm of complex
phrases. A terrible dream prophecy in Herodotus tells a man he
will be washed by the sun and anointed by Zeus. In the event, this
means he will be crucified.

But although ambiguity is everywhere—we might say that the
possibility of ambiguity is synonymous with language itself—stories of this kind have a very particular slant. They are often described as misunderstood warnings, and form a whole genre in
folklore and legend. The further implication is that they are supposed to be misunderstood, that the god is taunting the recipient

of the prophecy, the way the oracle at Delphi seemed to be taunting Nero. There is certainly an element of cruelty in most of these stories. But they can't really be warnings in any ordinary sense; they are too intricate and recondite for that. What is happening here, I think, in addition to the purloined-letter effect I have just described, is that a remote, secondary meaning of a name or phrase is being retrieved, not to save the god's credibility, and not as a rebuke to human interpretative hubris, but for the sake of vast recurring irony, a sort of joke that is like a pun on a metaphysical scale. *Nemea, Sicily, mother, victory, Jerusalem, sun, Zeus*: these and other words caught up in such stories will always have another meaning, and they won't even have to change their name. The world is a system of doubles, but the same actor plays both roles, as in many old Hollywood movies. What I said earlier about the idiom that describes oracles as coming true can also be said about their meaning one thing or another or both. The idiom makes perfect sense, and I have just used it six times, I hope unobtrusively. But strictly oracles don't *mean*. They play a verbal card, and the card is picked up by both the player and the whole universe of available names. When the player picks the wrong name, he hasn't exactly missed the oracle's meaning. He has chosen one meaning and ceased to look for others—a permanent risk even in the most anxiously examined life, and one of the gravest dangers of oracle consultation. We not only give up thinking but seem licensed to do so by an external authority, which turns out to have a canny verbal trick up its sleeve. In their widest implications stories of this kind suggest a form of casualty that could occur to any word at all: not misinterpretation but deportation, a second life beyond every speaker's control. It's the fact that they are recognizably the same words, even in this new life, that generates the irony, which would be funny if it were not so unkind. The gods get all the jokes, the first time as tragedy, the second time as farce.

What confuses you?

I suggested earlier that even a straightforward oracle response is not necessarily unambiguous, and we need to look a little more closely at this possibility. A university administrator of my acquaintance has on his desk, turned to face the usually intimidated visitor or supplicant, a boldly lettered block that says, "What is it about 'no' that confuses you?" The question invokes the very confusion it is trying to expel. It's not that the word *no* is ambiguous, in this or any other context, it's that ambiguity can surround even the clearest assertions. Everything depends on what the philosopher J. L. Austin calls "the total speech act in the total speech situation," the full context in which any question is asked and answered. This will include silent or implied questions and silent or implied answers.

Herodotus reports that the people of Cnidus, struck by all kinds of illnesses and misfortunes while working on a canal, asked the oracle at Delphi what they should do. The oracle answered, "Do not dig." Can't say plainer than that. The question was clear and so was the answer. The canal was a mistake, the illnesses were a sign; the oracle read the sign for the Cnidians, and they gave up digging. No ambiguity anywhere in sight, and many oracle situations are probably just like this.

But on another, more famous occasion, reported by both Plato and Xenophon, the oracle simply said, "No," as the motto on the desk is trying to. The question was, "Is anyone wiser than Socrates?" When the answer was transmitted to Socrates he, predictably, did not take this simple answer for a simple answer. He said, "I wonder what the god meant." Did Socrates think there was something confusing about the word *no*? No, but he did think that even the word *no* could be the start of a conversation, and more generally that even unequivocal monosyllables are signs—rather than emphatic speech or unbroken silence—and that signs have to be interpreted.

Socrates, in any case, went to work. He felt sure (or pretended to feel sure) that there were people much wiser than he was, and set out in search of them. He gradually discovered, though, that in spite of their claims, or the claims made for them, these people were certainly not wiser than he was, and perhaps not wise at all. So he accepted the god's simple answer as simply true—in the end. But of course the answer was true in Socrates' sense only when he had tested it and found out what it meant. The testing itself was part of the truth. The oracle did not mean that Socrates was wiser than anyone else; it didn't even mean, as it has often been taken to mean, that the truly wise man knows he knows nothing. There is something a little too grand and dogmatic about such absolute modesty: even an ignoramus can't be sure of knowing *nothing*. What the oracle meant, Socrates determines through his researches, is that really wise people don't delude themselves about their knowledge, as so many supposedly wise people do.

Was Socrates testing the god? Was he skeptical about the god's answer, putting the god's infallibility in question? Saving the god from a crass mistake, even? We may want to think Socrates is being pious and god-fearing, respecting what he knows to be the god's wishes for human self-instruction—think of the oblique teachings of Christ and of many an Eastern sage. Or we may prefer to think of Socrates as a mischievous humanist, treating the god's answer as the occasion for a little lesson of his own. But either way, from our point of view, the oracle spoke clearly and Socrates drew from it an unequivocal, although not uncomplicated message. Ambiguity got into the air in the form of a question—what can the god have meant?—and was then dissolved in the same air.

It may be there is always some ambiguity in the air where oracles are concerned—if we widen the frame or deepen the question enough. Some doubt or some need for a decision must have led to the consultation of the oracle, even if the question and answer are ultimately without mystery, and even if, as is surely so often the case, the consultant has made his or her mind up in advance, and is seeking from the oracle only a ratification of or a blessing on an action already chosen—rather in the way we seek advice on issues we have already mentally settled, or the way a modern state might wish to have the support of the United Nations for a policy it was determined to pursue anyway. An oracle would then be a remote reflection of an uncertainty, even if its job, in the event, is to settle the matter rather than raise the stakes or change the terms.

Isn't this just a manner of saying that uncertainty is everywhere? That ambiguity can be found in the fullest, frankest statement if you go hunting in the furthest reaches of its context? No, the suggestion is more specific than this. To find the ghost of an equivocation even in the clearest, simplest oracles is not to multiply doubt at random, it is to remember a significant feature of the oracles themselves. It doesn't make all oracles ambiguous, and it doesn't affect the clarity and simplicity of oracles that are clear and simple. But it does remind us of the job oracles have to do, and of the tension that lies at the heart of their very existence: the longing for certainty and infallibility in those areas of human life where they are characteristically least available. That's why the longing makes such sense, and why banished fallibility has a way of creeping back. As the dictionaries know in their uncomfortable way, an oracle is not a site of uncertainty *or* infallibility; it is a site of both.

The best example I know of an unambiguous oracle wreathed in ambiguity occurs in Herodotus. Most scholars assume this story is just that—a story rather than a datable historical incident—because the god speaks in his own voice rather than through a pythia or sibyl, and because the whole thing has the shape of a powerful

moral fable, "more interesting," one historian says, "than twenty reports of battles." H. W. Parke, however, doesn't see why the story
can't be true in its essentials. It certainly concerns historical figures
and returns us to the time of Croesus and the disastrous Lydian
campaign.

Pactyes, a Lydian on the run from the Persians, seeks sanctuary
with the people of Cyme. His presence creates a horrible quandary
for them. If they give him up to the pursuing Persians, they break
their own sacred rule of hospitality to the fugitive. If they don't
give him up, the Persians will turn the full weight of their wrath on
Cyme itself. The difficulty would be considerable for anyone, but
the Cymeans were proverbially supposed to be particularly stupid,
and that too is part of the story. They decide to consult the oracle
at Didyma, also known as Branchidae, after the family name of the
officiating priests, and the oracle says they should give Pactyes up.
The Cymeans are generally ready to do this, but Aristodicus, one
of their leading citizens, protests. There must be some mistake, he
says. The oracle can't have told us to break the rule of sanctuary.
Let's ask again. He offers to consult the oracle himself, and does.
The answer is the same. At this point Aristodicus goes around the
temple precinct, throwing from their nests all the birds who have
taken up residence there. Finally the god himself, Apollo, speaks
out in a booming voice and asks Aristodicus what he is doing.
Aristodicus says that since the god obviously has no care for those
who seek sanctuary, he won't mind if these creatures who have
sought shelter in his temple are driven out. Apollo takes the point
and explains. He had told the Cymeans to give up the man who
had sought refuge with them so that their thoroughly deserved disaster should come upon them all the more quickly. Their question
was so much—and so evidently—the wrong thing to ask that they
deserved the supreme punishment for even asking it.

Apollo here shows a finer feeling for principle than he often does, but the cruelty seems entirely characteristic. As in the story of Socrates and the oracle, the god's literal response and his ultimate meaning are perfectly unequivocal. The difference in the Cyme/Pactyes case is that what the god says so clearly is exactly the opposite of what he means. He has no advice for the Cymeans—or only bad advice in the form of withering sarcasm. He tells them to do what they obviously want to do—release Pactyes to the Persians—because he has already given up on them.

This is a god who speaks and remains silent and gives signs all at the same time, and I want to return briefly to Heraclitus' famous fragment. Joseph Fontenrose's reading of it, which I have already glanced at, is engaging because it is down to earth and dispels so much mystery. Or seems to dispel so much mystery. The god, Fontenrose says, does not speak—literally does not utter any words—but he doesn't keep silent either, because he doesn't refuse to answer questions. He shows his answer through his medium, the pythia: an answer that is neither his speech nor his silence but his answer all the same.

The trouble with this ingenious reading is that, plausible and even accurate as it may be as a description of Delphic practice, it's hard to imagine Heraclitus bothering to put such a proposition into words. Heraclitus' works are notoriously fragmentary, and I remember the attractive caution of my friend and colleague Helen Bacon, a professor of classics at Barnard College, who wouldn't teach Heraclitus to undergraduates, because she felt there was no way of knowing what he might have meant in his own context—or to put that another way, because we can make him mean anything we like. The rest of us are not quite so abstemious, and if Philip Wheelright is correct about the number of puns there are in the Greek of these fragments, and if Heraclitus' ancient reputation for obscurity—he was called the dark one—is not based on nothing, there are a couple of suggestions we can make. We can suggest that these fragments are likely to mean a little more than they seem to say, and that their purpose is unlikely to have been purely descriptive. "The way up and the way down are one and the same" is not about mountain travel when the roads are scarce. "You can't step into the same river twice" is not simply saying that water flows.

And in the fragment we are looking at—"The Lord whose oracle is at Delphi neither speaks nor remains silent, but gives signs"—it is plain that there are two things the god doesn't do and one thing he does do, however we turn the terms into English. There are of course many possible translations, but the modern relatives of the old words (*legei, kryptei, semainei*) are reason and law (logic, legislation), secrecy and code (cryptic), and sign and meaning (semantics). So paraphrasing very freely, we might say the god doesn't legislate or give orders, and he doesn't hide things or behave secretively. But his messages, whatever their medium, have a meaning.

Surely this hints at Heraclitus' own prose as well as specifying the god's practice. And Fontenrose must be right in this special sense. Heraclitus does not say the god is ambiguous and he is not ambiguous himself. But both Heraclitus and the god deal in signs, and signs need work: the sign is just the beginning of the labor of interpretation. Ambiguity, we might say, is the name impatient people give to language they don't want to work on. But it may also be the name others cling to until they find something better.

THE WAY BACK

Last night I saw the figures on the road again. They were agitated, talking rapidly, in overlapping speech, as if they were in a film by Orson Welles or Robert Altman. It was hard to catch what they were saying, and to piece together what had happened. They had obviously been talking furiously for days, and what I heard was a late fragment of a long conversation. The night was dark but the wind had dropped.

Gradually it became clear that their worst fears had been realized, and that the oracle had been closed when they arrived. Closed for good. Their plan to tell the story of their journey still seemed fine in principle, but they hadn't seen much on the way there, and they had spent the whole of the way back telling oracle-stories, invoking all the consultations they knew about, all the encounters that others had managed to have and that they had missed. So what account were they going to give of themselves when they got home?

One of them said, "You think we should claim that, open or closed, the oracle is a way of helping us to picture our choices?"

The other said, "Yes. Or our lack of choice."

The first said, "So our case would be that superstition is not to be scorned or condescended to, that superstition is a way of thinking, a way of working things out?"

The second said, "Who said anything about superstition?"

FOUR: The Death of the King

But why dissect destiny with instruments
   more highly specialized than components of destiny
   itself?

             Marianne Moore, "Those Various Scalpels"

Versions

Claude Lévi-Strauss suggests that interpretations of a myth are
themselves instances of the myth, prolongations or variants of its
narrative logic. He is thinking of the story of Oedipus, and Freud's
reading of it, but the point is a more general one, and I think the
proposition works backward too. All instances of a myth are interpretations of it, versions that insist on certain possibilities to the
exclusion of others. Some of these exclusions are very important,
and often need to be maintained. Sophocles' *Oedipus the King* and
Shakespeare's *Macbeth* are intricate and sophisticated arrangements
of words and events, and the student of drama will want to respect
those arrangements, and not be drawn into fabulous speculations
about plays the authors didn't write. But for us, who are interested
in the various logics of oracles, all the possibilities surrounding
these stories are significant, whether we find them in the plays'
sources or parallel versions or later interpretations and transpositions, or even make them up right now, as we are writing and reading this book. The Greeks knew many versions of the Oedipus

story, and went to the theater in the later fifth century B.C. to see, among other things, what Sophocles had made of it. They didn't imagine Oedipus would escape the fate the oracle promised him, but they didn't think he was wrong to try, and the play itself exacerbates both Oedipus' freedom and the intricate trap his very freedom manages to contrive for him. All kinds of legends shadow the plot of *Macbeth*, not only the Scottish history Shakespeare found in Holinshed, but also the folktales that Holinshed had included in his history, and still other folktales hiding behind them. In one of these, the witches are quite unequivocal about Macbeth's end. They tell him he can't be harmed by a living person, and everyone understands that this means he will last until a ghost or demon gets him.

The French classical scholar Jean-Pierre Vernant makes a rich and evocative distinction between myth and tragedy, where myth represents the full fund of early versions of a story, and tragedy a masterly concentration of it. Myth, Vernant says, brings us "responses without ever explicitly formulating the problem. Tragedy, when it takes up the traditions of myth, uses them to pose problems which have no solution." We could broaden the argument a little. Myth, we might say, is all the versions of a story, early and late: Sophocles, Seneca, Cocteau, Stravinsky, and Pasolini in the case of Oedipus; Holinshed, Shakespeare, Verdi, Smetana, and Kurosawa in the case of Macbeth. We have the responses, but we have to find the problem. What is helpful here is the chance of respecting the properties of the individual work of art, the particular case or version, while remembering the huge stock of alternatives that it dips into and makes possible, something like the murmur of voices the Chinese spy hears in Jorge Luis Borges's story "The Garden of Forking Paths," when he thinks of all the things that could have happened but didn't, and now can't, because he has set himself on a single road to assassination and death.

Once a story has started, its possibilities are not infinite, and they shrink in number as the story develops. We pass forks in the road and forget them, concentrating in memory only on the single road we took. This is how we understand stories, and we couldn't make sense of them if we didn't know how to do this. Even so, certain forks in the road may return to trouble or exhilarate us, and at crucial moments—crossroads, to get etymology to do a little work for us—the fork itself becomes the story, makes the difference between the continuing roads almost unimportant. This is a feature of stories, and not of life, where the chosen, continuing road is always essential. In life it makes a huge difference whether you crash your car and die or get married and live happily ever after. In a movie plot, for example, these are just two ways of resolving a heroine's (and a studio's) dilemma. Should Bette Davis be terminally punished for her forbidden love, or has she suffered enough to be rewarded now? In the latter case, her love would have to have been innocent after all, and of course even in a movie the two endings are different, and propose different meanings to us. That's why a studio might hesitate about its choice. But in this rather peculiar realm where possibilities as well as eventualities are our focus, we do see that these are two endings to the same story, a splitting of a road that was single so far. Every split we remember is a haunted place, where the taken and untaken roads both stretch out in front of us. Robert Frost's famous poem on this subject has an eerie little oracle-effect when the speaker announces not that the roads diverge in a yellow wood, or that they are different, or that they are "really about the same," but that he has his story lined up. "I shall be telling this with a sigh," he says, and "ages and ages hence" he will be saying he took the road less traveled by. He will have converted two actual possibilities into a single (brave, sorrowful) narrative destiny, and the choice he now describes will have made "all the difference." As indeed it will, once he has told the story a few times.

I remember being shocked, even outraged, when I read in Lévi-Strauss's book on totemism that what actually happens in any given situation is just one of the logical possibilities on offer. What happens is what happens, I thought. It is categorically different from what doesn't happen, and the difference is one of fact and practice and history, not one of logic. What doesn't happen is at best a phantom, a near miss or a source of regret. We can't place it on the same level with what actually does happen, as if the possibilities were all equal. It's true there is something dizzying about treating an event as a mere possibility even after it has occurred, but Lévi-Strauss wasn't denying the difference I was so keen on. He wasn't confusing the possible and the actual, he was inviting us to see the fork in the road, the point in the movie before the car crashes or the marriage is decided, the point in the poem before Frost's speaker has settled on his story. I would say now that there is a form of freedom in imagining even lost possibilities, especially lost possibilities, if we can avoid the forlorn nostalgia that so often goes with such exercises. In returning to the fork in the road, we are not seeking to relive our lives, or we don't have to be. We could be reminding ourselves that our choices are choices, and that not even an oracle can take this freedom from us.

The road to Delphi

Versions differ about the location of the event, but there are always three roads, and two of them appear in all the versions: the road to and from Delphi, and the road to and from Thebes. In a surviving fragment of a lost play by Aeschylus the chief character says, "We were coming to the crossroads where three carriage tracks meet at Potniae." Potniae is in Boeotia south of Thebes. But in Sophocles we are given another location, equally exact: a point in Phocis, where the road from Thebes branches toward Delphi and Daulis. The roads meet, the roads part. It's the second place that has the historical honors, or rather carries the myth into modern geography and history. But of course the name or siting of the spot where Oedipus killed his father matters less to us, and to the story, than the shape the roads make on the mythical map. Three roads, always. One too many for a predestined encounter, we might think. Or even two too many.

"About 5 miles to the south-west of Daulis," Sir James Frazer writes in his commentary on Pausanias, "the road, after skirting the eastern foot of the mighty mass of Mount Parnassus, turns sharply to the west and begins to ascend through the long, narrow, and profound valley which leads to Delphi. Just at the point where the road turns westward and before it begins the long ascent it is joined from the south-east by the direct road from Lebadea and Thebes." This place used to be called "the Cleft Way or Triple Road," and by Frazer's time was also called "the Cross Road of Megas (Stavrodromi tou Mega), after the gallant Johannes Megas, who met his death here in July 1856, while exterminating a band of brigands with a small troop of soldiers." At this point Frazer the scholar goes into high romantic literary mode:

Apart from any legendary associations the scene is one of the wildest and grandest in Greece, recalling in its general features, though on a vastly greater scale, the mouth of Glencoe. On both sides of the valley the mountains tower abruptly in huge precipices; the cliffs of Parnassus on the northern side of the valley are truly sublime. Not a trace of human habitation is to be seen. All is desolation and silence. A more fitting spot could hardly be found for the scene of a memorable tragedy.

Glencoe was the scene of an appalling massacre of a Scottish clan by a group of (also Scottish) soldiers who had previously been amicably staying with the family, so Frazer's unconscious also has its little say here. A comparison meant to indicate geographical resemblance turns out to have associations of treachery and violence: not parricide, exactly, but a betrayal of hospitality, a turning on those who have given you shelter, that has become legendary.

And of course what is striking in the evocation of both the Scottish and the Greek setting is the combination of emptiness and crowding. No trace of human habitation, all desolation and silence. Yet in Scotland a whole clan crowds into a gorge to get killed, and in Greece the road is not large enough for father and son to pass each other in peace. The spot is fitting for tragedy not because it's lonely, but because it's narrow, because the whole world dwindles to this meeting. In the ancient texts the loneliness is important, but has a different meaning: not grandeur or the stranding of mere humans in an awesome nature, but a total lack of witnesses. There is no human community here, and therefore no one to see what happens: just father, son, and the father's retainers, one of whom escapes to tell the tale. Well, there is another meaning to the loneliness of the spot, and one very pertinent to Sophocles' version of the story. It would be a good place for highway robbery and murder, as Johannes Megas discovered more than two thousand years later, and it has probably seen plenty of otherwise unwitnessed violence in the meantime. This was the initial assumption in Thebes about the death of Laius, Oedipus' father. "They say that Laius was murdered by foreign/robbers at the fork where three paths meet." Is it possible that Laius was killed by robbers, and that Oedipus killed another man at the same spot? Our only assurance that the son killed the father is the matching of two memories: that of Oedipus and that of the retainer who escaped.

No, no, we have the oracles. They told us this was going to happen, and it did. What else is there to say?

Let's go back a little. How did these two men, father and son, come to be on this road, in this cleft? Laius, we are told in various versions, was on his way to Delphi, to inquire of the god about a previous oracle: the one that said his son would kill him. The oracle has different forms in different tellings, and its message wavers between what we might regard as a stiff warning and an irrefutable prophecy. "Do not have any children, for if you do, your son will kill you" is what the oracle says in its mildest mode. Laius took the warning seriously, but one night, overcome by drink or lust or both, he gave up his bid for abstinence and slept with his wife, Jocasta. The rest is history, or mythology, or a mixture of the two. In another version, the oracle simply says, "Your son will kill you." It doesn't leave any options, and it presupposes the existence of the future murderer. It doesn't say, for example, "Your son will kill you unless you kill him first," or "Your son will kill you in spite of your attempt to get rid of him, because piercing the child's ankles at birth and abandoning him on a wild hillside is not enough to do him in." And in yet another version of the prediction, the oracle offers Laius a piece of advice that is situated somewhere between warning and prophecy: "If you have a son, he will kill you." Since Laius had gone to consult the oracle about his and Jocasta's childlessness, this answer might well have seemed like a consolation, a good reason for not having the son he thought he wanted.

So Laius is now on the road to Delphi, a bit late in the day, we might think, to ask, as Jocasta herself says in Euripides' play *The Phoenician Women*, whether "the child he had exposed/were still alive." In this play, rather neatly, Oedipus is also on his way to Delphi, planning to ask about his parentage—he has begun to suspect that the people who have brought him up may not be his biological father and mother. The two men meet where the roads meet, and where their stories meet: the father needs to know whether the son is dead or alive, the son needs to know who his father is. Both questions are answered with a single murder, and without Delphi's actual help. It was enough for them to be on the road. The road itself was enough, or rather the meeting of the roads.

In most of the other versions of the story, though, the movements on the ground and in time are a little more complicated. In Sophocles, Laius is on his way to Delphi, but we don't know what he plans to ask. And Oedipus is on his way from Delphi, having asked the oracle about his parentage and received what seems to be an appalling non sequitur in response. He is told not who his parents are but what he will do to them: he will beget children by his mother and he will murder his father. Even in the midst of his horror Oedipus does take this to be some sort of answer to his actual question, and he not unnaturally assumes the targeted parents to be the ones he has had so far, not the ones he wonders whether he has got, so he doesn't return to Corinth, the home of Polybus and Merope, the people we know to be his foster parents. As he journeys, not going anywhere, he comes to the place in Phocis, the Cleft Way, the meeting of the three roads, and an extraordinarily violent encounter ensues. Here is how he tells it:

> I was coming down the road, near the meeting of the three roads, the fork—when I met the herald, and a man on board a chariot . . . The herald and the man in the chariot ordered me aside. The driver jostled me—I struck him in anger. The old man saw this, and as the chariot came beside me, he struck me with a double goad. I retaliated, and struck him with my stick. He rolled out of the chariot.
>
> And then I killed them all.

For a predestined meeting, this seems horribly random and contingent: harsh words, jostling, a scramble, rising anger, a small massacre. Daniel Mendelsohn, in an essay in *The New York Review of Books*, wittily writes of Oedipus' "problems with road rage." But of course this is just how prophecies work: through the contingent, not against it or in spite of it. And the true contingency here is not whether the two men, meeting, have to fight, but whether they have to meet. This is where the seemingly trivial question of the two actual itineraries looms very large. Couldn't father and son have missed each other, simply by arriving at the crossroads earlier or later? They could if they were not living out a tale of brutal destiny. But then the destiny begins to look like a matter of time as well as space. The three roads in Greece are also two lives converging at a particular moment. The interesting thing is not that the lives do converge, but that destiny has left any apparent loophole at all.

When two roads meet, we think of the place as a crossroads. There are two roads but four directions: the cross is either a plus sign or some version of an *x*; St. George's cross or St. Andrew's. When one road meets another, we call the place a junction or a fork, perhaps adding the letter *t* or the letter *y* for greater descriptive precision. Two roads turn into one, or one road divides into two. But how can three roads meet, as the story so insistently says? Well, if you are standing at the junction, there are three directions you could take, and this is the sense of the three roads, locally and idiomatically. For the traveler, there is only the one road, which is joined by another, as Frazer describes the Daulis–Delphi road being joined by the road from Thebes, or as the road from Thebes to Delphi, for Laius, would have been joined by the road from Daulis. Or there is one road that divides. This is how the road from Delphi would look to Oedipus when he arrived at the fork and could have gone to Daulis instead of Thebes.

The point of this cartographical pedantry is not to insist on literal geography but to let us see a logic, and to underline the role of time. The ideal oracle, the one that left no leakages of causality and could only ever have been right in one particular way, doesn't need three roads, and indeed couldn't use them. As the defeated detective says in Borges's story "Death and the Compass," even a labyrinth needs only one line. He is thinking of Zeno's paradox of an infinitely divided space. This oracle, similarly, strictly requires just the one road, coming and going; the road from Delphi to Thebes for Oedipus and the road from Thebes to Delphi for Laius. On this road father and son cannot fail to meet. As they can't fail to meet if Oedipus takes the fork for Thebes. In these conditions, two roads or one, the question of time is irrelevant, and destiny looks like an irresistible engine. But as soon as there is another road, as soon as Oedipus could take the road for Daulis rather than the road for Thebes, time is essential. The option in space, in other words, depends on an option in time, because if Laius arrives at the crossroads either when Oedipus does or before he does, the two will meet: either right there, or between Delphi and the crossroads. There is one chance of avoidance of the encounter, a road manifestly not taken, because the encounter swallows up Oedipus' choice. Just think. Laius, on his way to Delphi, slows down a little, sees no one at the crossroads in Phocis, keeps going, arrives at the oracle, asks his question. Oedipus, arriving at the same crossroads a while earlier, pauses. He is quite alone. He could go either way. He decides to go to Daulis. He never gets to Thebes.

Does Oedipus kill his father in this alternative story? Of course he does. The oracle is always right. The question is not whether it is right but how. What we and Oedipus need to know is which father, and what counts as a killing. In Sophocles, when Oedipus learns of the natural death of Polybus he rather desperately tries to take this as the fulfillment of the oracle. "I did not kill him—unless it was his longing for me that destroyed him. In that sense, yes, he might have died because of me." But Oedipus can't really believe this. He knows better. He has always known better. Yet in the absence of any other fulfillment, this would have had to do. Just as Oedipus could have killed Laius at any time or at any place, even if he had missed him at the crossroads. The crossroads is where the murder happened, and also the place where it might not have happened. That is what the crossroads is: an intersection of contingency and necessity, the site of the irrevocable deed that wasn't irrevocable until it occurred. The timing of the event, similarly, is perfect in its ghastly synchronization; so perfect that it reminds us how easily things could have been different, what a tiny adjustment or mismatch of time would have been needed.

In trivio mortuus

I used the word *trivial* a moment ago, not entirely without an ulterior motive. The *Oxford English Dictionary* offers the definition "placed where three roads meet" as an obsolete and rare usage—although it must be pretty literal in etymological terms. How do we get from there to "paltry, poor, trifling, inconsiderable, unimportant, slight," which now seem to be the main meanings of the word, along with its mathematical and philosophical sense: this equation (or argument) yields a result that is not trivial. Since crossroads are only as important as the traffic they take or the places they lead to, there must be a story lurking in the shift of connotations, and the story of Oedipus seems a good candidate. What is trivial is not the crossroads but the third road itself, the one that lingers in the narrative when two roads, or even one, would do. It becomes paltry because no one takes it; remains more than paltry because no one forgets it. And perhaps *trivial* itself, the word, works in this way, quietly remembering what it is telling us to forget, restoring shadowy substance to what it calls trifles.

The most extravagant instance I know of this effect occurs in Stravinsky's "opera-oratorio" *Oedipus Rex*. This is a spectacular setting of a text by Cocteau, based on his rather lurid understanding of Sophocles, or more precisely of a Latin version, by Jean Daniélou, of that text. Stravinsky chose Latin, he says, because he "had no notion of how to treat Greek musically (or Latin, Latinists will say, but there I did at least have my idea)." The Latin is a little peculiar, but when sung it sounds, as the English composer Judith Weir says, like "a sort of ancient Italian"—or we might also think, given the reminiscences of Verdi and even Bizet in the score, like some generic Romance language. For Cocteau, Sophocles' play is about a "trap" set for the hapless Oedipus by the "heartless gods," and the language of the Speaker who introduces and summarizes (in advance) each scene of the work is emphatic on this topic. But it's not at all clear that Stravinsky felt the same, and the music seems to tell another story, more in accord with Stravinsky's enigmatic remark about contrasting kinds of fate: "my audience is not indifferent to the fate of the person, but I think it far more concerned with the person of the fate . . ." This second person (this second fate) has a more complicated program than traps and heartlessness.

Our first encounter with the three roads, and the word *trivium* and its relatives, is in the Speaker's announcement of what Jocasta has to say about Laius' death. "She does not believe in oracles," he says. "She proves that oracles lie. For example, it was predicted that Laius would die at the hands of one of her sons; but Laius was killed by robbers at the intersection of the three roads from Daulis and Delphi." The Speaker pauses, and then continues (in all the

versions I've heard) in a voice that, like the libretto, is full of exclamation marks: "Trivium! Crossroads! Remember this word."

Judith Weir says she vividly recalls this moment from the very
first time she heard the work ("There is something exciting and
sinister about the language of the prologues themselves"), but she
also thinks there is something "quite outrageous" about this
scene—"it is almost absurdist theater, almost Ionesco." Jocasta says
Laius was killed at a crossroads; Oedipus thinks, Gosh, I killed a
man at a crossroads—I wonder if this could be the same fellow.
The complicated ironies of Sophocles, where an elaborate argument against oracles turns into a confirmation of the very oracle in
question, are flattened out into a kind of philosophical slapstick,
and, most important for our purposes, the word *trivium* becomes an
arcane warning, a magical memory cue, literally naming three ways
but dramatically canceling out all but one.

And yet the music makes all this play a little differently, and it's
worth pausing over what happens. Singing over oboes, piccolo,
clarinets, and strings, very fast, the winds playing triplets, Jocasta, a
mezzo-soprano, tells us that oracles prove nothing, and that they
always lie: "*Ne probantur oracula quae semper mentiuntur.*" When she
sings "Oracula, oracula" on the same note repeated eight times (or
seven times before moving to another note) she seems to be citing
some Italian drinking song like "Funiculi, funicula," although there
is an undertow of menace. And she offers her example of the lying
oracle, the one that said her son would kill Laius, when in fact he
was killed by robbers at a crossroads, to a tune of truly lyrical exal-
tation, as if this death were a kind of triumph. She then repeats her
claim that oracles prove nothing—the mood is slower, more meditative now, but still confident, and the musical line sounds like that
of one of the great arias out of *Carmen*. She is certainly heading for
a fall, and wrong in everything she sings, but the tone is light, and

"the person of the fate" seems more amused than anything else. But as she returns to her statement about the crossroads, in a long, looping phrase heralded by harp and piano arpeggios—*Laius in trivio mortuus*—the Chorus begins to get it and joins her, first the tenors, then the basses, then the tenors and basses in harmony, singing over and over again the word *trivium*. It's a wonderful, eerie moment, but it's not dramatic or ironic, it's pensive. This is no arcane warning, and there are no exclamation marks. These people are wondering whether they have really heard what they have just heard, and whether it means what they think it means, and the music mimes their hesitation but also their insistence: they are not going to let go. Jocasta, either still in her own musical world or in denial, continues to sing about the lying oracles, and then Oedipus, according to Stravinsky's instructions a light lyrical tenor rather than a "large operatic voice," quietly begins to announce his fear, and asks if he heard correctly. Did she say something about a place where three roads meet? *"Locuta est de trivio?"* Jocasta knows what is happening now, but insists again, at a furious pace, that oracles always lie, and then she and Oedipus sing an amazing duet, a sort of double, contradictory soundtrack, with Jocasta very agitated and Oedipus curiously calm, at least as far their musical allocations are concerned, and with a kind of lyrical undercurrent to the panic, as if the duet carries memories of their married love before things began to fall apart. Her dismissal of oracles turns into a warning against oracles (*"Cave oracula"*) while he sings of his new fear. She sings about going home and not asking any more questions, while he repeats his confession: he killed an old man at the place where three roads meet, *"Nam in trivio cecidi senem."* The scene ends with Oedipus' determination to know the whole truth. I will know, he says. *"Sciam!"*

For Jocasta the place where the roads meet was, initially, trivial in its modern meaning, and the music makes this very clear. It is the place where her husband was killed, and also the place where the oracle came unstuck, but it's only a place, and has no importance in itself. For Oedipus the site is a memory, a scene of old violence, and trivial for him too in one sense, since it is not at the front of his mind, and he has made no connection between this murder and his later life. It's the Chorus, with their slow, staggered entry and their wondering repetition of the single word, who realize that the trivium cannot be trivial. But even they cannot see that a place where three roads meet must also be a place where three roads diverge. That is left to Stravinsky, and the sheer range of his musical invention, of his wit and playful quotations and parodies, moves us worlds away from the drama of destiny that Cocteau had in mind, and that monumental productions of the work always insist on. Stravinsky is not just setting scenes from a tragedy to music, he is creating and questioning the very idea of tragedy through music, and the score tells many more stories than words can recount. A composer who can sound as cool as Bach and as airy as Bizet, while remaining entirely himself, has to have a fairly flexible idea of doom. It's clear that Jocasta is wrong to sing that oracles always lie, but her error doesn't prove they always tell the truth, and "the person of the fate" remains ambiguous.

The Golden Legend

In his commentary on Apollodorus, Frazer, thinking of Oedipus, tells us that "some parallel stories occur within the folk-lore of other peoples," and sends us to an Appendix, where he recounts parricide and incest tales culled from Finland, Ukraine, and Java and, most interestingly, informs us that in the European Middle Ages the story of Oedipus was associated with Judas Iscariot.

In the Finnish tale a wizard announces to a peasant couple that the son they are about to have will kill his father and marry his mother. Unable to bring themselves to kill the child once he is born, they wound him in the breast, tie him to a table, and throw him into the sea. He is rescued and educated by the abbot of a monastery, and when he grows up, he leaves the monastery to seek his fortune. Needless to say, he arrives in his native land, and asking for work, is told by a peasant's wife to guard their fields against robbers. Not knowing who is a robber and who is not, he kills the first man who enters the fields—the woman's husband, of course. This is unfortunate but unintentional, and so "after weeping and wailing," Frazer says, "the widow forgave the young man and kept him in her service, and indeed married him." Some time later she notices the scar on her new husband's breast and begins "to have her suspicions." "Inquiry elicited the fatal truth that her husband was also her son." The son is "conscience-stricken" and confesses to two monks in turn, but when each tells him no expiation is possible he kills them both. A third monk is more accommodating, and turns out to be right. The man is to wait for a sign—a black sheep will turn white and water will gush from a rock—and is finally forgiven, but not before he has killed a mysterious figure who has tried to arrest him. This last homicide is justified by the third monk on the curious grounds that the man who was killed had offended God more than the killer had.

The tale from Ukraine is very similar, substituting only a barrel for the table, some sailors for the abbot, and offering a different source for the scar. The signs here involve an apple tree and the imprisoning of the sinner in a well, and there is no fourth homicide. But this story too ends in forgiveness. The tale from Java, more sketchily presented by Frazer, involves a woman who unwittingly marries her son, who in turn unwittingly kills his father—a neat reversal of the usual order of things—and there is also an act of identification by means of a scar.

The Judas story begins like the Finnish and Ukrainian tales. A woman living in Jerusalem, married to "a certain Ruben Simeon, of the race of David," dreams of the birth of a son "who would be fatal to the family." She immediately discovers she is pregnant, but the parents can't bring themselves to kill the child when it arrives, so they put it in a little ark and commit it to the sea. The ark washes up on the shore of the island of Iscariot, where the queen of that island finds the child and adopts it. Soon afterward, she has a son of her own body, and the boys grow up together. Judas, predictably enough, doesn't behave well, and is reminded that he is a foundling. In a rage, he murders his brother and takes off for Jerusalem. Here he finds a job with the Roman governor, Pontius Pilate, and one day, caught stealing apples for his master from a neighbor's garden, kills that neighbor by hitting him on the head with a stone. Rather mysteriously, or perhaps just sarcastically, Pilate rewards Judas by giving him the neighbor's property, and the hand of the neighbor's widow in marriage. The neighbor and wife are, of course, Judas's biological parents, and a few marital conversations serve to make Judas and his new wife aware of this. "Struck with remorse and anxious to comfort his mother," Judas flings himself at the feet of Christ and becomes his disciple. Unfortunately, his history or his character or his greed is too much for him, and he betrays Christ to the high priests for the famed thirty pieces of silver.

"The monkish legend," Frazer says, "may have been concocted by a mediaeval writer who, having read the story of Oedipus, turned it to the purpose of edification by casting a still deeper shade of infamy on the character of the apostate and traitor." "Edification" is Frazer being ironic about religion, but of course the propaganda point is persuasive. The betrayer becomes a parricide and an incestuous husband as well. He even, in the earlier part of the story, becomes a version of Cain killing Abel. But then earlier still he was a version of Moses being found by the Egyptian princess, so an aura of good luck surrounds this story, as it does all the others, even if only as a prelude to ensuing disaster.

Oedipus, Cain, Moses, Judas—surely the story is stretched too far now, spread across more meanings than it can take? Well, they are quite different stories, and Christian guilt doesn't sit well with Greek disgrace or Jewish destiny. But remembering the three roads, we could say that the place where Laius and Oedipus meet, like the gardens and fields in the various medieval stories, is the exiguous region where all alternatives end, the place on the narrative map where the oracle will always turn out to be right. It's a powerful, almost irresistible story; that's why the third road is not trivial.

FIVE: WHAT ARE SUCH THINGS?

Everything that has happened is here
there is no road away from it

Seneca, *Oedipus*

The father's tale

The scene is a small town in Italy in the 1930s. The camera looks across a quiet square and glimpses, through a half-shuttered window, the birth of a child: our hero. Then we see the child in a meadow, surrounded by a group of happy young women playing. The camera pans uncertainly and at length across a row of trees, as if looking up from the baby's point of view. We see the baby being breast-fed, in large close-up. We see the mother's calm and beautiful face, although the baby is now out of view. Her face clouds with a faint worry, then assumes another, less readable expression. A string quartet plays in the soundtrack. The absence of the child from the frame begins to seem less like a convenience of filming and more like the secret meaning of the whole scene. This is not an image of a mother and a child, it is a dreamy, idealized image of a mother—the child is notional, implied, perhaps imaginary. Or, if you prefer, the child is not really at the invisible breast as he is supposed to be—he is behind the camera.

The father is a handsome young soldier. We see him staring intently at the child in a baby carriage, and a title card emphatically reveals his thoughts:

> Here he is, the child who is gradually going to take your place in the world . . . He will kill you. He is here for no other reason. He knows it. The first thing he will rob you of is your wife . . .

Of course the child doesn't know it, except in the father's grim fantasy, although the writer-director, in his screenplay, can't resist the possibility of a "mysterious understanding" between the two. A little later the father, after "long and tranquil" lovemaking with his wife, steps into the child's room and looks down into the cradle. In a high-angle close-up we see his hands grasping the child's feet, squeezing them, and in the film's single most brilliant move we cut instantly to a bare mountainside that turns out to be in Greece and nearly three thousand years away. The work is Pasolini's *Oedipus Rex*, released in 1969. The smoldering father is Luciano Bartoli, and the haunted and haunting mother is Silvana Mangano.

On the distant and ancient mountainside a Theban slave is carrying the baby Oedipus slung on a stick, like a deer or a pig, and is about to leave him there, where a Corinthian shepherd will find him. The story now unfolds as we know it, but following the temporal sequence of events and not, as in Sophocles, the sequence of their discovery. Oedipus becomes the adopted child of Polybus and Merope, king and queen of Corinth, grows up, has a quarrel with a companion, is insulted about his birth, and decides to go to Delphi to consult the oracle. The oracle tells him he will kill his father and make love to his mother, and Oedipus stumbles away into exile, heading in any direction except that of Corinth. On a narrow road he meets and kills Laius and all but one of his companions. He arrives in Thebes, defeats the Sphinx, and is rewarded with the hand of the widow queen. Years later a plague besets the town and the film now matches Sophocles' tragedy pretty directly.

Of course Pasolini has made many contributions to the old story, notably by prolonging it very clearly into the twentieth century and by making the father the first aggressor, if only in thought. Before we see anything in the film except the credits, we hear a military band on the soundtrack, festive, cheerful, slightly out of tune, and we are mentally somewhere in the provinces in Europe, say in the late nineteenth or early twentieth century. But the first image we see is an ancient, Greek-styled milestone with the name of Thebes on it in Italian: Tebe. Then we see a small town from a distance, then a square with modern houses and a statue that looks like a World War I memorial. Soon we get clothes and uniforms and an Italian flag, and might guess we were in the 1930s even if the screenplay didn't tell us. A little later the extraordinary cut I've described sweeps us back into ancient Greece, where we remain almost until the end of the film, when the blinded Oedipus, leaving Thebes, abruptly finds himself in a large modern city with a vast cathedral and, to judge by the cars and the fashions, in the 1960s, say around the time of the making of the film itself. Oedipus and the boy wander into the outskirts of the city, but then end up in the little square we know from the beginning of the movie, unchanged except for two small Fiats parked at the back of the frame. Oedipus finds his way to a meadow and, shot against the backdrop of the row of trees we have already seen, says he has returned to his point of origin: "I have come back. Life ends where it begins." This narrative shape not only universalizes Oedipus' story, stretches it from ancient Greece to modern Italy, but locates its beginnings in life itself: one has only to be born to fall into the story.

More important, though, the story begins with the father's jealousy rather than the father's oracle. We do learn of this oracle in the film. As in Sophocles, Jocasta tells Oedipus about it to illustrate the inaccuracy of prophecy. But the dramatic effect is simply to make Oedipus wonder about the unknown man he killed, not to return us to the time and context of the oracle itself. And there just is no oracle for the young father staring at his son in the baby carriage. Or rather the child himself is all the oracle the father needs. He is not told, like the ancient Laius, that his son will kill him, as if this were an exceptional danger and required exceptional measures. He already knows what the relations of sons and fathers are like, as if he has completely internalized not only the story of Laius and Oedipus but the full set of stories of Uranus and Chronos and Zeus, where fathers eat or imprison their sons, and the sons escape these fates only by trickery and violence and with some assistance from their mothers. Oedipus in this version is not the hero of an exceptional and horrific story; he is the ordinary child of his father's hate and his mother's love, anyone's (male) child. The savage myth that occupies most of the film is the backstory, the explicit, lurid old tale we may not always recognize in its muted, polite, modern forms, but is there all the time anyway. When Oedipus insists, very much against the drift of the whole film, that everything that has happened was "willed, not imposed by destiny," he may have stumbled on the wrong truth. He didn't do much willing, but his parents did.

Pasolini's ancient Greece is very much that of the contemporary anthropologist rather than of the traditional classical scholar. He shot most of the film in Morocco, concentrating on burnt-out landscapes, dusty roads, and small tribal gatherings—the suggestion being, I take it, that living mythology is closer to us than we think. Corinth and Thebes are more like intricate desert fortresses than the cities we usually associate with those names. The people seem to be nomadic in spite of their city settlements, and they live much of their life outdoors. Being a king seems only a small notch up from a being a peasant, a matter of an ornate headdress or crown, and the right to give orders. And in such a world the oracle at Delphi doesn't inhabit a splendid temple of which the remains are even now still to be seen, or enjoy its fabulous location. There is no temple, only a tree casting a wide shade, a cluster of people, perhaps priests, perhaps just hangers-on, and the pythia, a large woman who orders food and messily stuffs rice into her mouth before pronouncing. She wears an extraordinary double helmet with two caricatural faces one on top of the other, and straw descending from it to cover most of her face. The suggestion is of witchcraft rather than religion, and of Africa rather than Greece. In the screenplay Pasolini has her deliver her verdict on Oedipus "in a species of dumb rage": "As he is doubtless guilty and loathsome to the god, he must therefore be just as loathsome to herself." But in the film, much more interestingly, she finds a ghastly amusement in her knowledge and laughs out loud, as if the prophecy, once spoken, broke the bounds of mere morality and religion. Oedipus himself almost laughs at the news, as if it couldn't be anything other than a joke. After all, he came only to ask a question, in this version, not so much about his parentage as about a dream he has had.

We don't know what the dream was, only that it was horrible and he can't recall it. He wanted to ask the oracle about the dream, to get the oracle to tell him, as he says, "what I can't remember." In Sophocles we don't know exactly what Oedipus asked the oracle, but we assume it is a question about his parents and therefore, effectively, a question about his identity. On this reading the oracle didn't evade the question, it answered it precisely: you are the person who will kill his father and marry his mother, that is who you are, that is what being Oedipus means. But to ask the oracle about a hidden memory is quite different, and if the oracle is telling the truth, the horror is double: these terrible things will happen and they have already happened in your mind. Later in the film Oedipus tells the story of his visit to the oracle, following the version that occurs in Sophocles, not the one we have seen, and the slippage is revealing. Oedipus, like his father, has an oracle in his head, a story of rivalry and love and death, quite independent of any external oracle he may consult. Does this mean that Pasolini's Oedipus, unlike most others, does have an Oedipus complex? It seems so, but the film as a whole suggests something else. It suggests that Oedipus, like many of us, has bad dreams, and that it takes a lot of work, on the part of fate, chance, the gods, or some other scriptwriter, to turn these dreams into lived facts.

There is a beautifully balanced image of the work needed, and the way it makes destiny look both inevitable and full of holes, in a game Oedipus plays with chance. Having heard the oracle's prediction and having exchanged his uncertain near-laughter for complete disarray and constant sobbing, he arrives at a milestone, or fork in the road. He covers his eyes, spins round several times, and continues in the direction he is facing when his spin ends. He does the same thing at three more consecutive forks in the road. This gives him four chances of not going to Thebes, three more than in any other version I know. But how do we read the result? As destiny annexing chance triumphantly, again and again, making Thebes the only place he can possibly get to? Thebes is the only place he can get to in this story, and certainly Pasolini wants us to be tempted by this interpretation, and perhaps to fall into it. But that's because we know the story, and we can take the repeated options and the abandonment of conscious choice in another way. The odds on Oedipus taking the road to Thebes are the same at each spin, they neither increase nor decrease. This is a perfect instance of undefeated chance. It's not destiny or prophecy that leads Oedipus into a world of horror, but sheer randomness, a crazy connection of dream and accident. The only patterns here are those made by chaos itself—a story we may well find scarier than the one about the prescient and malevolent gods.

Home again

"Trivialis," Roland Barthes reminds us, "is the etymological attribute of the prostitute who waits at the intersection of the three ways." Barthes's image of the writer is that of someone who waits at the crossroads of other people's languages. Waits and resists and persists. The writer's position is "trivial in relation to the purity of doctrine." Power is never trivial, and that is why certain trivialities may be intensely political. There is no prostitute (that we know of) on the road to Delphi, and no writer either. But there is the doctrine of the oracle and there is the road that could (but doesn't) contradict it. There are two men and an absent woman who will turn out to have been married to both of them. Perhaps a wife, as distinct from a prostitute, is a person who is not waiting at the intersection of the three ways, but is waiting all the same. At home. She *is* home, like Penelope, or in a less friendly version, Clytemnestra. Like Jocasta.

In another text and in a Lacanian mood, Barthes wonders whether all narratives don't "lead back to Oedipus." "Isn't storytelling always a way of searching for one's origin, speaking one's conflicts with the Law, entering into the dialectic of tenderness and hatred?" The father is the law, and Barthes is ironically mourning the old man's death and the new liberation of the 1960s: "We dismiss Oedipus and narrative at one and the same time: we no longer love, we no longer fear, we no longer narrate"—he is writing in 1973. "Death of the Father would deprive literature of many of its pleasures. If there is no longer a Father, why tell stories?" What's a father for, we might ask, if not to be killed? And what's a mother for, if not to be married—doubly married, always, to both son and father?

Freud's reading of the Oedipus story, much more subtle than it is usually taken to be, suggests not only that we all wish to kill our fathers and sleep with our mothers—Freud and the Greeks think of sons, but I don't see why daughters shouldn't have a shot too—but that we misrecognize these wishes because of our repulsion from them. "Horror and self punishment" follow, he says, not because these are primary impulses but because we can't bear to think of what is primary, and what our very socialization as domesticated creatures causes us to deny. It's fashionable to say these days, with Jean-Pierre Vernant and Jacques Schérer, that Oedipus himself "doesn't have the slightest Oedipus complex." He has no wish to sleep with his mother and he has no reason to believe that his mother is the woman he marries. I would think, myself, that a person who violently slays an older man on the road might not be entirely free of the other piece of the complex, but let's say there is nothing "Oedipal" about this bit of Oedipus' story either. There is no argument against Freud here. Freud is not suggesting that Oedipus has an Oedipus complex. Oedipus "merely shows us the fulfilment of our childhood wishes," and that is why, according to Freud, destiny in Sophocles' text lies not in the will of the gods but in the ancient and abiding psychological material the play works on. We might add that it's not Oedipus himself who keeps rewriting and restaging this story, it's us, and every version reenacts the recognition and misrecognition of the basic wish—nowhere better than in the insistence, in its way perfectly correct, on Oedipus' own exemption from it. We don't have to believe in the theory to see how many stories it generates, both in literature and in real life, and how hard it would be, in many cases, to do without it. If not science, it is a major myth, and if all narratives don't lead back to Oedipus—this seems like a bit of rhetorical dazzle rather than a real proposition—a great many narratives do find their way to him, by one road or another.

Here is Freud's summary of the Oedipus tale:

Oedipus, son of Laius, King of Thebes, and of Jocasta, was exposed as an infant because an oracle had warned Laius that the still unborn child would be his father's murderer. The child was rescued, and grew up as a prince in an alien court, until, in doubts as to his origin, he too questioned the oracle and was warned to avoid his home since he was destined to murder his father and take his mother in marriage. On the road leading away from what he believed was his home, he met King Laius and slew him in a sudden quarrel. He came next to Thebes and solved the riddle set him by the Sphinx who barred his way. Out of gratitude the Thebans made him their king and gave him Jocasta's hand in marriage. He reigned long in peace and honor, and she who, unknown to him, was his mother bore him two sons and two daughters. Then at last a plague broke out and the Thebans made enquiry once more of the oracle. It is at this point that Sophocles' tragedy opens. The messengers bring back the reply that the plague will cease when the murderer of Laius has been driven from the land . . . The action of the play consists in nothing other than the process of revealing, with cunning delays and ever-mounting excitement—a process that can be likened to the work of a psychoanalysis—that Oedipus himself is the murderer of Laius, but further that he is son of the murdered man and of Jocasta. Appalled at the abomination which he has unwittingly perpetrated, Oedipus blinds himself and forsakes his home. The oracle has been fulfilled.

This account is elegant, lucid, and accurate, and I imagine Lévi-Strauss, and Freud himself, would not call it an "instance"—the

Freudian instance would start with the psychoanalytic reading. But there is already quite a bit of interpretation here. First, Freud is following Sophocles—that is, accepting as his text Sophocles' powerful reading of the material—so that the oracle given to Laius is quite emphatic and clear, doesn't leave any of the options open in other versions of the story. And then, more subtly, Freud invents his own version of what the oracle said to Oedipus. We don't know, even in Sophocles, what "doubts as to his origin" Oedipus had, or how those doubts arose. We know he was insulted by a drunken man at a banquet in Corinth, who called him a bastard—literally said he was not his father's son—but we don't know where this person got the idea or why Oedipus took the insult seriously. It seems quite likely that in ancient Greece as in modern England and America the idea of illegitimacy could be used just as an insult, without any serious thought of anyone's lineage. However, Oedipus was perturbed and spoke to Polybus and Merope, the people he thought were his parents, the people who in all but the biological sense *were* his parents, and although he received an answer meant to reassure him, he wasn't reassured. Perhaps because Polybus and Merope were too visibly distressed: "They were furious at the man who had let such words escape him." This is how Oedipus continues the story when he tells it to Jocasta and the elders of Thebes:

> They reassured me, but I was vexed—it remained—the insult rooted, grew. And unknown to my mother and father, I went to the oracle.

> Apollo sent me away ignorant as to that matter, but he brought forth terrible utterances concerning me. He said that I would lie with my mother, that my family would be abhorrent to the sight of men, and that I would be the murderer of my own father.

Literally, the oracle says "of the father who had begotten me," as if it had another father in mind as well. But the chief point, of course, is that it doesn't tell Oedipus to "avoid his home." It doesn't mention home at all, and the assimilation of parents to home, the equation of home with parents, gives a wonderfully late-bourgeois feel to the tragedy, as if the scene had shifted not just to Vienna but to Ibsen's Norway or Eugene O'Neill's America. Home is where the Freudian heart is.

Freud's other contribution to the tale—the comparison of Oedipus' inquiry to the practice of psychoanalysis—does take us closer to the more ordinary idea of a "version," although we need to note that in this case, as in Freud's own, the analyst and the patient are the same person. In this light the unbearable verbal quibbles that swarm in the first part of the play, when Oedipus speaks "as a stranger to this story, a stranger to these events," or offers to avenge the slaying of Laius "as if he were my own father," and much more in this vein, cease to be the broad dramatic ironies they look like at first glance—appealing to the audience's knowledge of what Oedipus doesn't yet know—and become something subtler, and more frightening. They begin to look like the performance, the string of free associations almost, of a mind that both knows and doesn't know what it is really thinking; that stumbles into terrible truths as if they were puns, as if they were lurking not in a destiny or the foreknowledge of the gods, but in the words themselves, the combinatory chances of language. In this reading Oedipus would not have an Oedipus complex, in the sense of having unconsciously longed to do the things he has blindly done. But part of his mind would know that he was not a stranger in Thebes, and would place him, the killer of a man on the road to Thebes, on his own (repressed) list of suspects. This thought, or a relative of it, also occurs to the poet Gjertrud Schnackenberg, who sees the whole story of Oedipus as somehow waiting—for whom?—in the Greek alphabet.

I rescued the child

In Schnackenberg's book-length poem, *The Throne of Labdacus*, the story of the afflictions of Oedipus occurs in three places and three time zones: on Olympus, as the god Apollo tunes his lyre and composes the harrowing tale; in Thebes and Corinth and on the road to Delphi, as Oedipus lives out the marked events of his life; and in Athens, where an audience attends the first performance of Sophocles' play *Oedipus the King*. Various translations and transitions have to be imagined because the gods don't speak Greek (they speak the language of the gods), and Apollo is not writing a play. Oedipus isn't living a play either, he is walking into a destiny. But the play is already lurking in the god's music; lurking in Oedipus' travails too, the way the tale of Oedipus itself, the poem suggests, lies hidden in the Greek alphabet, waiting for its day and the right arrangement of letters. Stéphane Mallarmé once suggested that everything in the world exists in order to end up in a book. The proposition is pretty fanciful as it stands, but of course it is the case that many things in the world do end up in books (or in scripts, songs, performances), whatever their original purpose was, and it is possible that Mallarmé's French phrase—*"pour aboutir à"*—doesn't really mean "in order to end up in" but something like "finally comes down to." The last section of Schnackenberg's poem is called "The Premiere of Oedipus," but in it we still hear the squeaking of the pegs of the god's lyre as he tunes it before the whole story starts, and we hear the almost indistinguishable squeaking of the wheels of the cart that carries Laius to his meeting with Oedipus on the road. Three times, and too many destinies.

But the poem, like the god, chooses among these destinies, and its last words are: "I rescued the child." The poem is quoting itself at this point, and the god is making his own the words of the shepherd who found the maimed infant Oedipus on the snowy hillside near Thebes.

> I knew what the god had said.
> I covered my eyes with my hands.
>
> But there are things we do
> Not for the sake of the gods
>
> But for other men . . .
>
> At the sight of the infant's gaze
> I was riveted, chosen, beguiled.
>
> I knew what the oracle said.
> And I rescued the child.

This emphasis does very interesting things to our sense of the story. Knowing how it ends, we may feel we should say the child is saved in order to end up—*pour aboutir à*—killing his father and sleeping with his mother. The shepherd's kindness is a mere wrinkle or swerve in the longer tale that not only doesn't alter anything but ensures the fulfillment of the oracle's prediction. The shepherd's kindness puts everything back where it was, but in disguise, so to speak. It's as if Laius and Jocasta had not even thought of killing their child but had somehow just lost him. But seen from almost any other moment in the story—whether in the god's time or in play time or in Oedipus' lived time—things look very different. We remember that Laius was on his way to Delphi to ask the oracle precisely about this child—"Coming to inquire about the fate/Of the three-day-old he put aside," as the poem puts it. The scuffle on the road and Laius' death are the oracle's answer to this question; he didn't have to ask it, and he didn't have to reach Delphi to get an answer. So for Laius the saved child is a failed intention, the mark of an incomplete flight from a threat. For Oedipus himself his rescue is who he is, not only because he would literally have no life otherwise, but also because his maiming gives him his name—*Oedipus*, meaning "swollen-foot"—and because his foundling status makes him the child of no one and therefore potentially the child of everyone. For the shepherd himself the saving of the child is an immediate ethical decision, made in full knowledge of the oracle and the god's notional will. The shepherd chooses what is good in the present moment against the horrors of a past promise or a future possibility. But the very same words sound coolly cynical when they are echoed by the god,

The god who, delicately,

As if plucking a single fate
From a heap of entangled fates,

Touches a string and replies:
I rescued the child.

It's as if the god is saying he can do good deeds too—as if he didn't know where this particular good deed would take him and his song. The shepherd's bravery becomes the god's mockery.

But is it only mockery? Since the god and the shepherd have the last word in the poem, and the poem itself is far from cynical, we may need to think of the child's rescue in another way. Oracles do come true, the poem says, but in the past;

And not to fulfill a law. There is no need.
The laws are *there*, fulfilled or unfulfilled.

The god simply says,
I saw what I saw—

And again:

some blame the ignorance
Of Oedipus, some blame the gods' omniscience;

For some, the tragedy unfolds without a moral—
No how or why; no spelling out of fate

Or sacrifice or punishment . . .

And for others it is only an ancient folktale
About a guiltless crime:

Not a judgment, not a warning,
Not an example, not a command—

Merely a tale in which neither the gods
Nor the human ones can claim that they meant

To harm or to save, to kill or to stay their hands.
Merely a piling up of consequence,

With a bleeding-through of episodes and accidents.

These different assessments of the story are not just alternatives—they call out for and rectify each other. We blame Oedipus or the gods because we have to blame someone, because we can't accept the idea of a world so fully dedicated to the rule of crippling accident, the mere "piling up of consequence." We can bear the idea of chance in all kinds of things, large and small, but here, where what piles up is murder, incest, blinding, and suicide, we need a *story*, and if it's all accident, if none can claim to have meant to do anything, there just is no story. And yet blame doesn't seem the right story; and fate and sacrifice and punishment belong to a world where the maps are clearer, and where intentions can be firmly connected to deeds. "What are such things," Schnackenberg asks,

> What are such things, that even the gods can't repair?
> What are the gods, who can't repair such things?

In this context, the rescue of a child, and the claim to have rescued the child, the willingness to accept the act and perform it again in speech, might be the one unambiguous gesture in the whole story, and neither the horrible plot nor the god's mockery can blur the moral clarity of the shepherd's choice, his yielding to what Brecht, in the context of the saving of another child, called "the terrible temptation to goodness."

Oedipus in New York

For a series of evenings in September and October 1998, an actress stepped out into the stage space of the Blue Light Theater in New York's East Village, and began what looked at first sight like a scene from Euripides' *Hippolytus* or Racine's *Phèdre*. Here was an attractive, desperate woman racked by a love she could scarcely name, and certainly felt she should not allow herself. But didn't we catch the name? Weren't we listening? Or did we think it didn't matter? This woman calls herself Merope, and her companion calls her the same, several times.

Merope? Merope, as we have seen, is the person Oedipus thought was his mother, the person who was his mother for many years, the person who brought him up. She is the wife of Polybus and the Queen of Corinth. But she is also at this moment a metaphorical cousin of Phaedra, in love with a man young enough to be her son; with a young man who thinks he is her son, although she knows he is not. Hence her despair, and her horror at herself. Her crime is still only a crime of thought and feeling, and the crime is adultery, not incest. Or not exactly incest. But then something astonishing happens. Oedipus has gone to consult the oracle at Delphi, and now returns, with terrible news. He is to kill his father and marry his mother. He took neither of the roads he could have taken in Sophocles or Aeschylus; he took the one road he never traveled in any version of his story before this: the road back to Corinth. The audience, who so far have been invited to concentrate only on Merope in her emotional agony, are likely to think the oracle has granted her hidden wish, whatever it had in mind for Oedipus. And of course Merope thinks this too, although she can scarcely believe her ears. Oedipus, wiser at this moment than at any later stage in the play, says "the gods have told us our fate for a reason." They want us to choose, he says. "The gods have revealed our fate so that we can become human." Merope, horrified both at the possible fulfillment of her wish and at the thought that her wish might slip away after all, says, "The gods tell us our future so that we can premeditate our crimes."

This magnificent line, and everything else I have just described, appears in a play by the American writer Dare Clubb. It is called

Oedipus, and works through, in a series of brilliantly tangled and topsy-turvy moves, all the chief elements of the Oedipus story: exposed child, adoption, exile, the Sphinx, riddles, suicide, blindness, warring sons. In the performance I saw, Frances McDormand was Jocasta as well as Merope, and Billy Crudup was Oedipus, a man lapsing into innocence as his crimes piled up around him. When he says to Merope that the gods are perhaps mistaken in their prophecy about him, because they don't know everything, she tells him it is sheer impiety to entertain such doubts. "You can't fight the gods!" she says. She instructs him to leave, presumably expecting him to stay. He asks her if she is sure about the will of the gods. "Is there anything about the divinities that you doubt?" She says no. Oedipus, feeling appropriately rebuked and having no idea of her feelings for him, says he finds her commitment to the gods terrifying, but accepts its rightness. He goes into the palace and kills the father he loves: if this is his fate, he might as well get it over with.

Merope is horrified but Oedipus is now entirely serene. "How could I presume to think that I knew better than the gods?" he says, and he is ready to move to the other part of the prophecy: "For once, mother, let's do exactly what we want." Merope says, "I don't want this," and she doesn't. But of course part of her does, and Oedipus is not to be distracted by mere morality or personal preferences. "For once, mother, let's do something we don't want to do!" Merope gives in, and they leave the stage. A while later, Oedipus wants to marry his mother, not just sleep with her, because that is what the oracle said was to happen, and Merope, in the midst of so many disasters, makes one more dreadful mistake. "I can't marry you, Oedipus!" she says. "I'm not your mother!" There is a grimly intricate humor here, a twist on the logic of the old tale. She couldn't marry him if she was his mother—or not without committing incest—and she can't marry him if she is not, because a marriage without incest is not his fate. Then she tells him that Polybus is not his father, and the whole ghastly error is clear to him. Whatever the truth of the oracle, the story it foretold hasn't started yet. Oedipus has killed an innocent man and slept with . . . a woman. "So then," he says with unconscious cruelty, "you're truly not my mother? You're just a woman?"

There is no way back for Oedipus, of course. You can't abandon your fate just because you got it wrong once, and the rest of the play concerns Oedipus' rather Brechtian adventures in quest of his biological father and mother, the ones who gave him to a shepherd, the ones who abandoned him. There are many surprising moments and many fine lines, but I wish to insist here only on the work's original contribution to oracle theory. If an oracle is a form of words, and the fulfillment of an oracle consists in the match— some kind of match—between those words and an event, in the future or the present or the past, then the ultimate question about an oracle, as we have seen, is not whether it tells the truth but what we will allow to count as the truth. It is a matter of interpretation but above all a matter of reference, of how a particular piece of language hooks on to the world, in Wittgenstein's phrase. In Herodotus, there is a lovely instance of a man dreaming he has slept with his mother, but he doesn't think the dream indicates anything resembling a desire to sleep with his mother. He is an exile, he assumes the mother in question is his homeland, and he takes the dream as a promise of return. Similarly in Ovid, after a flood has destroyed the populations of the world, the one remaining couple, Deucalion and Pyrrha, consult the oracle of Themis. They are told to throw the bones of her mother behind them. They think, rightly, that the goddess cannot be recommending such impiety and therefore cannot be speaking literally. They decide that the mother in question must be the earth, and that her bones must be the stones that are lying around. They throw the stones over their shoulders, and a new race of humans is born from them.

These are success stories in interpretation, examples of catching the right reference, but in Herodotus, again, there is a spectacular instance of a mistake in this territory. This is an issue of general divination rather than of oracle interpretation in particular, but the failure is illuminating, and generates what is surely one of the funniest and most sinister throwaways in antiquity. Astyages, the king of Persia, has a pair of dreams that his Magi interpret to mean that Cyrus, Astyages' grandson, will one day become king in his place, and will rule all of Asia. Astyages orders the baby to be killed, and at one point it looks as if Cyrus is going to be exposed on a hillside and allowed to die, like Oedipus. But because of a switch with a stillborn infant, Cyrus survives and grows up in a village not far from the capital. When he is ten years old he is playing with his friends, and as part of their game they choose him as their king. One of the boys complains about the play-king's overzealous royal manner—he has his playmate whipped for disobedience—and Cyrus is brought before Astyages. The king is "visited by a kind of recognition," and establishes, by dint of a series of threats and inquiries, that this is indeed his grandson. He asks his Magi what it means that the boy should have been king in a game, and whether this counts as the fulfillment of the dream prophecy. They say, "If he is alive, and has already been a king by no contrivance of your own, then you may feel confident about him and need not lose heart. He has been king once and will never be so again. Even our regular prophecies are sometimes fulfilled in apparently small incidents, and as for dreams—they often work out in something quite trivial." "That is very much my opinion," Astyages says, adopting the confident tone that in Herodotus always signals some terrible error is brewing. Sure enough, grown to manhood, Cyrus raises an army against Astyages, and this is where the fabulous throwaway comes, as discreet and as absolute as anything in Virginia Woolf or Gabriel García Márquez. "Having first impaled the Magi who had advised him to let Cyrus go," Astyages arms all the Medes he can find and sets off for his last battle and decisive defeat.

In Sophocles and all the earlier versions of the story, Oedipus goes to Delphi because he fears Polybus and Merope may not be his parents, and he flees Corinth because he still thinks they are. The question of his parentage, and therefore of who he is, is central, and is answered by the intricate plot. The question of reference is settled by cross-examination of witnesses and recourse to memory, and results in Jocasta's suicide and Oedipus' self-blinding. In Dare Clubb's play Oedipus doesn't doubt that Polybus and Merope are his parents until he has killed him and slept with her, and he doesn't doubt that his biological parents are the only point of reference of the oracle. Like all Oedipuses he finds his identity in his frightful destiny, but rather than stumble into it he goes out to look for it, as if it were a vocation rather than a doom. He doesn't honor the gods or confirm their predictive powers, he creates the gods, they are his dogged desire to become what they said he was, and the fact that he has plausibly fulfilled the whole story before he even starts on his travels is irrelevant to him. He doesn't understand the problem of reference, or that reference could be a problem, and when Jocasta, late in the play, sounding very much like the Oracle in the Wachowski brothers' film *The Matrix*, tells him how the prophecy actually works, he initially dismisses her insight as merely a matter of words. What Jocasta says is that all prophecies contain, often invisibly but still substantively, the words *or not*. You will kill your father—or not. You will sleep with your mother—or not. In this form prophecies are invariably true, but not neutral, because they have named an agenda, and they may well have elided the escape clause. This is the Oedipal dilemma: not whether killing your father and sleeping with your mother is your destiny but what to do with the story once it has been proposed to you as an identity. Dare Clubb's Oedipus keeps running into people who think they recognize his type. "I'm not a type," he says repeatedly, eagerly asserting his individualism. "What is a life without a fate?" he asks, meaning a fate that would separate him from all other men. "I am not yet who I am," he cries out. What the play finally suggests, though, is that a deep and determining aversion to being a type, a longing for a fate that is all your own, is a form of the sleep of reason, and breeds monsters.

SIX: SIBYLS AND POETS

But if these words are heard
They will not be believed
I Ching

Sibylline

Patrick and I were sitting in a Paris café, going over the French text of a lecture I was due to give a little later in the day. Near the end was a phrase I was particularly fond of—I suppose because I liked its air of casual indirection, all the things it was not saying about not saying things. The phrase was, "according to a rather cryptic stage direction," "*selon une indication de scène assez cryptique.*" Patrick, a Frenchman in spite of his name, said, "Sibylline," pronounced "sibylleen." I said, "What?" "*Selon une indication de scène assez sibylline,*" he said. "Much better, much more idiomatic." *Cryptic* is fine in English, I think, but *sibylline* is wonderful in French, and the phrase has hung in my mind ever since, like a fragment of a tune or a piece of advice, even though I have long forgotten the stage direction itself, and most of what my lecture was about.

The hissing of the *s*'s is part of what is so appealing about Patrick's French phrase, a touch of snakiness and sneakiness in the language itself. But the general flow of the syllables is important too, as if being sibylline were a smooth and easy affair, a matter of casual elegance, where being cryptic is more like hard work, a matter of difficult transpositions and conscientious secrecy. This may be partly a question of French and English cultures, but both words come from another language and have ancient backgrounds. *Sibylline* suggests a sinuous mystery; to understand it you would have to hear its music, or catch its undertow. *Cryptic* foregrounds the act of hiding rather than what is hidden; to understand what is going on you would need to crack its code.

Cassandra's gift

Scholars distinguish very carefully between pythias and sibyls. Pythias answered particular questions, were literally inspired by the god, and spoke in his name and person. When they said "I" they meant "he." Sibyls offered generalized predictions, usually of disaster, and although provoked by the god, they spoke in their own name and person. It may be that these grammatical differences will seem smaller to us than they do to most scholars, and the distinction won't always hold. It certainly suffered a blow when the Sibyl of Cumae showed up in Rome offering to sell nine books of oracles to the ruler. Still, there are other, enduring differences, above all in the matter of dialogue.

Cassandra, the unhappy daughter of Priam, king of Troy, is the earliest prototype of the sibyl. Her predictions are more specific than most, but they unequivocally speak of disaster, and she is not prompted by anyone's question. Indeed, she is in one sense the perfect opposite of an oracle, and for this reason her story is immensely instructive. Not all oracles are ambiguous, but many of them are. Almost all oracles are taken to be truthful, even if difficult of interpretation. Cassandra's prophecies are entirely unambiguous, but no one believes her. This is not an accident, a matter of bad luck or incidental skepticism on the part of her hearers. It is part of the structure of her story: she has been blessed with fore-sight, cursed with the disbelief of others. She will always tell the truth that no one will ever hear: a bitter parable about the proxim-ity and distance of knowledge.

What exactly is this parable saying to us? Let's go back a little into the story. There are various versions. In one, Cassandra, along with her brother Helenus, receives the gift of prophecy when both of them are children and are licked by a snake in the temple of Apollo. In another version, Apollo himself gives Cassandra the gift of prophecy as part of his amorous campaign. But then she refuses his advances, either because she has changed her mind or because she didn't at first understand where the god's kindnesses were head-ing. In all versions of the story Apollo gets angry and annuls the gift, whatever the timing of its arrival. Well, he annuls the gift in a special sense. Although he doesn't—and perhaps can't—remove it, he makes it empty or useless, like a stopped check or a currency that is no longer recognized. But invalid checks and currency are only paper and coins, mere mementos, and the gift of prophecy in this story, particularly the gift of accurate prophecy, becomes a very special kind of curse, because it retains all its meaning, loses only its use. The god knows just what he is doing. He continues to lend his powers to Cassandra because he knows that those pow-ers will become a torment, that possessing them in vain is worse than losing them. How can he guarantee that no one will believe her? The short answer is that he is a god and can do what he likes. The longer, more interesting answer is that he must know how to program the failure to persuade into the message itself, that he has granted to Cassandra's speech a magical infliction, a signifying de-fect. We could imagine this as a form of autism. She hears herself speak clearly, but others hear only gibberish. Or she speaks her na-tive language to people who can't understand it. Or best of all, she speaks quite clearly in words everyone understands, but some curious, creepy quality in the total speech situation means the communication fails. Her hearers understand her, but also don't understand her—as if she were speaking in code when she isn't.

Or they think she is speaking metaphorically, or taking part in a play, when she is saying everything in deadly, literal earnest. There is a situation not unlike this in Luis Buñuel's late film *The Phantom of Liberty*, where a little girl is reported missing from a French school. The parents rush to the place, the headmistress explains what has happened, and they check out the classroom. The little girl is there after all, and answers to her name, but everyone proceeds as if she were still missing. A policeman is called, and takes down a description of the missing girl. He looks at the girl herself as he does so, and even, dizzyingly, asks if he can take the girl with him when he goes to look for her. This is a joke in Buñuel's best deadpan absurdist manner, and we should not overload it with interpretation. But it has a haunting pathos about it, undiminished by our recurring laughter, and it exemplifies perfectly a conversation in which all the ordinary conditions of communication are present, and inadequate. In twentieth-century France, where the film is set, the joke has mainly an antibureaucratic, even antiverbal tinge: these people are so hooked on the report of a missing person that they can't see the person herself, can't allow her mere presence to redeem her from the overpowering category she has been assigned to. But in other times and places we might think of the little girl as a small sister of Cassandra. She says "I am here," a statement that is perceptibly true, and that everyone understands, but no one pays any attention to her.

In her most famous performance in world history, Cassandra appears not in a film but in a play. Aeschylus' trilogy, *The Oresteia*, dramatizes the return of Agamemnon from Troy, his murder by his wife Clytemnestra, her murder by their son Orestes, and Orestes' subsequent madness and acquittal by the goddess Athena, after a hung jury in Athens. In the first play the returning king shows up in Argos with Cassandra, daughter of his defeated enemy, as his trophy and presumably his mistress. The stories about Cassandra, incidentally, are extraordinarily cruel, even misogynistic. She may have refused a god, but she wasn't given a chance to refuse Agamemnon, and another part of her tale has her raped by Ajax in a temple in Troy. Are the stories exacting vengeance because she refused a god, or because she knows too much?

In Aeschylus, Cassandra is silent as long as Agamemnon and Clytemnestra are present. Agamemnon says she is to be cared for, and both Clytemnestra and the Chorus tell her to go inside the palace for a ritual bath of welcome. In the face of Cassandra's silence, Clytemnestra wonders whether "the girl" is "crazed with shock?"

> Or grief? Or is she an idiot?
> Or is she locked up
> In some twittering language
> Like a strange bird, brought in a cage?

After a few more reflections—perhaps the girl is deaf and dumb or perhaps she's mad—Clytemnestra leaves the scene. Cassandra's first words are a scream addressed to a god and a goddess, to Apollo and to Earth, and the one word she says is no. Then she becomes more articulate and asks what "dreadful place" the god has brought her to, since this is "a house that hates God./A house that God hates." She has picked up the scent of the old murders in this family, reminding us that magical knowledge of the past can be just as important as magical knowledge of the future, although the Chorus rather dryly says, "We don't need a prophet/To tell us this story." But then Cassandra starts to see other things: a bath, a net, a knife, a body, pouring blood. She is seeing Agamemnon's death at the hands of Clytemnestra, and her own death too:

And I am there with him . . .
I roll in his blood.
Carved by the same blade.

Questioned by the Chorus, Cassandra finally begins to talk to them, tells them her story, how she correctly prophesied the fall of Troy and was not believed. The Chorus is now more impressed by Cassandra's knowledge of the ancient local murders, and tells her that although the god is punishing her through the disbelief of others they "believe every word you say"—because they know those words are true, and the events have already happened. They still don't believe—or don't get—what Cassandra is saying about Clytemnestra and the present murder, even when she says unequivocally that she is talking about "the dead body of Agamemnon." This can't be, the Chorus says, and they take refuge in the presumed obscurity of oracles—an extraordinary touch, I think, in which obscurity becomes a name for a clarity you can't bear.

"My Greek is clear," Cassandra says, "but still no one believes it." The Chorus says, "All oracles speak Greek and all darkly." Not darkly enough, obviously. Or not darkly in the right sense. We know the Chorus has understood Cassandra all too well because they have had the same premonitions themselves, caught something violent and threatening in the effusive, ostensible welcome Clytemnestra gave to Agamemnon, and in the king's cagey response. They sensed "a dark weight in the air":

Some horror is close. Some evil
Settling cold on the skin.

Knowledge of it
Is weakening my whole body.

"I knew it," they say. "I knew it before." "But now . . . the knowledge has darkened." This is the darkness of horror, not the darkness of obscurity.

Cassandra says her violent death will put an end to Apollo's
punishment. "This is where disbelief will finally desert me," she
says. This will be her "last gasp of the incredible." Of the incredible that is irreversibly true. Cassandra moves toward the palace, but
recoils, because she sees as already spilled, awash on the floors, the
blood that will be spilled within minutes; and she smells the reek
of massacre. The Chorus, now working very hard at its denial, says
the blood must be from the sacrifices of thanksgiving, the smell
must be that of the perfumes scattered for the banquet. Then Cassandra enters the palace, and we hear her no more.

Here the situation matches none of the possibilities I listed
above, although they all hover as dismissed alternatives: gibberish,
foreign language, code, metaphor, fiction. The Chorus understands
perfectly what Cassandra is saying, however hard they struggle
against their knowledge. What then has happened to the god's curse?
It has shifted its ground in an extraordinarily ingenious way. Or two
ingenious ways. First, Cassandra is making her prophecy to people
who are helpless, who can do nothing about it; to the old men of
Argos, left behind with their dreams, as they say, when all able-
bodied soldiers went to the war. It's true that when the murder of
Agamemnon occurs, the members of the Chorus feel they should
do something, and repeatedly say so. But they talk instead of acting,
and they even wonder whether Agamemnon's cry—"They have
killed me"—really is conclusive evidence that he is dead. A lesson in
the use of ambiguity for equivocation and delay, and a perfect prolongation of Apollo's curse on Cassandra. The point of the curse,

after all, is that the prophecy should be true, and heard, and useless. In this spirit, the inability to act will serve just as well as the inability to understand. Second, the god, or more precisely Aeschylus, has arranged the time frame so that what Cassandra reports as prophecy is barely ahead of the actual events, which are about to happen offstage. In technical terms, theatrically, she is one of those messengers who are ubiquitous in Greek drama—but one who knows the news as it happens elsewhere, and moments before it happens. The truth of her prophecy and the central action of the play are the same thing. What better confirmation of her gift? But of course none of the main protagonists hears her, it would be too late if they did, and her speaking to the helpless is compounded by her not speaking in time to anyone who could act. So that when Cassandra, in her last speeches to the Chorus, asks them to bear witness for her, to confirm, when everything happens as she has described it, that her "prophecies were all true," she is asking, like Hamlet and Othello as their plays end, for a story to be told that will set the record right. When she is dead, everyone will know she always spoke the truth. But of course in order to tell that story, we shall have to tell the other one too, the story of the woman who, in life, was never believed, because she had refused the attentions of a god, and whose truth can never be separated from our disbelief. That is who Cassandra is, that is what Cassandras are. The great nineteenth-century French scholar of ancient divination, Bouché-Leclercq, notes that Cassandra had several sanctuaries devoted to her memory, where girls were received who had been, in the scholar's delicate phrasing, "violated in their inclinations." Against their inclinations, more like. But there don't appear to have been any oracles given at these sanctuaries. "It was during her lifetime," Bouché-Leclercq concludes, "that Priam's unfortunate daughter cast her prophecies to the winds; her ghost inspired only Lycophron." The reference is to Lycophron's

Alexandra, a rather laborious late-Greek narrative poem, in which Cassandra foresees the contents of the *Iliad*, the *Odyssey*, the *Aeneid*, and much else.

The story doesn't end there—how could it?—and the poem is not only laborious. Lycophron has many distinguished fans, and we can read about him in *The Invention of Solitude*, a memoir by the contemporary American novelist Paul Auster. "A. remembers the excitement he felt in Paris in 1974," Auster says of himself in the third person, "when he discovered the seventeen-hundred-line poem by Lycophron (circa 300 B.C.), which is a monologue of Cassandra's ravings in prison before the fall of Troy." In this work, Auster continues, "nothing is ever named, everything becomes a reference to something else. One is quickly lost in the labyrinth of its associations, and yet one continues to run through it, propelled by the force of Cassandra's voice." As I write—well, maybe not just at this minute—Auster is at work on a novel called *Oracle Night*.

The old song

"The same old story," we read in Christa Wolf's novella *Cassandra*. "Not the crime but its heralding turns men pale and furious." In this book, perhaps the most interesting modern rendering of the ancient tale, and a fiction that bears a remarkable resemblance to Golding's *Double Tongue*, Cassandra narrates her own misfortunes, and like Arieka, she is both a sort of medium and a sort of unbeliever. "We have no name for what spoke out of me," she says. "I was its mouth, and not of my own free will. It had to subdue me before I would breathe a word it suggested." But although she (necessarily) believes in this nameless force, she doesn't believe in the gods, and her reasons are very eloquent:

I could not say how long I had been an unbeliever. If I had had some shock, an experience resembling conversion, I could remember. But faith ebbed away from me gradually, the way illnesses sometimes ebb away, and one day you tell yourself that you are well. The illness no longer finds any foothold in you. That is how it was with my faith. What foothold could it still have found in me? Two occur to me: first hope, then fear. Hope had left me. I still knew fear, but fear alone does not know the gods; they are very vain, they want to be loved too, and hopeless people do not love them.

But the future this Cassandra sees is not a privileged apparition. It is the future anyone could see if they could bear to look. She is the figure who reveals everyone else's denial of the truth, and the god's gift to her is a merciless clear-sightedness in a world in love with blurred vision. Of the Greeks she says, "If I tell them I know nothing, they will not believe me. If I tell them what I see coming, which anyone else could do as well, they will kill me." And of her own compatriots, the Trojans, she says, "Why are we carried away by the very wishes that are grounded in error? The thing they resented most about me later on was my refusal to give in to their disastrous wishful thinking." "This refusal," she adds, "not the Greeks, cost me my father, mother, brothers and sisters, friends, my people."

Cassandra herself is not immune to this fault, at least as far as her own life is concerned, and when she arrives at the moment we have already looked at in Aeschylus' version, she bleakly says

Now his wife is butchering Agamemnon.
Presently it will be my turn.
I notice that I cannot believe what I know.
That is how it always was, how it always will be.

And yet she, like her ancestress, wants her story to be told, or rather the story of her story. "I will continue to be a witness even if there is no longer one single human being left to demand my testimony." She bravely announces her "belief that a successful phrase—words, that is—can capture or even produce every phenomenon and every event, will outlive me." These claims are true only in a dark or deeply ironic way. Like all Cassandras, she can be a witness only to the failure or the irrelevance of (even true) vision, and she doesn't have any words except those storytellers give her. It is (in this case and in the case of Aeschylus) the writer's words that will outlive her, have outlived her, and it is the writer's words that will have captured and produced the phenomena and the events. The addressee of Shakespeare's sonnets is immortal, but he didn't know it, and we don't even know his name. Hamlet will never hear the tale that is told about him, and he probably wouldn't have liked Shakespeare's play.

Burning the books

Sibyls are very ancient, as ancient as pythias. They spoke without being spoken to, and as I have said, they spoke in their own person. And because they spoke mainly of disasters, they were easily associated, over time, with Hebrew prophets and apocalyptic Christianity. The chief known collection of sibylline utterances, the *Sibylline Oracles*, is a sixth century A.D. compilation of dire prediction, attributed in this case to a sibyl who identifies herself as Noah's daughter-in-law. Her sources include Bible stories, Greek legends, and various pieces of ancient history—mainly famous past events that could confirm the sibyl's gloomy wisdom. If she foretold the Flood, she was likely to be right about other matters. Or to put the matter more skeptically, if she kept on predicting disasters, she was going to be right much of the time, even if the predictions were random guesses. The oracles foretell, one of their German editors says, "much that has already happened or also perhaps will happen." "Or also perhaps" is excellent: a good range of possibilities.

The *Sibylline Oracles* are in Greek hexameters, and the sibyl, driven by the god, speaks of what is past, passing, and to come, like the golden bird in Yeats's poem "Sailing to Byzantium." She complains constantly of her pain and her task, but she continues.

> Samos too will become a heap of sand, and Delos will disappear,
> Rome will become an alley; then all oracles will be fulfilled.

She is particularly strong on the last days. A sword will appear in the evening sky. A cloud of dust will descend, hiding the sunlight. Blood will rain down in the moonlight, and the stones will begin to speak. The local seas will dry up, ships will not sail to Italy, and the whole of Asia will become an ocean. In one splendid formulation she says "the world is no longer world when humankind is destroyed." She foretells the coming of Homer and of Virgil, who will take their "words and measure" from her. She gives her own history. She left Babylon, stung with prophetic madness. But in Greece they called her the shameless woman from Erythrae, and others said she was an unrecognized daughter of Circe. They were all wrong. God told her everything that happened before her parents' time. At a certain dizzying intertextual moment the god—who is both Apollo and the Christian God—says

> Truly, I know the number of the grains of sand and the measure of
>   the sea,
> I know the hiding places of the earth, and know the darkness of
>   Tartarus,

I know the number of the stars, the trees, and how many kinds
   there are
Of quadrupeds, of swimming creatures, of rapid birds,
And also of humankind, who live now and in the future, and of
   the dead.

The editors send us to the relevant passage in Herodotus, but we
have probably already recognized it. The god through the sibyl is
quoting the pythia speaking for the god. The first line above is the
start of the answer she gave to Croesus' messengers on their first
visit. The trope must have been traditional even in Herodotus'
time, but the effect here, some ten centuries later, is unmistakable.
The claim to infinite knowledge of the world is itself borrowed
from a book.

Sibyls are oracular only in the broadest sense, and are not usually in dialogue with anyone. But one feature that appears in virtually all sibyl stories is worth noting, because it parallels, in another
key, the notorious ambiguity of oracles. Sibyls do not speak ambiguously, but they have all kinds of difficulties of transmission.
They write their prophecies on leaves, which are scattered by the
wind. They speak through the hundred mouths of a cave, so their
voice is distorted. There is much doubt about who they are and
how many there are—whether two different names for sibyls, for
instance, actually represent two persons or one. Some traditions
give us as many as ten sibyls: the Persian, the Libyan, the Delphian,
the Cimmerian, the Erythraean, the Samian, the Cumaean, the
Hellespontine, the Phrygian, the Tiburtine. Others, applying a
Mediterranean version of Occam's razor, suggest there is only one,
appearing in multiple guises. And in the most famous and haunting
of these stories, a sibyl destroys two thirds of the books of her
wisdom.

In Virgil, Aeneas asks the sibyl not to put her prophecies on leaves, and she doesn't. Indeed, although Virgil mentions the difficulty of understanding her as if it was going to be part of his story rather than just an aspect of her general reputation, for Aeneas she is "direct and perfectly clear," as the French scholar said of Apollo, an admirable guide to terrible regions. But then Aeneas, after his tour with the sibyl, leaves the underworld by the gate reserved for false dreams. The standard interpretation of this strange exit is that Aeneas, being still alive, is not a true shade, but this reading doesn't entirely clear things up, and a little cloud of trouble clings to the image, as if one just can't talk of sibyls without evoking some sort of Cassandra-like problem in communication. Leaves, holes in the cave, multiple identities, wrong gate, burned books: there is always something hampered or mutilated or scrambled about the wisdom the sibyl has for us.

One auspicious day the Sibyl of Cumae approached the Roman emperor with an offer. She would sell him her nine books of oracles for a certain sum. The emperor sent her packing. The sibyl burned three books and returned, offering the emperor six books for the same original sum. The emperor laughed. The sibyl burned three more books, and came back. This time the emperor wasn't laughing, and paid the full sum for the remaining three books. This is a striking cautionary tale, although I'm not sure whether it's about oracles or money in the first instance. The most important implication, in the context of communication and wisdom, is that whatever use the Romans made of their three books—and they made much, well-documented use of them, consulting them formally, carefully, whenever times were bad or unusual events occurred—they were six books short of the full set. If the emperor had not been so skeptical (or so stingy) they might have known everything, and ruled the world forever. It's true that the other six books probably exist only in legend, but then what a poignant instance they make of the formations of desire.

If oracle-stories offer us the image of a knowledge that might be perfect but is not quite attainable, that is hidden, just out of reach, like a poem we can enjoy but not fully explicate, then sibyl-stories show us a knowledge that was perfect in its original condition but is now lost or broken, a matter of fragments or remnants. The contrast resembles one I shall return to, between students who can't read the scripture they have and those who have lost the scripture they had. No great difference between the two sets, we might think, since neither of them is able to read the scripture. But there is a difference, and the size and nature of the difference is what these legends and images are asking us to imagine.

Sibyls abound in the buildings of Renaissance Italy, notably on the spectacular marble floor of the cathedral of Siena. There are four lovely Veronese sibyls in the church of San Sebastiano in Venice. They are rather sedate and matronly, and don't seem too troubled by their hectic charge, although one of them, the Samian, is younger and seems more meditative, as if she was giving some thought to the problem. But Michelangelo's sibyls on the Sistine Chapel ceiling are the ones that have drawn the most attention, both erudite and popular.

There are five of them, interspersed with seven Hebrew prophets, and Romain Rolland, in his life of Michelangelo, evokes them in this way: "disdainful Libyca; Persica, purblind and restless; Cumaea, with huge arms and pendent breasts; the beautiful Erythraea, strong, calm and scornful; Delphica, the virgin with the lovely body and fierce eyes." Each sibyl is accompanied by two small and rather muscular naked boys, engaged in various activities: reading, whispering, looking over the sibyl's shoulder, lighting what appears to be a tray of incense. This is not the place (nor am I the person) to go into the iconography or theology of these extraordinary figures, but I do want to pause over John Ruskin's comments on them, since they open up several interesting possibilities.

Ruskin was very disappointed with Michelangelo. He thought the artist had made the Delphic sibyl as beautiful as he could but had completely wrecked the Virgilian idea of the Cumaean sibyl, and had ignored the marvelous lesson of the burned books. "She might have had more than one book, at all events, to burn. She might have had a stray leaf or two fallen at her feet . . . It is by a grotesque and most strange chance that he should have made the figure of this Sibyl, of all others in the chapel, the most fleshly and gross. Thus he paints the poor nymph beloved of Apollo . . . as an ugly crone, with the arms of Goliath, poring down upon a single book." There is of course no reason at all why Michelangelo should have painted the picture Ruskin wanted him to paint, but like many great critics, Ruskin flagged something important through his prejudices rather than in spite of them. The Cumaean sibyl is a strange figure, and the contrast with the Delphic sibyl is instructive. I don't wish to slight the other three sibyls, but life is short and art is long.

We stare at the ceiling, and then at a reproduction of the figures in close-up. The Cumaean sibyl is indeed old and huge. If it were not for her large breasts and assertive nipples, she might be taken for a man. She wears a complicated white headdress, and her face is hard and gnarled like an ancient tree. She is reading a vast book, and her two boy companions, unlike the busy or unruly, often mischievous figures associated with the other sibyls, are, although rather sleepy, in close sympathy with their mistress. Because of her mannishness, she has been associated with the weird sisters in *Macbeth*, and there is something of the traditional European witch about her—or perhaps simply of the woman who has survived long hard times. Vasari thought she was beautiful. As Ruskin suggests, it's hard to imagine she was ever a nymph, but she is not the shriveled personage we find in Petronius either, the one who asked for eternal life and forgot to ask for eternal youth. This is a woman of extraordinary force, and she doesn't look as if she is about to retire—she won't retire until she dies. We might trust her not because she looks kind or helpful, but because we believe she knows things, because it would be hard to doubt her once we had started listening to her. But will she talk to us? She is not looking our way. She is reading her book. She is not aghast or perturbed, but she is concentrating, her intelligent gaze entirely on the page. What is on it that she doesn't already know, that holds her attention so firmly? We shall never find out. By a brilliant touch of perversity Michelangelo has pictured revelation as unmistakably in process, but closed to us. Other images on the ceiling tell other stories, but this sibyl has the scripture we lack, and there is no sense that her book is the Bible or any text we could get hold of. Indeed, the witch-appearance suggests it may not be a god-given book at all but a collection of spells. A heretical thought, which we need to banish as soon as we have it. We are in the Sistine Chapel, after all. But banished thoughts do linger in the mind, like the insinuations of Perry Mason, even when they have been struck from the record, and yet another heresy creeps onto the scene. What if she is not a witch but just a very wise woman? What if she has a book that belongs neither to Christianity nor to its enemies? What would she be reading then?

The Delphic sibyl is not reading but staring out at the world. Even so, she is not staring at us, but away toward our right, as if aware of something approaching. She has a scroll in her hand, presumably recently consulted and the source of her warning. Her boy companions seem to be otherwise occupied, one reading a book, the other staring at him over the top of the pages, neither of them in any way attentive to what is bothering the sibyl. She has a blue cape and headdress and Rolland probably thought she was a virgin because of the association of the color, in so many paintings, with the mother of Christ. I don't know where he got the idea of her lovely body from, since her gown is pretty loose, and her muscular arms suggest a male athlete rather than a delicate maiden. But the face is extraordinary, oval, pale, young, smooth, wide-eyed, and haunted. The scholar Edgar Wind says she is "moved by a violent inspiration which struggles in vain to become articulate," and there is something helpless about her, a sense not that she is announcing disaster but about to witness or even suffer one. So we can read this image, in a way in which we can't read that of the Cumaean sibyl— except as a metaphor for our exclusion from reading. We can read the Delphic sibyl's emotion, whatever we choose to make of it. But then the effect of this access is very curious. I can believe she is "moved by a violent inspiration" for the same reason I can believe she is the Delphic sibyl: because I have been told. But if I look at her face, I don't see inspiration and I don't even see a sibyl. I see a young woman who manages to appear startled and calm at the same time, terrified and yet unruffled. She doesn't know the things the Cumaean sibyl knows, and she doesn't appear to be driven by time or the god. She knows what is coming and she knows it is unalterable. But it is as if she had never learned anything like this before, and perhaps Rolland's idea of her virginity can be applied to her work as a sibyl: this is her first flight. She is close to us because of her surprise and remote from us because of her calm. But what has she read in her scroll, what is approaching from the unseen world beyond her portion of the ceiling? The end of the world or a local earthquake? The incest of Oedipus or the death of Nero? This too we shall never find out. A valuable reminder that sometimes the sheer feel of prophecy is more significant than what is prophesied. An impression of imminent revelation may linger in the memory as a form of truth even when the prophecies have failed or faded or worn themselves out through reinterpretation.

O our oracle

Gerard Manley Hopkins is the great English poet of pain. The pain is almost entirely mental, but none the less real for that. In one of his meditations on the Fifth Exercise of St. Ignatius Loyola—Hopkins converted to Catholicism when he was a student at Oxford, and soon after became a Jesuit—the poet noted:

> No one in the body can suffer fire for very long, the frame is destroyed and the pain comes to an end; not so, unhappily, the pain that afflicts the indestructible mind . . . Let all consider this: we are our own tormentors.

And in one of his most magnificent and most distressed poems he wrote:

> O the mind, mind has mountains; cliffs of fall
> Frightful, sheer, no-man-fathomed.

Hopkins's biographer Norman White uses the wonderful word *painscape* for this type of image.

Do we need poems about pain, of this or any other kind? Well, pain doesn't need poems, it has a life of its own, and whether we need poems about pain will depend on who we are. Hopkins offers a vivid argument based on experience—his and ours. Of the sheer mountains of the mind he says, with characteristic compression, "Hold them cheap/May who ne'er hung there." That is, if we don't know the mountains he's talking about, it will be easy to dismiss them and their terrors. Hopkins doesn't mean we're entitled to hold his experience cheap, just that the very possibility of thinking these mountains are not so terrible will be available only to people who have never been anywhere near them—rather as people who have never been depressed will not know the difference between clinical depression and a bad day. Does this mean we have to have hung on Hopkins's cliffs in order to know what he is talking about? I doubt whether all that many of us have been to his extremities. But we understand such things through proportion and relation, and we get some sense of Hopkins's mountains through the experience of our tiny hills. We can be "our own tormentors" even on the lower frequencies, as Ralph Ellison's invisible man would say, and poems can help us to see what we are doing.

The landscape of Hopkins's poem "Spelt from Sibyl's Leaves" is a darkening forest at evening, but it is also a pathway close to the city of Hell, and the scene pictured on the cover of this book. I would have wanted to write about this poem anyway, because it brings a very old story much closer to us in time, but until I began to explore its context I didn't know anything about the extraordinary role played by the word *oracle* in its writing, one of the many serendipities involved in approaching this subject.

Hopkins wrote the first ten lines of the poem—later he described it as "the longest sonnet ever made"—in late 1884, but then could go no further. "Here he seems to have stuck," his editors write, "as though his work of art had itself fallen victim to the crushing blackness which he had so powerfully described." The last words of what Hopkins had written so far were "O this is our tale too!" Two years later he took up the poem again and managed to finish it. The first new words were "Our tale, O our oracle!" The very word—not itself an oracle perhaps but a reminder of what oracles can do—appears to have released Hopkins's imagination from its trap. The sibyl's scattered leaves took two years to arrange themselves but now made stark sense. Or perhaps the oracle and the sibyl appeared at the same time, since facsimile versions of the poem suggest that the title is present only when the poem is being completed. The oracle, our oracle, turns out to be not only the instrument for ending the poem but the place where the poem changes, the point of passage from a descending darkness without distinctions to a black-and-white world of irreducible options.

Here's how the first part of the poem goes. The stress marks, and the marks for the pauses in midline, are Hopkins's.

> Earnest, earthless, equal, attuneable, / vaulty, voluminous, . . .
> stupendous
> Evening strains to be tíme's vást, / womb-of-all, home-of-all,
> hearse-of-all night.
> Her fond yellow hornlight wound to the west, / her wild hollow
> hoarlight hung to the height
> Waste; her earliest stars, earlstars, / stárs principal, overbend us,
> Fíre-féaturing heaven. For earth / her being has unbound; her
> dapple is at end, as-
> tray or aswarm, all throughther, in throngs; / self ín self steepèd
> and páshed—qúite
> Disremembering, dísmémbering / áll now. Heart, you round me
> right
> With: Óur évening is over us; óur night / whélms, whélms, ánd
> will end us.
> Only the beakleaved boughs dragonish / damask the tool-smooth
> bleak light; black,
> Ever so black on it.

The earth falls into darkness, disremembering, dismembering everything. The yellow light of evening dies; stars appear but they too will soon be gone as evening turns into black night. The language is violent, awkward, at times barely comprehensible, as if some disorderly and unnameable misery had latched on to what is after all a daily occurrence. The poem about the mind's mountains ends with this small comfort: "all/Life death does end and each day dies with sleep." In this poem each day's death seems to be death itself, with no promise of awakening, and the key phrase in this first part is perhaps the simple and dismaying "her dapple is at end." Dapple for Hopkins is color and light and difference, the sheer multiplicity and strangeness of the world. "Glory be to God for dappled things," one of his few cheerful poems begins. Dapple is "at end" in "Spelt from Sibyl's Leaves," not quite ended. It is "astray" or "aswarm," "all throughther" (the spoken form of "through-other," an Irishism meaning intertwined or mixed up), but this dishevelment is only an announcement of death, and perhaps more distressing than the thing itself. The poet's heart is right to tell him it's all over, and bleakness turns to blackness by the slightest of vowel shifts.

There is no mention of a sibyl here, though, except in the title, and no evocation of a Virgilian landscape, except in the sense of a generalized sorrow. But watch what happens when two years have gone by and the oracle makes its appearance.

> Only the beakleaved boughs dragonish / damask the tool-smooth
>   bleak light; black,
> Ever so black on it. Óur tale, O óur oracle! / Lét life, wáned, ah lét
>   life wind
> Off hér once skéined stained véined varíety / upon, áll on twó
>   spools; párt, pen, páck
> Now her áll in twó flocks, twó folds—black, white; / right, wrong;
>   reckon but, reck but, mind
> But thése two; wáre of a wórld where bút these / twó tell, each off
>   the óther; of a rack
> Where, selfwrung, selfstrung, sheathe- and shelterless, / thóughts
>   agaínst thoughts ín groans grínd.

The hectic stresses make this poem extraordinarily difficult to read aloud—and Hopkins did want it to be read aloud. Or even sung. "This sonnet should be almost sung," he wrote, "it is most carefully timed in *tempo rubato.*" Pretty violent music, but it's clear that Hopkins has pulled an amazing switch on his argument. Dapple is ending, he was saying, all that awaits us is the indiscriminate darkness. But hold on. There is worse than darkness. What happens at the end of the world is not that the multiplicity of earth and life vanishes but that it shrinks to two choices, and those choices not even ours: black, white; right, wrong; sheep, goats. This is what all that "skeined stained veined variety" comes down to. This is the moment of judgment, and Hopkins's editors refer us to the Dies Irae, the day of wrath, which is also the name of a medieval hymn that names David and the Sibyl as witnesses of the terrors attending the soul when its time comes.

The richer context, though, is the *Aeneid*, where the sibyl herself explains the landscape and the full harshness of the either-or decision even in a non-Christian world. Having instructed Aeneas to find and pluck the golden bough hidden among the ilexes of the forest, she leads him through the cave of Avernus and down into the world of Dis. They walk through the darkness, scarcely visible to each other, "*Ibant obscuri sola sub nocte per umbram,*" and if Virgil had had a word like *dapple*, he probably would have used it, since he literally says night takes away the colors from things. This is a passage Hopkins must be remembering, although as I have said, it is possible that he thought of it after rather than before he had written his own lines about the draining out of light. But the key moment in Virgil comes a little later. Aeneas is talking to a dead companion, slaughtered in the sack of Troy, who rather weirdly has the same unlucky name as the sibyl, or rather its masculine form: Deiphobus/Deiphobe, hated of the god. The sibyl reminds both men that time is running out, and says, in Robert Fitzgerald's translation:

> Here is the place
> Where the road forks: on the right hand it goes
> Past mighty Dis's walls, Elysium way,
> Our way; but the leftward road will punish
> Malefactors, taking them to Tartarus.

If Aeneas was dead, he would probably be allowed to take the right-hand road in any case, because of his many mournful virtues. But every soul must go one way or the other here, and the difference between Elysium and Tartarus could hardly be greater, indeed it looks almost like an image of the very idea of difference. What Hopkins is imagining is a court of judgment that sits every night and allows no middle ground or mitigation of sentence, a daily end of the world, and he resolutely locates it within the individual mind. There is a terrible declension from reflection to fear to torture in the sequence of words reckon-reck-rack, and all we hear at last is the grinding of thoughts against thoughts.

Everyone, whatever their religion, must fear the day of judgment if they believe in it, but Hopkins is getting the idea of the oracle and the memory of Virgil to do slightly different work. The horror seems to lie not in the threat of damnation or delivery to Tartarus but in the relentless collapsing of the world's multiple possibilities into the number two. The result is not only the obvious loss of variety and dapple but an endless conflict between the two remaining chances, as if they were after all a matter of individual choice rather than the decision of a god. But there is no choice, only the rack of oppositions. The two chances are all that count, the only things still talking—*tell* has both of these meanings—they need each other, and neither is going to leave. It's tempting to believe that each tells of the other, but Hopkins has the more mysterious "off," as if telling were like feeding or rebounding. This nightmare dialectic, this picture of dialectic as endless torment, is both signaled and enacted in the curious word *ware*, meaning either "aware" or "beware"—or rather meaning both, because we have no way of deciding which. This is how oracles work, and why the word *oracle* was such a find for Hopkins. "Aware" is milder, invites us to terrible knowledge but doesn't refuse the harsh order of this world. "Beware" suggests we should try to avoid this world, or this spiritual condition, as if there were another, as if evening could fall without these results. We are at the heart of Hopkins's poetry, where so many great moments hinge on this kind of ambiguity, where severe self-examination is hard to tell from pathological self-laceration, and there may even be a kind of perverse pleasure in the confusion.

Hopkins is a master of oracles in this sense, and can get double meanings even out of the repetition of the same word, as in "Carrion Comfort," another account of a nightly struggle with the angel of argument, which ends by evoking a night and a year "of now done darkness" in which "I wretch lay wrestling with (my God!) my God." And in "That Nature is a Heraclitean Fire and of the comfort of the Resurrection," a poem about the continuity of the amazing light and energy of the world while human beings and their works disappear, leaving no trace, Hopkins gets the indisputable proposition that a diamond is a diamond to produce an extraordinary revelation. Luckily, a manuscript exists for this poem, and we can see the lame phrase Hopkins wrote before he made his last correction. Judgment, as we have seen, is no answer to the loss of the world, but the doctrine of the resurrection might be, and that is what Hopkins seeks to show. He calls the resurrection a "heart's-clarion," and writes:

> Flesh fade, and mortal trash
> Fall to the residuary worm; / world's wildfire, leave but ash:
> In a flash, at a trumpet crash,
> I am all at once what Christ is, / since he was what I am, and
> This Jack, joke, poor potsherd, / patch, matchwood, is immortal
>   diamond,
> Diamond.

Great lines, but the repetition of *diamond* is just awkward emphasis, an echo of a single meaning. Hopkins then makes a small change and we get:

> since he was what I am, and
> This Jack, joke, poor potsherd, / patch, matchwood, immortal
>   diamond,
> Is immortal diamond.

Now poor mortals are not immortalized by death, they are immortal all along, already diamonds—the resurrection doesn't change them, it finds them out. The difference between the diamonds— the sense in which the diamonds are the same and different—allows Hopkins to grieve for the loss of what he calls nature's million-fueled bonfire, and even the trash and ash, since diamonds are discovered there, and also to celebrate the pure and final release of the resurrection. It is the work of an oracle, even when it doesn't appear by name.

But there are, in our context, two lingering questions about "Spelt from Sibyl's Leaves." What do we make of *spelt*, and what about the curious stress on *our* oracle? As we have seen, the Sibyl of Cumae traditionally wrote her prophecies on leaves and allowed the wind to scatter and confuse them—a kind of lottery of meaning. Hopkins is suggesting, I take it, that the physical world itself is a

kind of sibyl, and that its phenomena are leaves to be put together
and read, perhaps letter by letter, as the word *spelt* implies. What
looks like a description would then be a first stage of decoding,
and at this point the difference I evoked earlier between *sibylline* and
cryptic would be very faint. The world would be telling us, as I have
suggested, that earth's evening is a figure for our dying, but more
important, that nightly darkness hides a racking division from
which death would be a distinct relief. This is also the force of the
stress on *our* oracle rather than anyone else's. All oracles frame
choices, sometimes disguised as unequivocal propositions, but *our*
oracle, Hopkins is saying, thinking now no doubt of a Catholic
version of the "inward oracle" promised to us in Milton's *Paradise
Regained*, has none of the easygoing possibilities of the other vari-
eties. Is there a longing here for a different, kinder oracle, one that
would celebrate the world's profusion, for instance, rather than cut
it down to a binary battle? I think Hopkins finds it difficult to give
up such a longing, and this is particularly clear in the strange,
repeated stress of "Lét life," where there is surely a plea meeting some resistance. But he is not actively looking for another
oracle. We are our own tormentors, and he would say we are right
to be so.

Calling home

The light was better and I could see both figures fairly clearly now. They were wearing twentieth-century dress—trousers, bright scarves, woolen hats. What I had taken for cloaks turned out to be loose, heavy coats. One of the figures was talking into a phone. The other was carrying a computer bag. I still couldn't tell whether they were men or women.

The figure with the phone spoke slowly, as if dictating a report or anxious not to be misunderstood. "The whole thing," the figure said, "is to understand the logic of the consultation of oracles. Not the why or the what but the how. The way the questions solicit certain answers, the way the answers permit certain interpretations, the way the effect of closure is achieved."

The other figure said, "The effect of closure is just an effect," but the first figure paid no attention, just kept talking slowly into the phone. "You can refuse to accept the very idea of an oracle, and then the story is over. But if you concede that there is the faintest possibility of the oracle being right, you are caught in the game and can't get out. The only question is what will count as the fulfillment of the oracle, what event in life you will take as the ultimate match to the words it offered you. A question of reference, as the philosophers say."

The second figure nodded approvingly and murmured, "That's pretty impressive. What did they say?" The first figure turned off the phone and answered, "Not much. It was a wrong number."

SEVEN: THE DEATH OF ORACLES

The ancient gods always abandon ruins.

A. Bouché-Leclercq, *History of Divination in Antiquity*

Last orders

There are many haunting stories of the death of oracles, all of them testifying, in various curious ways, that death is not quite the end. Oracles announce their own present failure or cessation, they predict their future inefficacy; they die out instantly, all of them at once, on a single day, and are vividly remembered seventeen centuries later for this spectacular exit.

The most poignant of these instances are those in which the oracle describes its own demise. The people of Nicaea consult the god at Delphi and are told that he has lost his voice. Pytho is another name for Apollo.

Pytho's oracle can no longer find its talkative voice,
For now, destroyed by passing time
It has locked itself in a silence without predictions.
Offer to Phoebus, as is the custom, the sacrifices which lead the
gods to make known their wishes

The source here is the Christian apologist Eusebius and the quotation is part of his polemic against oracles. Parke and Wormell comment, "This is no doubt a genuine document, which belongs to the closing years of paganism, when the practice of giving oracles at Delphi had been abandoned, but the priests were unwilling on that account to give up the worship of Apollo or forgo the perquisites which they could claim from his sacrifices." The lines seem even sadder and more self-contradictory than this. The oracle is silent, a victim of time, the gods no longer make their wishes known by this means, so there is no point in putting a question. The priests invite the Nicaeans to make the old gesture, because the perks are all the priests have now, but also because even dead gods can be worshiped, and amputated limbs often make their continuing presence felt. These are melancholy survivals, though, pathetic memories that cannot finally pretend to be anything other than memories, and I wonder whether the Nicaeans made their offerings, "as was the custom," or decided the custom had had its day, and just went home.

Some time later, the Emperor Julian sends a doctor called Oribasius to Delphi, although we don't know what he was supposed to ask. Oribasius comes back with the message:

Tell the king, the fairwrought hall has fallen to the ground.
No longer has Phoebus a hut, nor a prophetic laurel, nor a spring
    that speaks.
The water of speech even is quenched.

These are reputed to be the last words of the oracle at Delphi. They are a description of ruin even more than a description of silence. No hall, no hut, no laurel, no water. The temple has collapsed and the very vegetation has disappeared. Certainly silence is evoked, but only in a mournful implied comparison: if the laurel is gone, and even the metaphorical chatter of the water has dried up, we know how much divine or human speech to expect.

Both of these oracles talk nostalgically of talking, remembering days when the god's talk was plentiful. But they also talk of time, of old splendors and present abandonment, as if the immortal gods had somehow become subject to history, as if the only time they now have is the past. Not only do these oracles not look into the future, they have no future. The future is not for them, and although ancient oracles knew many other things, like the measure of the sea and the number of grains of sand on the beach, to say nothing of what King Croesus of Lydia was cooking on a certain day in Sardis, an oracle that doesn't know the future and has no future itself is surely the ultimate image of obsolescence.

An oracle that describes its death is still alive, but only just. An oracle that correctly predicts its own defeat is in better shape as an oracle, no doubt, but not for long. When the Emperor Augustus consulted the god at Delphi, the pythia said, "A Hebrew boy bids (he who rules as god among the blessed) that I leave this house and go to Hades. Depart therefore from our halls and tell it not in the future." Augustus went to Rome and placed on the Capitol an altar inscribed "To the firstborn God." The oracle's response is curious, since its Christian authors are obviously trying to ventriloquize the language of another religion. The pythia understands who the Christ child is, and that he has become the risen God, but he is still a Hebrew boy to her, and he talks to her of Hades. She was wrong in any case, or a little premature, since there was a strong revival of paganism under Hadrian, and the pythias kept talking for a while. But in the end they were forced to do the Hebrew boy's bidding, as we have seen, and what is disturbing here, at the level of the story, is the pythia's, and by implication the god's, mild acquiescence in their demise. On the supernatural plane, this is a takeover, and yet no one seems to be shouting or complaining. Perhaps power is just power, on whatever plane. In another story of Delphi, Alexander

the Great is supposed to have tried to force an answer out of the
pythia. She kept refusing, he kept insisting, threatening all kinds of
violence, and finally she said, "You can do what you like." Alexander took that as his oracle. At the level of the writing of the Augustus story, of course, the effect is different. The Christians have
got the pagans to confess the absolute power of the Christians,
which must have been more of a wish than a probability, and no
doubt remained so even when the Christians had acquired the
power.

The most dramatic of all these stories, however, is that of the
sudden and total death of oracles at the birth of Christ, and its
most famous expression in English occurs in Milton's "On the
Morning of Christ's Nativity":

> The oracles are dumb,
> No voice or hideous hum
>   Runs through the archèd roof in words deceiving.
> Apollo from his shrine
> Can no more divine,
>   With hollow shriek the steep of Delphos leaving.
> No nightly trance or breathèd spell
> Inspires the pale-eyed priest from the prophetic cell.

Many scholars assume the precedent for these lines is an early an-
notation to Spenser's *Shephearde's Calendar* ("all oracles surceased, and
enchanted spirits, that were wont to delude people, thenceforth
held their peace"), but the scholar C. A. Patrides tells us that the
legend was in any case widespread in the Renaissance, and similar
lines appear in several seventeenth-century writers, including Hey-
wood and Cowley. There is even a much later reprise of the whole
scene by A. E. Housman:

'Tis mute, the word they went to hear
              on high Dodona mountain
          When winds were in the oakenshaws
              and all the cauldrons tolled,
And mute's the midland navel-stone
              beside the singing fountain,
          And echoes list to silence now
              where gods told lies of old . . .

It's a terrific scene, an extraordinary corollary to all the familiar pictures of what we now call Christmas Day. In Bethlehem there is the
child and the manger and the animals, there are Mary and Joseph,
and the shepherds coming to pay their respects, the whole iconography of Renaissance painting and the greeting-card industry. And
all around the Mediterranean, in mainland Greece and on the islands, in Asia Minor and along the coast of Africa, at Abae, Anti-
och, Argos, Delphi, Didyma, Dodona, Klaros, Lesbos, Olympia,
Tegyra, Thebes, and dozens of other places, oracles are closing,
universally struck dumb. How do we picture this? Questioners arrive, perform the required rites, ask their question. Nothing happens. Or the priestess starts to speak and suddenly goes mute,
abandoned by the god. Or the god is heard leaving the temple,
shrieking as in Milton. Or there is no one there. The questioners,
mysteriously, have all stayed away, understanding that the days of
divination are over. Priests and pythias linger on the thresholds of
their temples, bewildered by the deserted space around them.

Of course, it is just a story. As we have seen, oracles had a revival after the birth of Christ, and the Emperor Theodosius found
himself constrained to issue an edict against them in A.D. 391. But
then what is the story about? The pagan source of the Christian
legend makes interesting reading. A god is dead, but which god?

And are we talking about a birth or a death? Or a birth and a death? Here's how the story goes in Plutarch, in a dialogue significantly named "On the Obsolescence of Oracles."

The pilot of a ship drifting near the Echinades Islands in the Mediterranean is told by a mysterious voice, apparently from nowhere, that when he passes a certain spot, the island of Palodes, he is to "announce that Great Pan is dead." The pilot, Thamus, an Egyptian, is not sure what to do but decides that if there is a wind when he gets to the indicated spot, he will say nothing, but if there is "no wind and a smooth sea," he will make the announcement. The ship arrives at Palodes, there is no wind, and Thamus, looking landward, says, "Great Pan is dead."

> Even before he had finished there was a great cry of lamentation, not of one person, but of many, mingled with exclamations of amazement. As many persons were on the vessel, the story was soon spread abroad in Rome, and Thamus was sent for by Tiberius Caesar. Tiberius became so convinced of the truth of the story that he caused an inquiry and investigation to be made about Pan; and the scholars, who were numerous at his court, conjectured that he was the son born of Hermes and Penelope.

This conjecture probably goes back to Herodotus, who gives Pan the same parents, but who also says, in an interesting bit of early comparative ethnology, that Pan is one of the oldest gods among the Egyptians and one of the youngest among the Greeks. So is Thamus the Egyptian chosen as the speaker because of his culture's seniority? Is only one god dying or are there two? And who is doing the choosing?

The context in Plutarch is a discussion about whether demigods exist and whether they can die, and whether they are really any different from gods. The story at first seems to make the answer clear. These creatures—daimones, literally—are not gods and they can die. But then why the massive grieving, and what about the ancient Egyptian god hiding in the Greek half-god? The story takes on all kinds of meanings in the Christian era—one version equates the death of Pan with the death of Christ. The mention of Tiberius makes the date right for that, since he was in power at the time of Christ's death but not at the time of his birth. But lively mythologies don't worry all that much about dates, and the dominant Christian interpretation of the story is that Pan dies because Christ is born, dies exactly when he is born; that his death is the fallout, so to speak, of Christ's nativity. It doesn't matter whether he is a god or a demigod because all pagan deities and observances are obsolete now, and he represents all of them. That grieving, in the Christian reading, notably that of, again, Eusebius, is the sound of devils mourning the loss of their lord and their empire.

So many deaths

The prolific Plutarch lived from A.D. 46 to A.D. 119 or a little later. He was a Greek who was well connected in Rome, and from A.D. 95 he was Apollo's priest at Delphi. He is best known for his parallel lives of famous Greeks and Romans, and for his many essays and dialogues on various moral and philosophical subjects. Among the latter are three dialogues on oracles: "The E at Delphi"; "The Oracles at Delphi No Longer Given in Verse"; "The Obsolescence of Oracles."

Among the more familiar and more intelligible inscriptions at Delphi—"Know thyself," "Avoid excess"—was a freestanding single letter E. No one knew what this meant, and in Plutarch's dialogue a group of characters elegantly discuss the alternatives. They

are very comfortable with the idea of mystery, and one of them remarks, in Babbitt's translation, "Since inquiry is the beginning of
philosophy, and wonder and uncertainty the beginning of inquiry,
it seems only natural that the greater part of what concerns the
god should be concealed in riddles . . ." A little later another
speaker says, "That the god is a most logical reasoner the great majority of his oracles show clearly; for surely it is the function of the
same person both to solve and to invent ambiguities"—the word
here is *amphibolias*. Plutarch himself, as narrator of the dialogue,
makes the remark I quoted in an earlier chapter about Apollo's
helpfulness with "the problems connected with our life," as distinct
from those "connected with our power to reason," which the god
himself "launches and propounds."

It's all very leisurely, and speculation is more important than
doctrine. E is the fifth letter of the Greek alphabet and the second
vowel, and various opportunities for allegory arise from these nu-
merical positions. The text contains an ingenious rhapsody on
these opportunities, which Plutarch calls "the tale of arithmetical
and of mathematical laudations of E." The name of the letter E—
that is, the equivalent of our "ee" for E and "aitch" for H—is "ei,"
which also means "if" and "thou art." You can see what a set of ingenious philosophers could do with this. "If" indicates the questions asked of the god's oracle: people ask if they will succeed or if
they should do this or that. "If only" indicates the conditional
tense that belongs to wishes expressed to the god. "Thou art" becomes a phrase finally appropriate only for the god himself, because only he has real being, and in this sense "Thou art" is a
complement to "Know thyself," the first addressed to the unchanging god, the second to the uncertain human. This perspective
allows Plutarch's characters some wonderful Proustian lines. "Nobody remains one person, nor is one person." Nobody except the

god, that is. And: "We have a ridiculous fear of one death, we who
have already died so many deaths, and still are dying!"

The second of the three dialogues on oracles canvasses the
questions surrounding the bad verse of many oracular responses,
and the general shift from verse to prose in the responses over time.
Many of the arguments resemble those of modern literary criticism and literary history. If the verse is bad, should we say the answer is not the god's? Or shouldn't we rather reconsider our criteria,
and say the verse must be good if the god is its author? But then
why should we think the god is the author? The god gives the answer, but the pythia speaks it, and the verses must be hers. Does
prose necessarily represent a decline from verse? The old oracles
spoke in prose and verse, apparently. And in fact some oracles are
still given in verse. In any case, prose could be appropriate for the
time, without requiring us to deprecate the time, or speak of a
falling off. Perhaps life has got plainer, and that is not a bad thing.
"History descended from its vehicle of versification, and went on
foot in prose, whereby the truth was mostly sifted from the fabulous." Philosophers used to write in verse but now don't, but we
still have philosophy. Do we complain that Socrates and Plato
didn't speak or write in verse? Finally, it seems strange that where
people used to complain of the obscurity of oracles, they now
complain of their "extreme simplicity." These people are like children who prefer rainbows to the sun and the moon; they "yearn for
the riddles, allegories, and metaphors which are but reflections
of the prophetic art when it acts upon a human imagination."
Again, the suggestion is that the god is not difficult unless we want
him to be. And again, there is a sense of leisure about the dialogue,
of the good life being lived among friends, and there is a deep and
unlikely air of calm about the whole proceedings. "There is, in
fact, profound peace and tranquility; war has ceased, there are no

wanderings of peoples, no civil strifes, no despotisms, nor other maladies and ills in Greece requiring many unusual remedial forces." The Pax Romana was fine if you were in the right place.

"The Obsolescence of Oracles" is perhaps the richest and most interesting of these three dialogues. It begins with a nice little swerve out of mythology into the historical or anecdotal. A story tells that certain birds (eagles or swans) flying from "the uttermost parts of the earth towards its center" met at Delphi. Is the story true? An ancient oracle implies that the truth of the story is neither here nor there, and that the attempt should not be made "to investigate an ancient myth as though it were a painting to be tested by the touch." In any case, Plutarch says, we do know that two travelers met at Delphi, one coming from Britain and one coming from Egypt—that is, "from opposite ends of the inhabited earth"—and we do know their story. With that, the conversation starts, and takes in questions like whether it is or is not absurd to draw large inferences from small phenomena, whether the gods ever did any of the extravagant things myths attribute to them, whether the concept of infinity makes any sense, and whether the spiritual powers of the gods depend in any way on the material capacities of humans.

As we have seen, this dialogue also recounts the death of Pan, and explores at length the possible nature and the possible existence of daimones as distinct from the gods. We also learn a great deal about the actual practice of consulting the oracle at Delphi. There used to be three pythias at the temple at the same time, for instance, two working, one in reserve. Now one is enough. The growing obsolescence is real, and one lovely, mournful sentence (in parenthesis) speaks louder than most of Plutarch's serenity: "The god's abandoning of many oracles is nothing other than his way of substantiating the desolation of Greece."

In this context the following oracle-story becomes particularly poignant. Demetrius, the traveler who came from Britain, now listening to various tales of oracles becoming idle or mute, says he doesn't know how things are at present because he has been away for a long time, but certainly the oracles of Mopsus and Amphilochus were still flourishing when he last visited their region. The ruler of Cilicia, Demetrius says, was "an arrogant and contemptible man" much influenced by the Epicureans, but "of two minds towards religious matters." Demetrius uses a marvelous phrase to describe the man's condition: "his skepticism lacked conviction." He couldn't quite bring himself to believe in his doubt. The ruler sends a freedman to the oracle of Mopsus bearing a sealed tablet with a question in it that no one except the ruler knows. This was a dream oracle, apparently, with a response induced by so-called incubation—after performing certain rites, the consultant sleeps in the temple precincts, and the answer to the question appears in a dream. In this case the freedman dreamed that a handsome man stood beside him, said the one word "Black," and disappeared. That was it. The ruler of Cilicia, however, was much impressed by the answer, since his question had been "Shall I sacrifice to you a white bull or a black?" It's hard to think of a better instance of an oracle satisfyingly at work, and yet of course, as Demetrius says, he doesn't know the present state of affairs, and all he is actually offering is a brave memory. The suggestion is that oracles are dying not because they are false or ineffective but because no one wants them anymore. What the devout Plutarch describes as the god's abandonment of the oracles, others might describe as the world's abandonment of the god. The world had other places to go.

The business of lies

How did those Greek daimones become Christian demons? This is an intricate and fascinating story well beyond the scope of this book. Let me just cite Patrides on the "widespread Christian belief that the pagan gods were fallen angels, and the oracles their instrument of delusion." Patrides adds that "Justin Martyr was the first, but certainly not the last, to admit this theory; thereafter the notion appears in such diverse thinkers as Tertullian, Origen, and Lactantius, and continues uninterruptedly until the Renaissance." The linguistic clue, apparently, lies in the fact that early translations of the Hebrew Bible rendered *idols* as "daimonia" in Greek and "daemonia" in Latin.

What is important for the oracle world is the extravagant logic of this shift, a sort of anticipation of what is more familiar to us as Cold War thinking, where the present enemy not only is everywhere but always was everywhere, absorbs all previous enemies as mere prefigurations or disguises. There can be no pluralism in such a world; the one true religion is all there ever was or will be. Anything that looks like another religion is really just the bad side of our religion. When our angels fall they become other people's gods, but we know the truth. There are no other gods, only idols; and those idols, it turns out, are only rebels, ragged and arrogant members of a doomed resistance movement.

I'm simplifying hugely, and I don't want to hide what is bullying and unattractive in such a claim. But I do want to say there is a touch of collective genius in it too. What a move. All other cultures become multiple versions of a single error, and we have a single enemy in Satan, however multifarious his masks and antics. "All things are full of gods" becomes "Satan is everywhere"—but this also means God is everywhere, since even Satan is part of God's scheme. The power is in the extraordinary simplicity and concentration of this doctrine, of course, but the interest is in the details.

What happens to oracles, for instance? They are struck dumb on the morning of Christ's nativity, but when they were still talking, what was happening? Was it always Satan who spoke through them? Did the Father of Lies always lie, or did he tell the truth now and again by accident? Was he forced to tell the truth occasionally, converted into God's unwilling messenger? Could Christians use ancient oracles as foreshadowings of Christ, or were all oracles to be scourged as forms of idolatry? Debates on questions of this kind raged for centuries, all the way into the witchcraft trials of the seventeenth century, where the oracles had turned into instances of Satanic possession, and we hear an echo of them in Banquo's wondering, as he hears the first of the weird sisters' predictions for Macbeth accomplished, "What, can the devil speak true?"

The orthodox line, stemming from St. Thomas citing St. Chrysostom, is not that a devil can't speak true but that he is not to be believed when he does. *"Daemoni, etiam vera dicenti, non est credendum." Etiam vera dicenti,* even telling the truth. A very nice distinction, and an elegant piece of theology. This would exclude all oracles from Christian consideration, but a number of the Church fathers took another view. They needed pagan support for Christian revelation and were content to find it scattered about the ancient world. They didn't believe the oracles were struck dumb at the birth of Christ, only that God allowed them to die out when they could no longer serve any purpose of his. In a sinister and extreme variant on this argument, the exorcists of witchcraft at Loudun insisted that a devil, "when duly constrained by a priest of the Roman church," was "bound to tell the truth." Now the devil not only can but must tell the truth.

It's quite a range: from truth that isn't to be believed to truth that can be believed to truth that must be believed. But what happened to error and the Father of Lies? Well, this is the problem, and a sign of Satan's subtlety, one of the ways in which multiplicity and complication creep back into the marshaled Christian world. As Pascal says, if error was always error, we could rely on it and it would be a form of truth. If Satan just told lies, no one would listen to him, and the lies he does tell wouldn't do any damage.

This whole dilemma is wonderfully staged in Milton's *Paradise Regained*, although I have to admit that Satan does seem to have much the best of his bout with the Son of God. Am I saying, as so many have said of *Paradise Lost*, that Milton was of the Devil's party without knowing it? I'm saying, to put it all too bluntly, that Milton thought that the truth belonged to God while Satan had most of the arguments. Not an easy situation for a person who believes in both truth and arguments—who knows, as a believer, that truth doesn't need arguments, but who would like to see some arguing all the same.

There is a moment early in the poem where, with an ingenuity we might find diabolical in itself, Milton makes a fallen angel not only the power behind idolatry, but the power behind all ancient lust, as if sex itself had to be caught up in the conspiracy theory. Satan, taking a stern and unlikely moral tone, rebukes Belial ("the dissolutest Spirit that fell") for his interest in "womankind": "their shape, their color, and attractive grace." Since before the Flood, Belial and his "lusty crew" have been "roaming the earth" and seducing beautiful women:

> Some beauty rare, Calisto, Clymene,
> Daphne, or Semele, Antiopa,
> Or Amymone, Syrinx, many more
> Too long, then lay'st thy scapes on names adored,
> Apollo, Neptune, Jupiter, or Pan,
> Satyr, or Faun, or Sylvan.

So they were innocent, all those Greek and Roman rapists? Just scapegoats? It was Belial all along? Well, they were nonexistent, just

disguises. Belial was the reality behind the fanciful old story. However lovely and imaginative the tale, it was always the same randy
old demon. Laying the scapes becomes a fine joke in this reading,
since you can't really blame a fictional figure, only pretend to. The
fallen angels have had a whole fabulous mythology as a smoke
screen. And since human beings have told and retold these stories,
we are also part of the plot. This would be one of the things it
means for Satan to possess the universe, as he says he has since
Adam and Eve left paradise.

But the heart of the secret Christianity of the pagan world in
the poem lies in the management of oracles. Tempted by Satan in
the order described by St. Luke—he is invited to turn stones into
bread, to accept the kingdom of the world at Satan's hands, to cast
himself down from the temple and be caught by angels—the Son
of God listens to all kinds of talk from his enemy, and says relatively little himself. The adverbs tell a large part of the story. The
Son of God speaks "sternly," "temperately," "patiently," "calmly,"
"sagely." Only once, by my count, does he say anything "fervently."
This is a cool and proper response to the Devil, of course, but it's
a little static, and the adverbial phrases describing Satan are full of
moral and psychological action. He is "inly stung with anger and
disdain," "doubting," "malcontent," "mute confounded," "murmuring," "inly racked," "perplexed and troubled," "impudent,"
"with fear abashed," "quite at a loss," "swollen with rage," "in
scorn," and much more of the same. The Son's position is made
more delicate by the fact that he is not representing a modern skepticism about the powers of prophecy but the true God's scorn for
false divination, so that he and Satan agree about the principle of
prediction, but are in dispute about the practice. And in an extraordinary move, revoking the old legend, the Son turns out to be
saying not that the oracles were struck dumb at his birth but that
the old oracles of error are to be replaced by a new oracle of truth.

The question, for us although no doubt not for the Son, is whether
the new oracle will inherit the ambiguity of the old ones. How can
it, if it is the truth?

Satan opens this part of his campaign by boasting of his success in the oracle field. He deviously says he doesn't know why he is
regarded as the foe of mankind, when he has nothing against humans and has done so much to help them. This is rather like W. C.
Fields saying he likes children—as long as they are properly
cooked. Humans are not the problem, Satan insists. God is.

> They to me
> Never did wrong or violence, by them
> I lost not what I lost; rather by them
> I gained what I have gained, and with them dwell
> Copartner in these regions of the world.

He gives them "aid" and "advice"

> by presages and signs,
> And answers, oracles, portents and dreams,
> Whereby they may direct their future life.

There is a splendid, sinuous irony in the presentation of this cynical operation as if it were a modest form of counsel, and of course
everything Satan says is true in its way. His aid and advice will indeed direct the future life of anyone who heeds them—direct it to
hell.

The Son is very firm in return. He says lying is Satan's business,
"thy sustenance, thy food." "Yet thou pretend'st to truth." Can the
devil speak true? He can claim to. "All Oracles/By thee are given,"
the Son says. Not just some, and not just the bad ones. Satan is behind every oracle just as Belial is behind every seduction. Satan's

"craft" is that of "mixing somewhat true to vent more lies"; and he's had a lot of success. "And what confessed more true/Among the Nations?" That is, what has been more thoroughly accepted by humans than these packs of lies supported by small doses of truth?

But then the Son shifts his position rather suddenly, and attacks on the grounds of obscurity what he previously attacked on the grounds of deception.

> But what have been thy answers, what but dark
> Ambiguous and with double sense deluding,
> Which they who asked have seldom understood.

"Have seldom understood" can mean two things here; either have seldom got the right meaning, and so been led into error like Croesus and Macbeth, or have seldom made any sense of the thing at all. Here the Son editorializes a little more about obscurity. "And not well understood as good not known." But then he suddenly turns back to the question of deception. Is the devil deceiving people with vacuous double-talk, cheating by giving them nothing instead of something? Or is he actually leading them astray?

> Who ever by consulting at thy shrine
> Returned the wiser, or the more instruct
> To fly or follow what concerned him most,
> And not run sooner to his fatal snare?

That last line is the real kicker. The logic suggests that ambiguity itself is devilish, a temptation to ruin; not merely an absence of clarity, but an open invitation to get everything wrong. Yet at this point the Son switches to the older interpretation of oracles. If they did occasionally tell the divine truth, Satan can take no credit for this, he was just the messenger.

For God hath justly given the Nations up
To thy Delusions; justly, since they fell
Idolatrous, but when his purpose is
Among them to declare his Providence
To thee not known, whence hast thou then thy truth,
But even from him or his Angels President
In every Province . . .

And in any case this possibility is closed now, or is about to be closed.

But this thy glory shall be soon retrenched;
No more shalt thou by oracling abuse
The Gentiles; henceforth Oracles are ceased,
And thou no more with Pomp and Sacrifice
Shalt be enquired at Delphos or elsewhere,
At least in vain, for they shall find thee mute.

That "at least" suggests the Son is only just beginning to understand how complicated the new arrangements are. People won't consult oracles anymore—well, they may consult them, but they won't get any answers, not even falsehoods. So have the oracles ceased or not? They have ceased in their old pagan form, they have been taken out of the domain of the devil, but there are now two modern oracles, more familiarly known as Christ himself and the Holy Ghost.

God hath now sent his living Oracle
Into the World, to teach his final will,
And sends his Spirit of Truth henceforth to dwell
In pious Hearts, an inward Oracle
To all truth requisite for men to know.

It is striking, and perhaps a little odd, that of all the many possible attributes or descriptions of Christ he should be called an oracle. Christ disperses the pagan oracles only in order to replace them, to take over their job and do it right, to teach God's "final will." But then how do we consult this oracle, and why is it an oracle and not just the simple voice of truth? Well, we listen to our protestant hearts and we consult the words of Christ. Will that remove all ambiguity and uncertainty? Manifestly not, I'd say, and I assume Milton would say so too. Is the poem pitting one sense of oracles (divine infallibility, as long as you get the right oracle) against the other (devilish ambiguity and endless deception), and telling us that the first is going to win out? It does seem so. But it can't quite be doing that. Milton is returning us, I take it, to Pascal's dilemma, but reading it through a strenuous Puritan lens. The new oracle is an improvement on the old one because its province is the whole truth rather than appetizing or seductive half-truths devoted to the service of lies. But it is an oracle, and it doesn't give simple edicts or dictations. The "living oracle" speaks to us, and the "inward oracle" lives in our hearts. It redeems us from systematic error but it doesn't save us from work. The labor of interpretation is all before us.

History of a fallacy

In 1687, some sixteen years after the appearance of *Paradise Regained*, Bernard Le Bovier de Fontenelle published the most famous single work on oracles, and a book quite different in tone from anything we have looked at so far. This was a translation and revision of two Latin treatises by the Dutch Protestant Anthony Van Dale, although Fontenelle made clear that much of the writing was his own: "I have sometimes argued differently from him," he said. "I have not scrupled to insert many arguments that belong only to me." With a style and delivery that anticipate those of Enlightenment thinkers like Voltaire and Diderot, Fontenelle crisply argues that oracles were not given by demons and that oracles did not cease at the coming of Christ. "Oracles ended when paganism ended, and paganism did not end with the coming of Jesus Christ." This is certainly historically sound, but the brusque good sense hides another program. "Looking at things closely, we find that these oracles, which seem so marvellous, never existed." Fontenelle is saying that oracles can't have ceased, because they never started. They weren't oracles at all; they were never anything but frauds. And—a lovely touch—they can't have ceased for another, exactly symmetrical reason: fraud itself hasn't ceased in the world, and isn't likely to.

Fontenelle insists on what he calls the trickery of the ancient oracles, their "fourberies," and at one revealing point, late in the book, he says he is "so tired of uncovering the trickeries of pagan priests." Usually he is cooler, though, and often very funny. To the argument that perhaps the oracles did cease at the birth of Christ but the priests faked them for four hundred years or so after that, he replies by asking, with a fine deadpan, why the priests couldn't have been faking them before. Citing the oracle I mentioned earlier about Alexander ("You can do what you like"), Fontenelle says it's one of the "prettiest oracles there have ever been," allowing the little word *joli* to do the work of pages of scathing comment. The translation, here as elsewhere in this section, is mine. When the ancients were short of explanations, Fontenelle says, they turned to their demons. "Everything they found surprising and extraordinary, they attributed to the devils they had in hand." "In hand" is wickedly dismissive. Fontenelle is witty and sarcastic about Eusebius, who he thinks should have known better than to allow the pagans any place in his theology. "I can say that all oracles may have been nothing but trickery," Fontenelle pictures Eusebius as thinking, "but I don't wish to believe it. Why not? Because it suits me to get the devils in there. Now that is a pitiful enough kind of reasoning." And when Fontenelle pretends for a moment to believe in oracles, it is only to evoke a form of groveling. "If the demons gave oracles, the demons did not lack sympathy for rulers who had become powerful, and one notes that hell showed the greatest deference to [*l'enfer avaient bien des égards pour*] Alexander and Augustus."

Fontenelle's reading of the oracle of the torn vine, given to the Emperor Trajan and reported in Microbius, is worth quoting at length for its ingenuity and its brilliant conclusion. This oracle, Fontenelle says, is

> allegorical and so general that it couldn't fail to be true. For if Trajan returned to Rome victorious but wounded, or having lost some of his soldiers; if he was defeated, and his army put to flight; if there was merely some division in the army; or some division in the Parthian army; or some division in Rome in the absence of the emperor; if the Parthians were totally defeated; if they were partially defeated; if they were abandoned by some of their allies—the broken vine would fit all of these different cases wonderfully, it would be very unfortunate if none of them happened; and yet I believe that the bringing back to Rome of the bones of the emperor, which was accepted as the explanation of the oracle, was the only thing the oracle had not thought of.

The creature Fontenelle is stalking is human credulity. His Christianity is quite orthodox, or at least he makes the right assertions. The human spirit, he says, "is not capable of adding anything real and solid to the work of God," and a little later he affirms that we can't add truth to the true religion or lend truth to religions that are false. But of course it's hard to confine credulity to the pagans, and the real trouble is the phenomenon that Fontenelle calls "the marvelous." "If one has studied the human spirit a little," he says, in the voice of one who has studied it a lot, "one knows what power the marvelous has over it." Can we tell God's marvels from the factitious marvels of the devil? Fontenelle thinks so. His project is not to explain what really exists, marvelous or not, but to chase away the nonexistent wonders of human history, at least those that have to do with oracles, and by implication, many others as well. He offers us this beautifully skeptical definition of ignorance—ignorance as a fabulous form of invention: "I am convinced of our ignorance not so much by those things that are, and of which the reason is unknown to us, as by those that are not, and for which we find the reason." It's as if Fontenelle had been listening to Macbeth, who, letting his mind race toward a fantasy of murdering his king, says that

Function

Is smothered in surmise and nothing is,
But what is not.

Even the line break makes an argument. "Nothing is": there is nothing here anymore, everything has been swallowed up in the murderous fantasy. "But what is not": wait a minute, there is something, there is the fantasy, the thing that hasn't happened and yet already has eclipsed the world. Such fantasies are precisely Fontenelle's target, and his discreet but withering irony hits dozens of them. He is writing the history of oracles, he says, with the same precision as if he was following "the natural and historical order" of things. It's as if he has leaped into the twentieth century and taken his place among anthropologically minded historians: fallacies, too, have their history.

But can we be sure even of our ignorance? For all his refined intelligence, Fontenelle digs some wonderfully interesting holes for himself. Like Milton, he is deprived of the rich resources of modern atheism—rich at least when it comes to extending the territories of doubt. Just as Milton is not about to question the general possibility of oracling, Fontenelle can't quite get rid of the demons who didn't give the oracles, and is thereby robbed of the one argument that would close the case: that the demons didn't give oracles because there are no demons. But there are. "The devils have, beyond contradiction, the power to tempt humankind." So we need to separate the devils from the oracles but look out for the devils anyway, and there are moments when Fontenelle's otherwise elegant logic becomes desperate. "Thus, if oracles had been given by evil spirits, God would have told us, so that we wouldn't believe he had given the oracles himself." He did tell us, Milton would say, but only with the coming of Christ. Fontenelle continues to worry about earlier instances, though. What about Job? "It is possible that God sometimes permitted demons a few real effects." Why would God do that? Fontenelle is helpless here. "If that happened, God had his reasons, which are always worthy of profound respect." No doubt, but then why raise the question? It may be true, Fontenelle says, that "God allowed the devil to burn Job's houses, to waste his fields, to kill his flocks and to strike his body with a thousand sores, but that is not to say that the devil has been released on all those who experience the same misfortunes . . . The case of Job is a particular case . . ." A particular but extremely compelling case, we might add. God's playing games with the devil is a problem for most believers, and disastrous for anyone trying to dispel the darkness of superstition.

Perhaps Fontenelle's irony is at work here, too, and a discreet agnosticism lurks beneath a merely token piety. Hard to tell. But it is certainly to his intellectual credit that he allows himself to get into such trouble, and like most pieces of writing of more than polemical or documentary interest, the *History of Oracles* has slips that look like occluded insight. The Greeks, Fontenelle says, were witty and intelligent, "*avaient extrêmement d'esprit,*" but they were "very casual, curious, restless, incapable of moderation," and "to say what I really think about them, they were so intelligent that their reason suffered a little." It's hard to think of a judgment that is further off the wall by modern standards, but Fontenelle goes on:

> I would not be surprised if the Greeks, without thinking about the consequences, had . . . made sacrifices while still arguing about whether sacrifices could reach the gods, and had consulted oracles without being sure that oracles were not pure illusions.

The reason of the Greeks "suffered a little" because they knew how to believe and disbelieve at the same time, and understood, far better than any thinker in the European seventeenth century, that credulity is not going to go away, and shouldn't. As I have already said in other terms, and as I shall suggest more fully in relation to Adorno and astrology, credulity and suspicion are not entirely opposed concepts. We often need a dose of one to get the full benefit of the other.

eight: Can the Devil Speak True?

We will always be there to your call
the old witches said
always said   always saying
something else   at the same time
Audre Lorde, The Marvelous Arithmetics of Distance

Oracles and history

Greek oracles, or certain combinations of Greek oracles, have a so-phistication that surpasses a good deal of modern thinking, and I want to begin this chapter, which concentrates on Scotland and witches and ends in the Japanese cinema, with a backward, Western glance.

The Greeks had oracles, at least in their mythology, long before the birth of Apollo, the god who came to assume knowledge, or partial disclosure, of the human future as his special domain. They had oracles even before Apollo's father, Zeus, assumed full control of the universe, and became the all-mastering figure who is now fa-miliar to us. These oracles were associated initially with the earth and then more particularly with the goddesses Themis, who was Earth's daughter, and Metis, who was the daughter of Ocean. Both of these goddesses were omniscient, and Zeus married both of them. Why both, we might ask, if we think these stories have a logic and are not just fanciful expressions of a folk imagination?

Because Themis and Metis were omniscient in different ways, and Zeus needed the help of both of them, the powers of both of them, in order to become Zeus. Here is what the classical scholars Marcel Detienne and Jean-Pierre Vernant have to say about this setup:

> The omniscience of Themis relates to an order conceived as already inaugurated and henceforth definitively fixed and stable . . . She spells out the future as if it was already written and since she expresses what will be as if it were what is, she gives no advice but rather pronounces sentence . . . Metis, by contrast, relates to the future seen from the point of view of its uncertainties; her pronouncements are hypothetical or problematical statements. She advises what should be done so that things may turn out one way rather than another; she tells of the future not as something already fixed but as holding possible good or evil fortunes . . . Themis represents the aspects of stability, continuity and regularity in the world of the gods: the permanence of order, the cyclical return of the seasons . . . Metis, on the other hand, intervenes at moments when the divine world seems to be still in movement or when the balance of the powers that operate within it appears to be momentarily upset.

Detienne and Vernant add in a note:

> Seen from the point of view of men rather than from that of the gods, one could say that these goddesses correspond to opposite aspects of the oracular function. The divining words of Themis express the necessity, the irrevocability of divine decrees that men can do nothing to avoid. When Metis is consulted as an oracle she speaks of the future from the point of view of a trial between men and gods, seeing it as a subtle and dangerous

game where nothing is fixed in advance, in which those consulting the gods must know how to time their questions oppor-
tunely, accepting or rejecting the oracle and even turning into
their own advantage an answer given by the god in favor of their
adversary.

It's true that this brilliant analysis makes the ancient Greeks
sound like lucid modern Frenchmen, and of course the Greeks, like
the members of any culture inhabiting a world of stories, would
understand the logic of their own myths without having to behave
like logicians—just as the native speakers of any language respect
the grammar they may not be aware of. But we need to see that
there is a logic of myth, and in these stories of Themis and Metis
some very difficult possibilities are being negotiated. For the gods
the world is both stable and unstable, unchanging and erratic; for
humans it is fixed and not fixed, fated and free. And Zeus, having
married these two goddesses, knows and represents all this. As Vernant says in another book, "Greek gods are powers, not persons,"
and Zeus's power has both "an aspect of regularity, of constancy,
and an aspect of unpredictability, of the benevolent and the terrifying." These different views of the world and destiny are not contradictory, for gods or for humans. Both views are manifestly
true—and also true, I would suggest, for cultures quite different
from that of the ancient Greeks. Things are not either fixed or not
fixed, they are both. But the views are not both true at the same
time, and once Zeus has taken on the very different forms of
knowledge of Themis and Metis, mere humans can never know
which aspect he will show at any given time, which card he will
choose to play.

In one sense there is a philosophical trick in such thinking, a
sleight of narrative I have already evoked. Themis, or her husband
thinking like Themis, "spells out the future as if it was already

written and . . . expresses what will be as if it were what is." In matters of the deep regularities of the universe, like the law of gravity or the inevitability of unemployment under capitalism, this is what we would call science, rational prediction rather than magic. The "as if" in such a context is scarcely a figure of speech, because the future, barring miracles, is as good as written already. But in more transitory and volatile human affairs, like love and war and World Cup soccer, any invocation of the knowledge of Themis is going to look like hindsight masquerading as foresight—even if, as I have also suggested earlier, the outcome in question was actually foreseen. Only the addition of hindsight to foresight is going to make this into a destiny. But such thinking is not always a trick.

Conversely, Metis works with what we now call probabilities. We consult her about the odds, and if we are superstitious, we may pretend the odds are a little better than she actually says they are. This is where the equivocations mainly arise. We find ambiguities in Metis's language that seem to tilt her oracles in our favor, or we (later) accuse her of misleading us through such ambiguities. But Metis's perspective is after all a little too close to our own, and we can see why Zeus needed another wife in his early days. What Metis doesn't know, and what Themis knows all too well, is the aspect of divine and human happening that really is inevitable—not because it is magically predetermined, or because the Three Fates say so, but because the multiple grounds of the event have long been in place, and it takes only ordinary, if unseen and complicated, causality to bring it about. We still need hindsight to confirm this knowledge, but a goddess might be pretty confident about the ultimate arrival of the confirmation. When historians who are not Marxists say that the Mexican Revolution of 1910, for example, was inevitable, they mean that once the reasons for the revolution are fully understood, it is hard to see how it could *not* have happened. This is not an absolute inevitability, perhaps, and stops short of the rather bleak certainty of Themis. But it goes quite a bit beyond any odds Metis could have given us.

These questions, famously, are Tolstoy's topic in his epilogue to *War and Peace*. What historians offer as causes for the Franco-Russian War of 1812 are insufficient, he says. That is, they don't explain, and they are not enough in number. "The causes that suggest themselves are legion," he says. And he reaches a (surprising) first conclusion by saying, "And so there was no single cause for the war, but it happened simply because it had to happen." This sounds like fatalism, but Tolstoy introduces this view only to attack it. "We inevitably resort to fatalism to explain the irrational phenomena of history (that is to say, phenomena the reasonableness of which we do not understand) . . ." Tolstoy's parenthesis gives the game away, or part of the game. What he calls a "law of coincidence" is not a law of coincidence at all but a law of collision or conjunction, or a law of coinciding perhaps, which says that lots of things happen, ineluctably, at the same time. Napoleon and Alexander were "never . . . so subject to inevitable laws" as when they thought they were acting freely. "Consciously man lives for himself, but unconsciously he serves as an instrument for the accomplishment of the historical, social ends of mankind . . ." The apparently free acts of Napoleon and Alexander are "in the historical sense, not free at all, but . . . connected with the whole course of history and determined from eternity." As I understand him, Tolstoy is here confusing, with great skill, several entirely different states of affairs: that events have many causes; that once things have happened they cannot be undone; that historical consequences often far outrun anyone's intentions; that events usually acquire their meaning after they have happened; and an assumption of what looks like flat-out determinism.

What is he up to? A trick worthy of Zeus himself. He evokes "the mysterious forces which move humanity (mysterious because the laws determining their action are unknown to us)" and goes on to say that words like *chance* and *genius* are only ways of saying we don't know what we are talking about. And then he produces his hidden card, a canny mixture of modesty and overreaching, as if Metis and Themis were one person after all. If we renounce all our claims to knowing historical causes in any familiar way, we shall have to admit—here's where the card slips out of the sleeve—not that there are no causes, or that there are merely multiple, contingent causes, but that there are deep and final causes that we don't know. "Only by renouncing the claim to knowledge of an ultimate aim immediately intelligible to us, and admitting the ultimate purpose to be beyond our comprehension, may we discern the logical consistency and expediency of the lives of historical personages; the cause of the effect they produce, which is incommensurate with ordinary human capacity, is then revealed to us . . ." Revealed to us, that is, as a reminder of our ignorance. And again: "As the sun and each atom of ether is a sphere complete in itself, yet at the same time only a part of a whole too vast for man to comprehend, so each individual bears within himself his own purpose, yet bears it to serve a general purpose unfathomable to man . . . The higher the human intellect rises in the revelation of these purposes, the more obvious it becomes that the ultimate purpose is beyond our comprehension." It's a dazzling performance: cause and purpose are completely unknown and therefore permanently intact, beyond the reach of narrow human reason and therefore untouchable by our faith or our doubt. Of course, only the deepest longing for cause and purpose would make you believe such a thing.

But we need a story to make clearer what is happening in such discussions, and perhaps a story that is not quite so classically mythological. Once upon a time . . .

Once upon a time

Once upon a time, and a very turbulent time it was, there was a king who had come to the throne by violent means, murdering his predecessor in his bed. He reigned for many years and brought peace to the land, although the threat of violence was never entirely absent, and he made many enemies. When he named his eldest son as his successor, this very act served as a provocation to one of the king's leading generals. The general murdered the king in his bed and mounted the throne himself. He reigned for many years. There was not much to choose between the two kings. They were men of their time, they were courageous and cruel, they lived in a world of perpetual vendetta.

Once upon a time, the same turbulent time in fact, there was a weak king who badly misgoverned his land. His sudden nomination of his eldest son as his successor seemed to guarantee the continuing national disarray, so one of the king's foremost generals murdered the king and mounted the throne himself. The new king reigned for fourteen years, settled the quarreling factions within his country, defeated the country's external enemies, and was hugely admired, in his lifetime and long after his death, as a national hero.

Once upon a time there was a king who, after a long and peaceful reign, decided to nominate his eldest son as his successor. The nobles were a little surprised but took no counteraction. Except for one of them, who had long coveted the throne. Soon after the king's announcement, this lord found an opportunity to murder the king and blame the murder on the king's eldest son, who promptly took flight to another country. The old king was mild and gentle; almost saintly; the new king was driven by the most naked longing for earthly power and glory.

The new king had scarcely begun his reign when the other nobles rebelled against him, and he was killed at the end of a sequence of fierce battles.

We can imagine all kinds of other variants. The new king
doesn't act alone against the old king, he has a coconspirator, or a
whole set of coconspirators. His motive is neither ambition nor the
honor of the nation but quite different: a preemptive strike, for instance, since he has grounds for believing the old king is out to get
him; insane jealousy; a long-resisted compulsion to crime. And of
course we can add other kinds of players to the story—witches, for
example—as we shall do in a moment. But let's just stay with what
we've got, and imagine we have consulted both of our goddesses
about this story, now that we know as much as the goddesses do
about its ending—or its endings. The oracle of Themis will have insisted in each case on the turbulence of the times, the inevitability of
violence, and the relative brevity even of long human reigns. It will
have nothing to say about the timing of events or opportunities
taken and missed, or about the ethical matters that are so central to
so many of our stories: Was the old king a good man? Was the new
king a good ruler? Did anyone here deserve what happened to them?
The oracle of Metis, by contrast, will have spoken of just these
things, and will have emphasized particular occasions, the moments
when events could have turned out differently but didn't: the day of
the nomination of the successor, the repeated murders in the beds,
the details of conspiracy and war and practical rule. And both oracles will have been right. It is true that violence breeds violence, and
that even in peace death cannot be indefinitely postponed. It is also
true that human beings (some of them) survive times of violence,
and that although someone dies every day, that someone doesn't have
to be me. We must, I think, as the Greeks did, believe in Metis till
our time is up, our story over. Then we shall have no choice but to

see that Themis was right all along, but only because we and Metis
played our parts, took the chances that led to what now looks like
necessity, followed the roads that led to a conclusion that was not in
any sense narrowly determined but that cannot now be undone.

The equivocation of the fiend

> May they not be my oracles as well
> And set me up in hope?

This is Banquo's question about the weird sisters in Shakespeare's
Macbeth. They may be, indeed they are his oracles, but they can't set
him up in hope. They reveal, in a long show or shadow play, a line
of Scottish kings descended from him, reaching almost, but not
quite, to Mary Queen of Scots and her son, James VI of Scotland
and James I of England, reigning monarch of both countries at the
time the play was first performed. But Banquo can't see or enjoy
this sight because by this moment in the story he is dead, and his
murdered body is itself part of the spectacle. All he has during his
lifetime is the sisters' initial, elliptical pronouncement:

> Lesser than Macbeth, and greater.
> Not so happy, yet much happier.
> Thou shalt get kings, though thou be none.

My oracles as well. Mine as well as Macbeth's, Banquo means,
and of course Macbeth does get to see the display Banquo is denied, although it can't set him up in hope either, because it is designed to do the very opposite. "Show his eyes and grieve his
heart," the sisters say in chorus with considerable cruel relish.
Macbeth sees a line of eight kings, with "many more" projected

through a magic ball or mirror. Even halfway through he thinks the procession seems endless. "What, will the line stretch out to th' crack of doom?" "The blood-boltered Banquo" brings up the rear, and indicates that all these kings belong to his lineage ("points at them for his"), smiling at Macbeth to make the pain more exquisite. Macbeth has murdered his king, defiled his mind, as he puts it, solely to establish Banquo's family on the throne of Scotland for as far as the future can be seen.

This crisscrossing of oracle and recipient—Banquo can't see his own scarcely confessed hopes fulfilled, but Macbeth can see with despair what Banquo would have seen with delight—suggests a kind of malevolence in the system, a structural cruelty in the design of the oracles and their delivery. This is entirely compatible with the play's repeated assertion that the sisters are the agents of the devil, and with what many have seen as Shakespeare's attack on the very idea of equivocation, or what Macbeth calls "lying like truth"—that is, telling the truth in a technical sense but making huge mental reservations or actually meaning something quite different. "The unnatural thing," Garry Wills says in his book *Witches and Jesuits*, referring to the sisters' equivocal prophecies about a moving wood and Macbeth's freedom from the possibility of being harmed by anyone "of woman born," "is not Birnam Wood's moving or Macduff's nonbirth birth but the unnatural (Jesuitical) language of the witches, the destruction of reality in *words* misused."

Banquo himself says, when he and Macbeth first meet the sisters,

> And oftentimes, to win us to our harm,
> The instruments of darkness tell us truths;
> Win us with honest trifles, to betray's
> In deepest consequence.

The immediate context is the sisters' second salutation of Macbeth. First they call him Thane of Glamis, which he is. Then they call him Thane of Cawdor, which he isn't. Within moments Macbeth learns that Cawdor has turned traitor to Duncan, has been captured, and is about to be executed, his title falling to Macbeth as a reward for his loyalty and feats in battle. As soon as he hears this news, Banquo says, "What, can the devil speak true?" The lines quoted above are his more reflective commentary on this exclamation. In one of the ancient histories that lie behind Raphael Holinshed's *Chronicles*, Macbeth is said to be the son of the devil, and diabolical associations surround him in the play. "By the pricking of my thumbs," one of the sisters mutters, "Something wicked this way comes." Macbeth appears. When Macbeth names himself on the battlefield, his opponent says

> The devil himself could not pronounce a title
> More hateful to mine ear.

And in another (comic) register, the porter of Macbeth's castle at Inverness famously compares his job to that of working at hell's gate. The moral of the story appears to be that if you deal with the devil (or with Jesuits), you must expect to be cheated. This is Macbeth's own final view, when he says

> And be these juggling fiends no more believed
> That palter with us in a double sense,
> That keep the word of promise to our ear
> And break it to our hope.

Within minutes he is dead. A little earlier he has said that he begins

To doubt th'equivocation of the fiend
That lies like truth.

Doubt here means both "suspect" and "wonder about"—that is, Macbeth both suspects that the fiend is equivocating rather than telling a single or plain truth and thinks he knows how the equivocation works.

But is all equivocation the work of the devil, and must all claims to know the future be the devil's work? Aren't there other oracles as well?

Consider this sequence of propositions, which I will put back into their context in a moment:

None of woman born shall harm Macbeth.
Macbeth can be harmed but only by a man not born of woman.
Macbeth is slain by a man but not one born of woman.

The slither here—and the drama, and much else—lies in the subtle movement of altered logic: "none" becomes "only this kind" and then "only this man." In that slither an open promise becomes a closed prophecy. I want to suggest that this is how prophecy typically works and also that this motion meets a very particular human need, what we might call a pathology of promising. Promises are kept, but promises are also often not kept, and we need to be prepared for that eventuality. The pathology arises when a promise is manifestly not kept but we can't bring ourselves to believe this. Our favorite strategy in this situation is to reinterpret the promise so that what looked like its breaking was a hasty illusion; on reinterpretation we see the promise has been kept after all, we have not been betrayed. Whose promises do we cling to in this way? Those of God or the gods; of our parents and loved ones; those of anyone whose reliability is more important to us than any truth contained in their apparent defection.

Here's another oracle with a subtle slither.

The king shall have no heir if that which is lost be not found.
The king shall have no heir until his lost daughter is found.
The king has an heir because his lost daughter has been found.

The oracle appears in Shakespeare's *The Winter's Tale* and is delivered by the god Apollo. He has various other things to say, and it has seemed surprising to many that he is emphatically clear about some things and riddling and oracular about others. In fact, what's surprising is the almost clumsy clarity with which Shakespeare's Apollo exercises the double function of oracles: to tell us a certain truth and to remind us how uncertain truth is. The oracle says emphatically that the king is "a jealous tyrant," that his wife and friend are faithful, that the child suspected of illegitimacy is undoubtedly his own, and then slips without warning into a riddle, in fact a phrase taken verbatim from Robert Greene, Shakespeare's source: "and the King shall live without an heir if that which is lost be not found."

This riddle is not impenetrable but it is curiously open-ended. If the king never has an heir, the oracle is fulfilled anyway. It doesn't matter what he lost, all that matters is that he didn't find it. If he remarries and has an heir, he will need to have lost and found something nameable, but almost anything will do. A ring, a crown; or something more moral or metaphysical—his faith, his nerve, his dignity. But this king has lost a daughter; her very name, Perdita, given to her by her despairing mother, tells us this. If Perdita stays lost, and the king has no other heir, the oracle is still fulfilled. If she is found, and the king has no other heir, the oracle is also fulfilled. But her being found was not part of the oracle's prediction. It spoke only of the consequences of *not* finding her—indeed it didn't speak specifically of her at all.

In *The Winter's Tale* the oracle that actually promises Perdita's return, and takes over the plot of the whole play, is not given by Apollo at all, but is produced by a strong rewriting of what Apollo said. First, "that which is lost" is identified as Perdita and no one and nothing else. And more drastically, the oracle's "if not" becomes an "until." Paulina, a lady-in-waiting at the king's court, and chief agent of the play's resolution, exclaims,

> For has not the divine Apollo said,
> Is't not the tenor of his oracle,
> That King Leontes shall not have an heir
> Till his lost child be found?

Well, no, that wasn't what Apollo said. It's true that Paulina thinks this development is impossible: "his lost child be found? Which that it shall,/Is all as monstrous to our human reason/As my Antigonus to break his grave/And come again to me . . ." But her language is more hopeful than she is. "Till," in its way, is quite emphatic, surely an implicit promise that the child will be found sooner or later. So it looks as if the oracle that was fulfilled was the rewritten oracle—a promise, not a riddle. In fact, both were fulfilled, and this is where we enter the territory of what I am calling slither.

When a character in the play says "the oracle is fulfill'd; the king's daughter is found," it sounds as if the oracle promised Perdita's rediscovery, and certainly only the rewritten oracle promised that. And when Perdita's mother says she stayed alive because the oracle gave her hope of seeing her daughter again, she must also be taking the rewritten oracle as her guide.

I,

Knowing by Paulina that the oracle
Gave hope thou wast in being, have preserv'd
Myself to see the issue.

But of course the original oracle didn't say these happy reunions
would not occur; it merely didn't say they would.

When Macbeth goes to consult the weird sisters, they produce a
series of apparitions for him. Macbeth is told to "beware Macduff"
and to "beware the Thane of Fife"—these are not two people, although they might well be, given the switching of thanedoms that
goes on in this play. Macbeth is not surprised by this warning, merely
thanks the spirit for the "good caution" and says, "Thou hast harped
my fear aright." The second apparition tells him that he may

Laugh to scorn
The pow'r of man, for none of woman born
Shall harm Macbeth.

Macbeth is reassured, but thinks he probably should have Macduff
killed anyway, to "make assurance double sure." Macduff thwarts
this plan by fleeing to England. What's interesting here—this was
the point of my joke about Macduff and the Thane of Fife not being two people—is that, as with Perdita and "that which was lost,"
an equivocating game of reference is being played. "None of
woman born" looks at first as if it's simply a hyperbole for "no
one," but quickly takes on the more specific apparent reference "not
Macduff, or not even Macduff." The second apparition, that is,
seems to counteract the first. But of course what the prediction
turns out to mean is "only Macduff, Macduff and no one else."
Both apparitions are talking about Macduff; Macduff is the refer-
ent of both stories.

If Macduff had stayed in England and Macbeth had died in his bed at a ripe old age, the prophecy would still have been fulfilled, as it would if he had been killed by a bear, or any other nonhuman agent. The sneaky part of the prophecy is that it does seem to rest on detailed knowledge of the Macduff family history—as we learn when Macduff tells Macbeth that he was "from his mother's womb/Untimely ripped."

The oracle logic, the subtle slither of the argument, is even clearer in Holinshed than it is in Shakespeare. In Shakespeare, Macbeth recites the prophecy to Macduff, who tells him about his birth. In Holinshed, Macbeth says he is "not appointed to be slain by any creature that is born of woman," and Macduff, responding to some kind of magical knowledge of the story script rather than Macbeth's speech, says, "I am even he that thy wizards have told thee of, who was never born of my mother, but ripped out of her womb." This resembles the movement of interpretation in *The Winter's Tale*, because the wizards ("a certain witch," actually—Macduff's magical intelligence is not quite accurate) didn't tell Macbeth of anyone, they told him of no one. "Not appointed to be slain by any creature that is born of woman" becomes "appointed to be slain by precisely this person, this never-born man." It is as if Macbeth had been told that nobody could kill him, and Macduff is saying I am that nobody, or my name is Nobody: a ghastly joke, which has its echoes in the *Odyssey*, and in *Alice in Wonderland*. The second prophecy—that only Macduff can slay Macbeth—is the one that gets fulfilled most obviously and most particularly, in Holinshed and in Shakespeare. But the other, earlier one is fulfilled too. It said none of woman born would harm Macbeth; it didn't say he wouldn't be harmed.

There are all kinds of interesting distinctions to be made here: between the initial prophecy and its rewriting, between prophecy and event, and especially between what remains a possibility and what has become a plot—that is, between the prophecy as prophecy, where the appropriate question is always one of interpretation, of what will count as fulfillment, and the combined prophecy and conclusion, which now looks like, and indeed is, a form of absolute necessity, not because it had to happen, but because it already has.

An analytic philosopher would need to clear these matters up, and it's worth remembering J. L. Austin's warning: "it is not enough to show how clever we are by showing how obscure everything is." It is not enough, but I think we can pause over the blur and speed of the slither and try to show the work it does. It is Austin who, on another occasion, speaks of "the innumerable and unforeseeable demands of the world upon language," and among those demands must be an acknowledgment of the hunger for certainty and of the fact that promises are kept, which nevertheless will not deny the repeated recurrence of uncertainty and the world's many unkept promises. We can acknowledge these demands as perhaps necessary contradictions; but the idea of contradiction doesn't get us quite close enough to what is happening.

This is where we need to see the metaphor of slither as an image of a kind of cultural work, a functioning mythology that allows logical alternatives to haunt each other incessantly, without ever seeking or finding a middle space or resolution. On ordinary days, or if we are not especially interested in the intricate machinery of oracles, we are not supposed to notice the slither—that's how it works.

The oracle in *The Winter's Tale* says, in effect, I do not promise the king an heir, but you may choose to find a promise in my riddle. Once Perdita is found, this initial speech act is interesting only as a forsaken horizon of possibility, a memory of choice. But the memory of freedom haunts the closed, finished plot. In *Macbeth* the weird sisters say, in effect, we promise you will not be killed except by a miracle, but we do not promise the miracle will not take place. The miracle itself, even as it confirms the necessity of Macbeth's doom, underlines the more open order it is subverting.

But Macbeth gets yet another revelation. A third apparition says,

> Macbeth shall never vanquished be until
> Great Birnam Wood to high Dunsinane Hill
> Shall come against him.

This sounds promising, and is ultimately, as everyone knows, deeply deceptive. Birnam Wood moves to Dunsinane because the Scottish and English soldiers led by Macduff and Duncan's son Malcolm are instructed each to take a bough from a tree as camouflage. We may wonder, if we are stubbornly literal-minded, why they couldn't have found their camouflage in a forest a little nearer to Dunsinane, but to think this is to stray from the point of the deceptive promise, where the awkwardness of interpretative accommodation is actually a boon, a reminder of how strange and intricate these things are.

The witches' promises turn out not to be promises at all but riddles—quite a different animal. A riddle often gives you help if you can crack it. But if you don't know it's a riddle, you can't even try to crack it—what would there be to crack? By a hideous, mounting irony, as Macbeth's allies defect and his enemies rise against him, he needs more and more for the promises to be magical after all, and it becomes clearer and clearer that no promises were made. Now we may feel that Macbeth has got what he deserved, but we also surely feel he has been tricked. How exactly has this happened? Let's return to the pagan modes of equivocation, like the Delphic oracle's answer to Nero.

Suppose the witches in *Macbeth* have not read the whole play and don't know how it ends—don't know about the trees used for camouflage or Macduff's untimely nonbirth. Or to put that less frivolously, suppose the witches, at the time Macbeth consults them, don't know the future—or don't know all of the future. This time the oracle guesses wrong. By "none of woman born," it means no one; by "until/Great Birnam Wood to high Dunsinane Hill/Shall come against him," it means never. Macbeth is to be consoled about his own long life, and crushed with the repetition of the news about Banquo's children: a balanced account. When Macduff kills Macbeth both prophecies have to be revised. They can't be revoked but they can be reinterpreted, although it takes some fancy footwork. One key phrase has to be remodeled in a rather strained way—do we usually think of cesarean births as not births?—and the other requires some strenuous plot action to convert it from an easy figure of speech into a crude military maneuver. And—this is the truly tricky bit—these reinterpretations have to be inserted into the text so that they will seem part of the events themselves rather than a crafty afterthought. It mustn't look as if the oracle rewrote the story, it must look as if the rewritten story is all there ever was, and Macbeth himself must understand the equivocations that misled him, the riddles that he took for promises. In the language of modern philosophy he must see that he was playing the wrong game, the promise game. In the promise game, you know what the words mean and you hope the promise will be kept. In the riddle game, you have to find out what the words mean before you can know what to hope for. "Fear none born of woman" as a promise means fear none born of woman. As a riddle it means: work out who will count as not being born of woman, and that will be the person who will kill you.

Thrones of blood

Now let us imagine *Macbeth* set in medieval Japan. We don't have to work very hard at this, since a great film director, Akira Kurosawa, has already imagined it for us. The film is *Throne of Blood*, more literally translated as *The Castle of the Spider's Web*, and also known as *Cobweb Castle, Spiderweb Castle,* and . . . *Macbeth*. There are no devils here except those of human rapacity and ambition.

The politics of this world are those of the first of the versions of *Macbeth* I evoked earlier. The film's equivalent of Duncan, the lord of Kumonosu, Cobweb Castle, has become supreme ruler by killing the previous lord, and Miki, alias Banquo, says confidentially to Washizu/Macbeth that "dreams are the expression of our five desires. Frankly speaking, every warrior has dreamt of becoming lord of the castle." A little later, talking to his wife, Washizu evokes this dream as if it were ultimately unthinkable, only to get a determinedly realistic answer from her. "The lord of Kumonosu Castle," he says. "To have such an inordinate desire . . ." She says, "You shouldn't say that it's an inordinate desire . . . You know well there's no warrior who does not crave it."

By this stage Miki and Washizu have met a strange androgynous figure in the endless forest, who has told them pretty much what the weird sisters told Macbeth and Banquo: that one of them will become the supreme lord, and that the other one's son will take over the lordship in the further future. Miki and Washizu, like the hearty, unreflecting samurai that they are, think this is a huge joke, and kid each other about it. But of course, although they are not in the habit of thinking, they can brood, and this is what brings Washizu to his conversation with his wife, the redoubtable Asaji. She reminds him that the current lord "ascended the throne by killing his previous lord, as you well know." Washizu says "the previous lord distrusted our lord and tried to kill him! Our lord trusts me! I say, he treats me most kindly." Asaji says that is because "he doesn't know what's at the bottom of your heart." In the translated screenplay Washizu replies, "At the bottom of my heart? Why, there's nothing shameful in me!" but in the English subtitle of the version most often screened, he says, as if in an eerie, distorted echo of Macbeth's own play with the word, "At the bottom of my heart? There is nothing." This might be true, but then there is no reason why a such a heart couldn't give a home to a bottomless ambition, and in any case Asaji says she knows otherwise.

The crux of the argument for Washizu at this stage—later he will worry about Miki's son, and have Miki killed and see his ghost—is that Miki knows the prophecy and may perhaps tell their lord about it. There is nothing like this in Shakespeare, and Asaji insists on the point. In this world, she says, "parents kill their children and children kill their parents. This is a corrupt age when we must kill others to avoid being killed." In such a climate, overthrowing the lord and taking his place would be more of a preemptive strike than an act of treason. Washizu tells her not to be so distrustful.

It's far from clear that Asaji is right, and her later cool complicity in the murder of the lord plunges her deep into the film's idea of evil, but it's not clear at this stage that she is entirely wrong about the world they live in. The supreme lord is arriving as a guest at their castle, the occasion a hunting expedition. What if this were a feint, a prelude to an attack? It is a feint and a prelude to an attack, but on a neighboring lord, not on Washizu. He is right for the moment, but couldn't she be right next time? A question for an oracle.

The story continues as in Shakespeare's *Macbeth*, and we need only to pick it up at the moment Washizu visits the strange figure in the forest again. The figure has all kinds of things to say—"you finally came to the last step of delusion," she remarks—and as-

sumes various more and more warlike and more masculine disguises. But as an oracle she concentrates on just one of the weird
sisters' prophecies: the moving forest. Exactly the same equivocation occurs here. The promise seems to say that Washizu can be
conquered only when the Cobweb Forest moves toward Cobweb
Castle—that is, never. It turns out to mean he will be conquered as
soon as the forest moves, whenever that is. But there is a difference
surrounding this identical equivocation. First, this forest has already played a huge part in the film. It is a forest that is supposed
to baffle all enemies and protect only those who know it well, like
Washizu and Miki and the locals. Except that when they leave the
strange figure the first time, Washizu and Miki get lost in this place
that they claim to find so familiar. They are caught up in thunder,
lightning, and rain, as if to mirror the witches' language in *Macbeth*,
and they hear the mocking laughter of a spirit among the trees.
Kurosawa represents this altered relation to the forest by shooting
the two men through screens of branches that look like cobwebs or
miniature labyrinths, and by having them finally ride their horses
toward us out of the mist and up to what seems the edge of the
cinema screen, then return to the depths of the mist and become
invisible, only to come pounding back into view, bewildered, again
and again. This process goes on longer than you can quite believe.

And second, Washizu and the witch are in the forest when the
prophecy is made, surrounded by trees as real as cinematography
can make them. Shakespeare's Macbeth underlines the figure of
speech, as if to question and confirm it. "Who can impress the
forest, bid the tree/Unfix his earth-bound root?" No one, is the
answer to the rhetorical question, although Macbeth himself earlier
seemed to think trees could speak, and if they could speak, why
couldn't they move? Washizu asks the same question, but also looks
around him at the thick and undeniable trees, as if to say, you're
telling me I'm safe until this very forest moves? This glance is not a

rhetorical question, not even an implied one, it is the frank contemplation of an impossibility, and that is how the film plays out. What Kurosawa shows us is not the easy subterfuge of Malcolm and the English—well, he does show us the same subterfuge adopted by Washizu's enemies, but only later, after the forest has moved—but the literal accomplishment of a miracle. Washizu is confronted by what looks like a revolt of nature, as if the physical world itself had risen up to resist his tyranny.

In Shakespeare, Macbeth doesn't even see the moving forest, and there is a distinct spookiness in the language of his realization of what has happened. A messenger tells him of "a moving grove," prefacing his news with the acutely cautious phrase "I should report that which I say I saw"—two removes from perception, and three removes from the thing itself. Macbeth twice uses *if* about the prophecy's apparent fulfillment—if this is true, he doesn't care if he starves to death; if this is true, "there is no flying hence nor tarrying here"—but never verifies the fact. This is extraordinarily effective dramatically, since it makes Macbeth's mind the real location of the prediction and its accomplishment. He doesn't need to see the moving grove, because he knows it's there—because in some sense he has always known it would be there one day.

In Kurosawa, Washizu is told about the moving forest and goes to look himself. He sees it clearly enough, but more important, so do we. It's as real as anything else in the movie, as real as Washizu himself, the estimable and physically solid actor Toshiro Mifune. It just is a moving forest, whatever the details we later learn of the trick. It's true we have had some subtle earlier clues, which will have helped us if we know the story. Soldiers in Washizu's castle hear chopping sounds in the night and think the enemy is perhaps making fences. Birds invade the castle, unhoused, we later realize, by what is happening to the forest. But when Washizu sees the forest move, we are with him, and there is nothing else to see. The forest fills the screen, tall conifers waving in the mist, not a soldier in sight, and whole trees are shifting magically toward the castle, not a few branches or paltry pieces of camouflage. The forest itself is moving, no doubt about it, and in the cinema we can't unsee what we have seen. We realize almost without thinking that Washizu misunderstood the oracle not because it paltered with him in a double sense but because its single sense was an unimaginable truth, and he dies, in a ferocious storm of arrows unleashed by his own men, without overcoming his entirely legitimate surprise. As in *Macbeth* the hero's undoing is all his own violent work, but in *Throne of Blood* the cosmos itself seems to sign the verdict. The fiend was not equivocating, and probably not a fiend. If Washizu were a Greek, he would know that he had fallen out of the arms of Metis and into the unyielding grasp of Themis.

NINE: VESTIGES

Reality is under no obligation to be interesting.
 Jorge Luis Borges, "Death and the Compass"

Plenty of hope

Walter Benjamin writes of "a sort of theological whispered intelligence" in the work of Franz Kafka. Is it the god whispering or only the rustle of the trees? Kafka is afraid it is just the trees but has to write as if it were the god. There is an excellent introduction to this fraught and familiar situation in the correspondence between Benjamin and his friend Gershom Scholem. Benjamin, in an essay, had described Kafka's world as, among other things, a place in which the students in the prayer house have lost the scripture. "The door to righteousness is study. And yet Kafka does not dare to link this study to the promises which the tradition connects to the study of the Torah." In response, Scholem wanted to distinguish between students who have lost the scripture and students who cannot decipher it. The problem, he said, is not the absence of revelation but the impossibility of its completion. Benjamin (of all people) answered that he couldn't see the difference. "Whether the students have lost it or whether they are unable to decipher it comes down to the same thing, because, without the key that belongs to it, the scripture is not scripture but life." Scholem was distressed. "I certainly cannot share your opinion that it doesn't matter whether the students have lost the scripture or whether they can't decipher it, and I view this as the greatest error that could happen to you." Translating this dialogue into oracle-talk, we find these alternatives. The god speaks, Benjamin says, but no one understands him, and this is just the same as if he didn't speak at all. On the contrary, Scholem says, what's important is that the god speaks, whether we understand him or not. To imagine that a god who speaks is the same as a god who doesn't speak is to imagine that it doesn't matter whether the god is hidden or never existed at all. Precisely my point, Benjamin says, or would say if he were reading my script rather than his own. What Benjamin actually says is so rich it has to be read in full. It appears in a letter from Paris, dated June 12, 1938, which includes the phrase I've already quoted about the theological whispered intelligence.

Benjamin says that in Kafka there is no question of wisdom, but only of the products of the decay of wisdom. He cites the famous story told by Kafka's friend and biographer Max Brod about Kafka's idea of hope. Kafka remarks that we are "nihilistic thoughts that came into God's head." Brod mentions the Gnostics and their idea of the demiurge, but Kafka suggests we are not as important as that:

> "I believe we are not such a radical relapse of God's, only one of his bad moods. He had a bad day."
> "So there would be no hope outside our world?"
> He smiled. "Plenty of hope—for God—no end of hope—only not for us."

This last sentence, Benjamin surprisingly says, really contains Kafka's hope, and "is the source of his radiant gaiety." A moment later, in a slightly different register, Benjamin adds, "One might say: as soon as [Kafka] was sure of his ultimate failure, everything else succeeded for him like a dream."

No success like failure, as Bob Dylan used to moan, and these paradoxes are apt to make your head spin. Benjamin doesn't let up, though, and in a letter written the following year (February 4, 1939), he mischievously compares Kafka and Brod to Laurel and Hardy and picks up his own image of the key to the scripture: "I think the key to Kafka would fall into the hands of the person who could find the comic side of Jewish theology." What's important to understand, I think, is the closeness and the difference of the positions on offer. Both Benjamin and Scholem are talking about a world haunted by theological need, although that world may see itself as thoroughly secularized; about a place where even absent or nonexistent revelation is still a major player. But Scholem is arguing for the presence of an (at times) unintelligible god, while Benjamin is insisting on the god's complete absence as a kind of modern fate. How does Benjamin find hope in Kafka's apparently hopeless joke? There is the smile, of course, which Brod insists on, here and elsewhere in his biography. But Benjamin also thinks that in a radically troubled world—the world of Kafka is determined, Benjamin says, by mystical experience on the one hand and by the experience of the great modern city on the other—all certainties have their charm, even entirely negative ones. A perfect lack of hope is a (comic) form of perfection, and God's hope, we might say, is merely the extravagant accumulation of all the hope we haven't got.

The work of Kafka is the great modern elaboration, executed with ironic lucidity and desolate, breathtaking humor, of the oracles of the possibly nonexistent god. Not all of Kafka's writing fits this description, and indeed some of the most famous parts of it belong to quite different regions of doubt. The notion of the Kafkaesque, for instance, doesn't ordinarily include the oracular.

Gregor Samsa, in "Metamorphosis," doesn't consult anyone about becoming a giant insect, he just wakes up that way, to his and everyone else's surprise. If Joseph K, in *The Trial*, calls down the court authorities upon himself, he does so unwittingly, and through some kind of ghastly, magical sympathy that is in the nature of the court. These are visitations, attacks, not trips to any kind of Delphi. The same is true of the father's onslaught in "The Judgment," which leads directly to the son's unambiguous suicide.

But once Joseph K's case has begun, he consults a number of authorities, and a dizzying kind of oracle-writing, characteristic of all Kafka's late work, sets in. Think of the brilliantly hairsplitting distinctions the court painter Titorelli makes among the options available to K once his case has been set in motion. "There are three possibilities," Titorelli says, "definite acquittal, ostensible acquittal, and indefinite postponement." Definite acquittal would be the best, of course, but for that you would have to go through the whole trial and get the right result. Nothing in the novel suggests this is a probability, and a great deal suggests that in this system worrying about the trial *is* the trial. In any case, the painter says, he can't influence that kind of verdict, and has actually never encountered such a case, so they are left with the other two options. But what is the difference between them? Well, "ostensible acquittal demands temporary concentration, while postponement taxes your strength less but means a steady strain."

For ostensible acquittal the painter would get an affidavit of innocence endorsed by a series of judges, and when enough signatures had been accumulated the accused man would be pronounced free. "But only ostensibly free, or more exactly, provisionally free," because the judges who signed the affidavit belong to a lower court, whose ruling could be overturned at any moment. A long time may pass before this happens, and the case may even be forgotten or lost. But it is also possible, the painter says, "for the acquitted man

to go straight home from the Court and find officers waiting to arrest him again." Of course the man could then start the process all
over again, and get another ostensible, but only ostensible, acquittal. And then, the painter says remorselessly, "the second acquittal
is followed by the third arrest, the third acquittal by the fourth
arrest, and so on. That is implied in the very conception of ostensible acquittal." K says nothing, and the painter wonders if postponement, the other option, might suit him better.

"Postponement," we learn, "consists in preventing the case from
ever getting any further than its first stages." This has the advantage
of staving off "the terrors of sudden arrest," but of course the accused man has to work on his case all the time, to submit to regular interrogations, for example, in order to stop his case from
actually coming up in court. You can be acquitted, in other words,
but not really acquitted; and you can be accused, but not finally accused. You can't be unaccused once the accusation is made, once
the process (the German title of the novel means both "trial" and
"process") has begun; you can't be completely released; and you
can't be finally tried. The very provisions for deferment make an actual acquittal impossible, as K gloomily realizes, and says. "You
have grasped the kernel of the matter," the painter replies.

In the strict logic of this scheme you can't be sentenced either,
but in this respect Kafka's novel eludes its own logic, and K is executed by two men in frock coats and top hats. "Like a dog," as he
says to himself before dying. "Logic is doubtless unshakable,"
Kafka writes a sentence or two before this, "but it cannot with-
stand a man who wants to go on living." Or a novelist who wants
his character to die, who momentarily prefers a brutal certainty to
all the dizzying uncertainties in which he has become an expert.
Because of course what is painful and wonderful about Titorelli's
options is the subtle way in which they invite the argument between
Benjamin and Scholem. If definite acquittal is unknown in the

world of the court, does it still count as a real, but undecipherable scripture? Or is it lost, irrelevant, an old mirage, even a hindrance to freedom? Do the distinctions between ostensible acquittal and indefinite postponement really matter, if what you want is for your case to be over rather than eternalized? Titorelli is a failed oracle for K in one sense, a successful one in another. He fails to give him any help or comfort, but not because he says too little or is too ambiguous. He is lucid and even garrulous about the world's ambiguity, and K understands him all too well. This is not Heraclitus' oracle of the god who certainly exists but only gives signs. This is the oracle of a god who may or may not exist, and whose signs therefore may not be signs at all, and who almost certainly will not show up on Judgment Day. For the Hopkins of "Spelt from Sibyl's Leaves" this might be a kind of consolation, but for Kafka it is a desolate joke, what Kafka's beloved Flaubert called the comedy that doesn't make us laugh.

Except that sometimes it does make us laugh, and especially in *The Castle*, Kafka's magnificent last novel, where the hero is not accused or transformed, but arrives of his own volition in a village, seeking admission to the aloof and arcane Castle that dominates it. I am the assailant, he says; the aggressive, if also timid consultant. The Castle itself is not an oracle, of course, but everything else is if it can help the hero understand his chances, and he converts the most casual configurations—a voice on the telephone, a look on a face, a letter, silences, departures, a nighttime encounter—into clues for his future, messages from the god, if there is a god. K can't carry out Pascal's wager, he is too nervous and self-conscious for that. In place of Pascal's suggestion that we should bet on the Christian God's existence, because if he does exist we win, and if he doesn't we don't lose anything, K has only a desperate modern prudence. If the god exists, why wouldn't these be his messages? K can't possibly lose as much by trying to interpret them as he could by trying to ignore them.

The god here is not a traditional or institutional deity, a figure of power or of scrutable or inscrutable intentions, but he is not exactly a metaphor either—at least, not a metaphor as an atheist usually understands a religious image, a figurative representation of something that doesn't exist. Kafka's god is the very possibility of a future in any way consistent with one's plans or desires—the future fact, we might say, of having got some things right now. This is particularly poignant, because K seems to get so many things wrong at every turning. By the time he came to write *The Castle*, Kafka was a master of this bleak but hilarious comedy, where the reader literally wants to yell a warning at the chief character, as he sets out again and again to step off some spiritual or intellectual cliff. It's as if the Marx brothers had swallowed Kierkegaard, or vice versa.

Soon after his arrival in the village, K receives a letter from a Castle authority confirming his appointment but not saying what that appointment is. His immediate superior, however, is not a Castle official but the village mayor. K ponders the letter carefully and sees himself as being offered two clear alternatives. He can be "a village worker with a distinctive but merely apparent connection to the Castle," or he can be "an apparent village worker" whose real instructions come from the Castle. An honorary appointee, let's say, or a secret agent. The oracle has spoken, or K thinks it has, and he doesn't hesitate in going for the first option: "It was only as a village worker, as far from the Castle gentlemen as possible, that he could achieve anything at the Castle." This seems to me exactly and emphatically the choice most of us wouldn't make if we were trying to make headway with the Castle—although of course I could be wrong, we are in strange territory here. I'm not saying K really is mistaken—how could I know?—or that the style of his thought is unfamiliar. There are many circumstances where only outsiders manage to have any impact on the inside. My suggestion is just that Kafka is playing brilliantly with our usual preferences, even our ideas of practical wisdom, on the subject of appearances. Superman is apparently the mild-mannered Clark Kent, just as all kinds of famous figures, real and imaginary, were apparently the guy next door. But it would be a devious comic touch to argue that it is only as a fumbling journalist, far from any magical powers, that Superman is really able to do anything for the American way; that next door is the only place to be if you want to be famous. The comedy rests on a sudden, symmetrical uncertainty, and is itself an image of uncertainty.

These minimalist oracles—omens desperately converted into oracles by the person reading them—are everywhere in *The Castle*, and represent a radical moment in the story we are exploring. Omens are signs full of meaning, and we may see the writing of the gods in them, but they are not institutions, and have nothing like the structure of authority that ordinarily goes with oracles. Omens are prolific and particular; anything can be an omen. Kafka is suggesting to us that anything can be an oracle, and this is also true, but with a proviso. We shall need to invest the sign not only with exceptional or magical meaning, but also with a whole apparatus of intention and rules for consultation. We shall need to invent the institution we no longer have. Just before he lays out for himself the alternatives he sees in the Castle letter, K swiftly excludes the possibility that the ambiguities he finds in the letter might be unintentional, sheer confusion, or ineptness. "The idea, crazy in relation to such an authority, that indecision may have played a part here scarcely occurred to him." If K was looking only for an omen, such confusion or indecision wouldn't matter. But he is not. He is looking, we might say, for a message rather than a sign; for a word of authority, a mark of the god's will and not just a hint of good or bad luck.

Among the many such moments in *The Castle*, I want to pause over two more, which add significantly to our sense of what modern oracles may be like. In the first of these moments K tries to force a silent oracle to speak and is left only with a picture of the full scope of his attempt, a bleak idea of what it means to live in a world without oracles. In the second instance the oracle speaks, volubly, but K is asleep.

Castle officials often spend time at one of the village inns, and K thinks he may be able to press his case by waylaying one of them before he returns to the Castle. He waits in the courtyard by the official's sleigh, and feeling tired and cold, gets into the sleigh, and has a nip of the brandy he finds there. An official appears—not the one he is waiting for—and tells K to follow him. K says he is waiting for someone and doesn't want to miss him. The official says K will miss the person either way, whether he goes or stays. K, in another of those moments that seem to anticipate the Marx brothers, says in that case he would rather miss him by staying here. He is left alone in the courtyard. No one else comes, the horses are unharnessed from the sleigh, and the sleigh is put away. K feels he has won a victory, but "a victory that gave no joy." He has forced the Castle into a retreat, so to speak, but he didn't want a retreat, he wanted an encounter. All the lights are turned out, and K feels "freer than he has ever been," because he knows he can stay here as long as he likes. But his freedom is the freedom not to be spoken to, even by an oracle, especially by an oracle, and the chapter ends with these haunting words:

> It seemed to K . . . as if he had fought for this freedom for himself in a manner almost nobody else could have done and as if nobody could touch him or drive him away, or even speak to

him, yet—and this conviction was at least as strong—as if there
were at the same time nothing more senseless, nothing more desperate, than this freedom, this waiting, this invulnerability.

Toward the end of the novel, K finally gets an interview with a
Castle official who, it seems, might really be able to help him, indeed seems to want to help him. The man's name is Bürgel, and K
has met him, in a characteristic Kafka touch, by stumbling into the
wrong room at an inn. Is any room ever entirely the wrong room?
Another question for the oracle.

Bürgel describes, with exhaustive philosophical patience, as if
they were both elsewhere and he was merely offering an example,
the precise conditions of their encounter. "There are sometimes
opportunities that are almost not in accord with the general situation, opportunities in which by means of a word, a glance, a sign of
trust, more can be achieved than by means of lifelong efforts." K is
very tired, almost asleep, and is not too interested anyway—he has
been in the village too long, taken on too many of its assumptions,
to believe in such opportunities anymore. Bürgel goes on, "But,
then again, of course, these opportunities are in accord with the
general situation in so far as they are never made use of. But why
are they never made use of?" The scene continues, with Bürgel getting more and more eloquent and K getting more and more dozy,
until Bürgel makes an unmistakable, if complicated offer of help.

And now, Land Surveyor, consider the possibility that through
some circumstances or other, in spite of the obstacles already
described to you, which are in general quite sufficient, an applicant does nevertheless, in the middle of the night, surprise a secretary who has a certain degree of competence with regard to
the given case . . . You think it cannot happen at all? You are
right, it cannot happen at all. But some night—who can vouch

for everything?—it *does* happen . . . It is a situation in which it quickly becomes impossible to refuse a request . . . The applicant wrings sacrifices from us in the night.

This is "the official's hour of travail," Bürgel says, and waits for K's response. Kafka's next words are "K slept," "*K schlief*," a terse, ironic consummation of the whole scene.

The man K was actually supposed to see now knocks on the wall and says K is to come right away. K wakes up and staggers out, dimly aware of what he has missed through sleeping. Bürgel consoles him with the thought that everyone has a limit. "Who can help the fact that precisely this limit is significant in other ways too? No, nobody can help it. That is how the world itself corrects the deviations in its course and maintains the balance. This is indeed an excellent, time and again unimaginably excellent arrangement, even if in other respects cheerless." Excellent and cheerless, "*vorzüglich*" and "*trostlos*": a dizzying combination of attributes, and no pronouncement from Delphi ever stretched the range of interpretation any further than this. The whole pattern of Bürgel's thought follows this scheme. There are exceptional opportunities but no one ever makes use of them—that's how exceptional they are. The things he is describing can't happen, but they do happen. Although even when they happen they don't actually happen, for the reason just given: the opportunities are too exceptional. Kafka has a little parable about crows that tells this story beautifully. "The crows maintain that a single crow could destroy the heavens. There is no doubt of that, but it proves nothing against the heavens, for heaven simply means: the impossibility of crows."

K's sleepiness is weariness of heart as well as physical fatigue. He doesn't believe in his chances of success with the Castle, and he may be right—perhaps Bürgel is just playing with him. The Castle and the village have defeated him by teaching him the odds, and getting him to treat the odds as reality. But here is the subtlety of Kafka's desolate social vision. The scene with Bürgel suggests to us, even if only in mockery, that a revolt against local customs, indeed any challenge at all to the settled way of the world, is not impossible, or deluded, or doomed, just a very bad bet. It could always succeed in theory, although none has ever succeeded in practice. In a terrible variation on most of the oracle-stories we know, there is no silence or ambiguity here, and no difficulty of interpretation. The oracle speaks clearly to K, and by extension to Kafka's readers, but we are lost in sleep. Plenty of talk, only not for us.

Elms and ashes

Ludwig Wittgenstein wrote the work later published as *On Certainty* in the last year and a half of his life. His editors describe it as "a single sustained treatment of the topic," "not a selection," and tell us that "the last entry is two days before his death on April 29th 1951." G.E.M. Anscombe is "under the impression" that Wittgenstein wrote the first twenty pages in Vienna, where he was from Christmas 1949 to March 1950, but says, "I cannot now recall the basis of this impression." Very nice touch for a book about certainty.

In this work Wittgenstein wonders whether he is right to be guided in his actions by the propositions of physics, whether he has "good ground" for this. He answers this skeptical question with another: "Isn't precisely this what we call a 'good ground'?" It's what *we* call a good ground, the argument now goes, but what about other people?

> Supposing we met people who did not regard that as a telling reason. Now, how do we imagine this? Instead of the physicist,

they consult an oracle. (And for that we consider them primitive.) Is it wrong for them to consult an oracle and be guided by it?—If we call this "wrong" aren't we using our language-game as a base from which to *combat* theirs?

Wittgenstein underlines *combat*, as if to suggest the violence that so often goes with the refusal of doubt, and indeed this is the situation he explores further. He asks again whether we are right or wrong to combat the language-game of the oracle users, and says, with barely perceptible sarcasm, "Of course there are all sorts of slogans which will be used to support our proceedings." And then:

> I said I would "combat" the other man,—but wouldn't I give him *reasons*? Certainly; but how far do they go? At the end of reasons comes *persuasion*. (Think what happens when missionaries convert natives.)

"At the end of reasons comes persuasion": what a line. It's an extraordinary description of our desire not to know whether we are right or wrong, which is where Wittgenstein's current set of questions started, but just to be right—to have been and to continue to be right, itself a mentality that belongs to the world of oracles. "The very wish to be right," Adorno wrote a few years earlier in *Minima Moralia*, is an expression of that spirit of self-preservation which philosophy is precisely concerned to break down." He tells the story of "someone who invited all the celebrities in epistemology, science and the humanities one after the other, discussed his own system with each of them from first to last, and when none of them dared raise any further arguments against its formalism, believed his position totally impregnable." "Such naïveté," Adorno adds, anticipating Wittgenstein's view, although Wittgenstein obviously thinks more than naïveté is involved, "is at work wherever

philosophy has even a distant resemblance to the gestures of persuasion." We may think Adorno himself was not quite exempt
from the wish to be right, and that philosophers should perhaps
try to understand the spirit of self-preservation as well as break it
down, but the point is a good one. You can't ask serious or even interesting questions if you're only ready to hear one answer; and you
can't give good reasons if you're only offering them as gunshot.

In the last entry, already mentioned, Wittgenstein says, "We
might speak of fundamental principles of human inquiry," where
the immediate inquiry might be, Could you be mistaken? What
would it mean to be able to say you were, or to say with certainty
that you weren't? His example is flying to a part of the world where
people know little or nothing about the possibility of flight. He
tells them how he got there, and they ask him if he could be mistaken. He says he can't be mistaken, but realizes this is not enough.
"That won't perhaps convince them; but it will if I describe the actual procedure to them. Then they will certainly not bring the
possibility of a *mistake* into the question." "But for all that," Wittgenstein adds, always ready to ruin an argument, his own or anyone else's, "they might believe I had been dreaming or that *magic*
had made me imagine it."

He then asks one of his vast skeptical questions—"If I don't
trust *this* evidence, why should I trust any evidence?"—and tries
again with his flying example, and adds another, more domestic one
to it:

> If someone believes that he has flown from America to England
> in the last few days, then, I believe, he cannot be making a *mis-
> take*.
>
>   And just the same if someone says that he is at this moment
> sitting at a table and writing . . .

J'écris, donc je suis. Or I sit, therefore I am. But this isn't what Wittgenstein means, it turns out. I could be deluded, or dreaming, or hallucinating through drugs, so my not being mistaken doesn't mean my sense of things is a proof of their empirical truth. It means only that if I am wrong about this, something is wrong about the whole situation, I couldn't be wrong just about this, and it wouldn't be just me that was wrong. The very possibility of a straightforward mistake would have been cancelled. This is where Wittgenstein gets with his final examples. If I am drugged, "if the drug has taken away my consciousness, then I am not now really talking and thinking." I can't be mistaken because I am not in a realm of acts or thoughts where mistakes can even arise. And this is also true of getting things right, even when they are right. Wittgenstein's final dizzying picture, the last words of his last work, are:

> Someone who, dreaming, says "I am dreaming," even if he speaks audibly in doing so, is no more right than if he said in his dream "it is raining" while it was in fact raining. Even if his dream were actually connected with the noise of the rain.

The point, as I understand it, is that the language-game of being right and being mistaken has certain rules; and dreaming or hallucinating the truth (or a falsehood) takes us outside the rules. In order to be right or to be mistaken, you would have to be conscious and living in a world where certain verifications (not the right word perhaps) could take place. A world where you could be right because you could also be wrong, and because you would have some sort of means of knowing the difference. Means that are imperfect but good enough, as good as these things get. Wittgenstein has an elegant little discussion earlier about whether one could be mistaken about having eaten or knowing one's own name. "I can't see how it would be possible." This surely is exemplary phrasing. The first question is not whether the thing is possible, but how we would see whether it was—or not. If I say I've just eaten, someone "may believe that I am lying or have momentarily lost my wits but he won't believe that I am making a mistake. Indeed, the assumption that I might be making a mistake has no meaning here." Are we safe now? We are never safe. Wittgenstein opens the case yet again. "But that isn't true. I might, for example, have dropped off immediately after the meal without knowing it and have slept for an hour, and now believe I have just eaten." Although Wittgenstein doesn't say this, he would be mistaken in this instance only about the timing of the meal and not about the meal itself. But he would be mistaken.

The notion of a language-game, Wittgenstein's most famous and most abused contribution to philosophy, goes back to the 1930s and to the works known as *The Blue and Brown Books*, and plays an important part in *Philosophical Investigations*, the first part of which was completed in 1945, where it brings together a whole complex of insights, best indicated by rapid quotation: "You need to call to mind the differences between the language-games"; "Lying is a language-game that needs to be learned like any other one"; "One must always ask oneself: is the word ever actually used in this way in the language-game which is its original home?"; "We remain unconscious of the prodigious diversity of all the everyday language-games because the clothing of our language makes everything alike."

A game has rules that can be learned and mislearned, applied without thinking, forgotten, and broken. If we are interested in how it is played rather than merely who wins, the moves are what are important and need to be understood. A game is itself part of a culture, and we may think of it as a small-scale representation of that culture. Sometimes Wittgenstein thinks of language-games in just this sense as models, invented instances, strenuous simplifications of linguistic practice. They are "*objects of comparison* which are meant to throw light on the facts of our language." "The term 'language-game' is meant to bring into prominence the fact that the *speaking* of language is part of an activity, or of a form of life." But at other times, particularly in his later work, Wittgenstein comes close to equating language-games with whole cultures, as in the instance of the physicist and the oracle. The facts of our language can scarcely be disentangled from our larger form of life; and sometimes language-games seem to be forms of life themselves. Wittgenstein's list of examples of language-games includes giving orders and obeying them, describing the appearance of an object, reporting an event, speculating about an event, forming and testing a hypothesis, making up a story, guessing riddles, telling a joke, translating from one language to another—and in a wonderfully miscellaneous conclusion, a kind of poem of behaviors—"asking, thanking, cursing, greeting, praying." The games are related to each other not by some single essence—the deep meaning of the word *game*—but in "a complicated network of similarities overlapping and criss-crossing." These sets without a single essence or single shared common feature Wittgenstein pictures as connected by "family resemblances," "for the various resemblances between members of a family overlap and criss-cross in the same way: build, features, color of eyes, gait, temperament, etc." The sheer multiplicity of the language-games being played in ordinary life is a rebuke to all logicians yearning for simplicity, Wittgenstein thinks, including himself in his earlier work.

So when we use one language-game to combat another, what are we doing? We are failing to respect another culture, obviously, but we are also misunderstanding our own. Just before his remark about the oracle culture, Wittgenstein asks, "But what if the physicist's statement were superstition and it were just as absurd to go by it in reaching a verdict as to rely on ordeal by fire?" We consult the physicist and other people consult the oracle. The physicist is our oracle.

But Wittgenstein doesn't want us to make the easy move from here. The point is not to disparage or disbelieve our physicist or to elevate the oracles of others: no ready-made cultural relativism. "The difficulty is to realize the groundlessness of our believing," Wittgenstein writes, and his way of getting us to realize this is to question all certainties so remorselessly that only the toughest remnants will survive the questioning. So in spite of the appearance of being all about doubt, this haunting little book really is about certainty. Doubt is the method, certainty is the subject. The work explores many of the ways in which our reasons run out or run aground, but it is about reasons.

A strange pragmatism winds through the book, suggesting that the reasons for belief, or at least for giving up doubt, just have to do with getting things done. "One cannot make experiments if there are not some things that one does not doubt. When I write a letter and post it, I take it for granted that it will arrive—I expect this." The postal services of our day make the letter example seem wishful rather than down-to-earth, but that only shows how pragmatic the whole argument is. "If I make an experiment," Wittgenstein continues, "I do not doubt the existence of the apparatus before my eyes. I have plenty of doubts, but not *that*. If I do a calculation I believe, without any doubts, that the figures on the paper aren't switching of their own accord . . ." This is a pragmatism of necessary certainty, but there is also a pragmatism of doubt. We don't have to doubt everything just because we theoretically could. Doubt is selective, opportunistic; a possibility, not an obligation. "Doesn't one need grounds for doubt?" "If you tried doubting everything you would not get as far as doubting anything." "Doubt gradually loses its sense. This language-game just *is* like that."

But then the pragmatism turns into something else before our very eyes. "Doubt itself rests only on what is beyond doubt": still pragmatic enough, perhaps, but already edging into questions of method and logic. Surely the following is scrupulously logical, would be true whatever the practical conditions of its application: "A doubt that doubted everything would not be a doubt." And here Wittgenstein enters the territory that is so specially his own. "There are cases where doubt is unreasonable, but others where it seems logically impossible. And there seems to be no clear boundary between them." I associate this with one of his very last, hair-raising questions: "Is it not difficult to distinguish between the cases in which I cannot and those in which I can *hardly* be mistaken? Is it always clear to which kind a case belongs? I believe not." Could I be mistaken in thinking I have just typed out that quotation? I could certainly think I had typed it out when I hadn't, but could I be mistaken if I have typed it out and also think I have? No? Hardly?

"A doubt without an end is not even a doubt." This crisp, de-mystifying sentence, a sort of anticipatory critique of the looser kinds of deconstruction, identifies endless doubt as both unreasonable and logically impossible. But it doesn't say it is nothing. It says it is not a doubt, and the proposition chimes exactly with what I take to be the deepest moments in *On Certainty*, the places where, if we were not too dazed or drowning, we might begin to fathom the riddle of the physicist and the oracle. The first moment is an apparent throwaway, or mild analogy; the second tells a story.

Someone makes an argument, and we say, if we are English or living in England, "O, rubbish!" This, Wittgenstein says, is not to reply but to admonish—different language-games, as he would also say. "This is a similar case to that of showing that it has no meaning to say that a game has always been played wrong." Why does it have no meaning to say this? Because a game that was always played wrong would either be another game or no game at all. Imagine that everyone else plays tennis on a court and we play without lines and without a net. This might, just, still be a form of tennis—using rackets and balls, played in the London suburb of Wimbledon, strawberries offered in the intervals—but it would be interesting to know how points are scored. Yet even if it wasn't tennis, it would still be a game, not played wrong but having its own rules. If on the other hand we habitually ignore the balls and use our racket to beat our opponent, that is hardly a game at all. I remember long ago complimenting a student in one of my classes in a particularly tough school in East London on his performance in the hundred-yard dash. "Pretty good, Malcolm," I said, "especially since you're wearing those heavy boots." "Yeah," Malcolm said, "I didn't get them for running, really. I got them for kicking people."

Wittgenstein's story, the second of my deep moments, is even more dramatic, at least in terms of linguistic dissonance.

> I once said to someone—in English—that the shape of a certain branch was typical of an elm, which my companion denied. Then we came past some ashes, and I said, "There, you see, here are the branches I was speaking about." To which he replied "But that's an ash"—and I said "I always meant ash when I said elm."

Had Wittgenstein always been playing the game wrong? No, he had been making one repeated false move in the game of trees and names, at which he was quite proficient otherwise. To get the name of a tree wrong is quite different from confusing the name of a tree with the name of beetle, for instance. And the matter is easily settled, as it is in the tennis example. If English speakers usually call this particular tree an ash, and German speakers call the same tree an *Esche*, and each word is usually translated as the other, there is no problem, Wittgenstein has just got his trees wrong, like the person in Nabokov's *Ada*, who says to the heroine, "I guess it's your father under that oak, isn't it?" Ada says, "No, it's an elm."

But suppose—returning now to the physicist as our oracle—it is a question not of local phenomena but of whole systems of nomenclatures and proofs, mixtures of demonstrable facts and propositions we take to be self-evident: forms of life, in short, belonging to large populations whose whole languages are versions of saying elm where others say ash. Or saying elm where others say elm, but meaning something different, as with the word *sparrow* in England and America, or the dozens of "false friends" found in French and English: French place for English square, French deception for English disappointment. Each culture is playing the game wrong by the other culture's criteria, and playing it right by its own.

Can we get beyond this perception without lapsing into combat and persuasion on the one hand, or lazy tolerance on the other? Well, we could describe our culture in detail, see how all its games are played, and we could start to see how many related and urgent questions come up in the process, about authority, consensus, advantage, history, and much else. Who plays or controls the games, who is excluded from them, whose interest do they serve, how much unexamined history lies around in them? "(My) doubts form a system," Wittgenstein says, and we could compare the system of our doubts with our various systems of certainty, and then compare those systems with those of others. It would be like explaining to people who know nothing of the very possibility of air travel how you got from England to America in seven hours. Magic would be one explanation—not that magic had made me imagine my flight, as Wittgenstein suggests, but that what we know as physics and engineering are forms of magic. This might not be a very good explanation—for us. But a sophisticated and well-established system of magic might explain physics and engineering and much else quite well for those who lived within the system. It's true it wouldn't enable them to build airplanes, but I can't build airplanes either, and although my explanation of how I flew is not based on magic, it might as well be, as far as I am concerned. It doesn't involve aerodynamics; it involves buying tickets and trying to get upgraded.

This is not to confuse physics with magic, only to recall that the real question here is not the availability of certainty—it is and it isn't available, in all kinds of specifiable areas—but the forms of certainty we take on trust, because they are the language of our culture. Wittgenstein's insight complements Kafka's, in a slightly more cheerful fashion. There can be oracles without gods, and we don't have to sleep through our oracle's message. But we do have to see that understanding its speech, measuring its proportions of proof and faith, of readily disclosed evidence and calls for leaps of faith, may be much harder than we thought.

Beyond the Matrix

Slavoj Zizek, the Slovenian philosopher, says that when he saw *The Matrix* he "had the unique opportunity of sitting close to the ideal spectator of the film—namely, to an idiot." He doesn't mean the film is idiotic, only that it's inconsistent, and a terrible temptation to the kind of pseudo-philosophy the idiot is immune to. In fact, much of what seems new and surprising in the film is very old, and the chance of talking about Plato and the movies in the same breath seems to have helped *The Matrix* to displace *Blade Runner* as the academic's smart cultural reference of choice.

But Plato is not the most interesting forebear here. What appears to be reality in *The Matrix* is virtual and secondary, but unlike the shadows in Plato's cave it is not a reflection of the real but a full-scale replacement of it. We are in the year 2199 or thereabouts—no one knows the exact date for sure because the sense everyone has of being in the year 1999 is so convincing—and the bodies of all but a few human beings are tucked away in vats of liquid and used as batteries to provide energy for a population of intelligent machines. The minds of these same millions of humans are connected to a computer program that simulates life as it looks and feels in our world at the end of the twentieth century. The Matrix is that life, "a neural interactive simulation"; "a computer-generated dream world, built to keep us under control." The self people think they have is a "residual self-image," the mental projection of a "digital self," and they know nothing else. And again, in a fine twist of idiom that combines world and wool, our hero is told that the Matrix "is the world that has been pulled over your eyes to blind you to the truth."

But there are a few individuals who have freed themselves from this illusion, and who form the slender resistance to the technological occupation. They are led by Morpheus, an imposing African American. And there are others who have moments of intuition, hunches that something is awry. One of them is Neo, a computer programmer who has begun to wonder about the Matrix. "You feel," Morpheus says to him, "that there is something wrong with the world. You don't know what it is, but it's there, like a splinter in your mind, driving you mad." But even these hunches fall far short of the truth, either of the elaborate simulation or of the blasted gray planet the earth has actually become. Members of the resistance, or the members we see, live in a vast hovercraft called the Nebuchadnezzar and keep moving to escape the machines that are constantly hunting them. They can hack into the Matrix by means of telephone lines, and there they appear as simulations like everyone else—well, slightly more gothic and stylish, since the leaders are played by Carrie-Ann Moss and Laurence Fishburne, and much leather clothing is involved. Neo is Keanu Reeves. Outside the Matrix these people look like simulations too, only in scruffier dress, but that's because *The Matrix* is a movie after all.

The most memorable image in the film is a picture of what I think we must take as the actual running of the Matrix: not the visible simulation but the fast-changing codes, ciphers, and numbers streaming down the screen like heavy green rain. The codes at first seem to be a version of Japanese kanji, but then turn into blocks of numbers. We see them at the start of the film, but also every time we get a glimpse of a computer screen on the Nebuchadnezzar. That's what the world has become: an inhabited DVD rather than the more familiar film or video. Behind the appearance is not a studio or a location with its cameras and cables but a world of numbers, a pattern of combinations, nothing else. The film gets a little edge of faint plausibility from the fact that such virtual constructions are indeed possible, and we do often feel that the digital rebuilding of sounds or images is eerily different from copying them, even if the results seem much the same.

Only faint plausibility even so. The energy of the film, and the pleasure all that hokey talk gives us, come from well-tried science fiction tropes and stories that depict the world as a manipulation or a model rather than the real and only thing. In Borges's story "The Circular Ruins," a man dreams up another man, only to discover that he himself is the figment of someone else's dream. In a remarkable 1950s story by Frederick Pohl, a sort of forerunner to the film *Groundhog Day*, a man wakes to find each day the same, an exact repeat of the previous one: he is living inside a miniaturized model of the world, designed to test the success of certain advertising techniques. Philip K. Dick's novel *Time Out of Joint* is even closer to *The Matrix*. The date is 1998 but a small group of people is locked into a near-perfect simulation of the 1950s. This time the reason is political, a means of hiding the facts of civil war from a

person who would otherwise go over to what his captors think is
the wrong side. And there is *The Truman Show*, of course, a film in
which the hero discovers his life is a television program and his
world is a set.

The man sitting next to Zizek in the cinema kept shouting,
"My God, wow, so there is no reality." Not quite. But all these stories do suggest that reality is not what or where we think it is, and
more important, that someone has an interest in hiding reality
from us, or hiding us inside a fake reality. Dream, model, simulation, television show are not only derivations or deviations of the
real, they are the product of minds and intentions, and in these
stories the minds and intentions are not ours, or not those of our
protagonists and representatives. So that although several characters
in *The Matrix* often talk as if the lack of reality was the chief problem with the simulated world, and many viewers of the film talk
this way all the time, the more difficult and interesting question is
a political one: Who controls reality and why are we prisoners of a
program? When Neo first sees the withered world as it is outside
the Matrix, Morpheus ironically says, in a now much-quoted
phrase, "Welcome to the desert of the real." But he also says, "As
long as the Matrix exists, the human race will never be free." This is
a little grandiose, and he may simply mean that truth and freedom
are the same: we are free if we are not deceived. This is an attractive
notion, and a traditional feature of much radical thought, from the
English dissenters of the eighteenth century to Bertolt Brecht in
the twentieth. But the power relations in the film, the struggle
against the intelligent machines and their agents, suggest a closer,
grimmer reading: we need to be free even to be interested in the
truth. There is a difference between resisting illusion because it is
an illusion, and resisting it because you don't want the world to be
pulled over your eyes. In this light freedom is not an abstract value,

however estimable, but a contested, particular right: the freedom from precisely these schemes, the ones that other people have wrapped around you.

With this we arrive at the Oracle. She inhabits the Matrix but she works for the resistance movement. Here as elsewhere the Oracle represents both destiny and freedom, deeply entangled in each other, only here she is a witty, ironic African American woman wonderfully played by the late Gloria Foster. She lives in a run-down housing development, graffiti and trash all over the halls, bead curtain closing off her kitchen, children's letter magnets on the fridge. She is baking cookies, a neat allusion to the fumes that are supposed to have arisen from the ground to inspire the pythia at Delphi, and her assistant/receptionist speaks the language of the doctor's or the dentist's office. "The Oracle will see you now," she tells Neo. The Oracle is smoking a cigarette and drinking from a tall glass. Greeting Neo, she remarks on the cookies ("Smell good, don't they?") and performs a couple of small acts of precognition as a warm-up. She says, "I'd ask you to sit down, but you're not going to anyway. And don't worry about the vase." Neo says, "What vase?" turning around and knocking to the floor a vase of flowers as he does so. The Oracle says, "That vase." Then she adds, "What's really going to bake your noodle later on is, would you still have broken it if I hadn't said anything?"

Things get pretty complicated after this, and hard to describe without telling the plot of the whole movie. But essentially Neo has come to find out whether he is the One, the figure who has been foretold as the ultimate leader of the resistance, who will finally destroy the Matrix and undo its masters. Is he? He doesn't think he is, and the Oracle doesn't undeceive him. She says enigmatically, "You already know what I'm going to tell you." He takes this to mean he is not the One, and the Oracle says, "Sorry, kid." She then tells him, in an unambiguous act of prediction, that one day he will have to choose between his own life and that of Morpheus. She is right. But that very choice, when the time comes for Neo to make it, alters the meaning of the prediction. Morpheus devoutly believes Neo is the One, and is about to die, to sacrifice himself to the enemy, in order to protect Neo and the future of the resistance. Neo, knowing, as he thinks, that he is not the One, can't let this happen, can't let Morpheus die in this error, and saves him. The powers Neo displays in the attempt reveal him to be the One. Wait for the sequel. Or sequels, since two of them are planned for release in 2003.

Did the Oracle know the future? She knew the contradictions of the present and the crossroads they would have to lead to. She knew that Morpheus believed Neo was the One and that Neo thought he wasn't, and that these views would have to come to a showdown sooner or later. Did she know the result? She could guess, and so could we. The trick is her role in Neo's progress toward heroism, and that's what the joke with the vase is about. Did she know he was going to break it, or did she cause him to break it by alerting him to it? Let's say she knew the odds, just as she knows Neo's doubt is a part of who he is. She is the authority for his doubt, so to speak, and she knows he can't get anywhere without it. I hate to allow Plato back in here, but the logic of this development is precisely that of Socrates' response to the oracle's announcement that no one was wiser than he. You doubt the oracle, but your doubt is what makes the oracle right. And your doubt, in the context of the film, is the equivalent of your political freedom. It makes your destiny a choice rather than a doom, even if, looking back, there seems to be no possibility of your having taken the other road.

In a recent book called *Welcome to the Desert of the Real*, Zizek tells a joke from the old East Germany. A German worker has got a job in Siberia, and anticipating Russian censorship, works out a code with his friends. Everything he writes in red ink will be false; everything he writes in blue ink will be true. Pretty soon his friends receive a letter written in blue ink, saying how wonderful life is in Siberia: plenty of food, well-heated housing, beautiful girls, western films. Just the one snag: no red ink. "Is this not," Zizek asks, probably not making a pun at this state, "the matrix of an efficient critique of ideology—not only in 'totalitarian' conditions of censorship but, perhaps even more, in the more refined conditions of liberal censorship?" "We 'feel free,' " Zizek continues, "because we lack the very language to articulate our unfreedom." Except that as the joke suggests, we can name the red ink we don't have, and thereby get the code to work. We can't tell the truth, but we can signal the falsehood, and it is possible to cheat the Matrix in its very own language.

DEAD OR ALIVE

The figures had reached the outskirts of a modern city, anonymous enough to be almost anywhere, but small shops were open, and there were people on the streets. As far as I could tell from the light, and a certain sleep-laden look on many faces, the time was early morning. Very early morning perhaps.

The first figure said, "Did we ever talk about Schrödinger's sparrow?" The other figure said, "Schrödinger's cat." The first said, "No, Schrödinger's sparrow. Well, it's Aesop's sparrow, but you'll see the resemblance. A man arrived at the oracle of Delphi holding a sparrow hidden in his hands. His question for the oracle was whether the bird was dead or alive. The oracle refused to respond." The other said, "Not much of a story." The first said, "Wait a minute. The oracle explained its refusal, which I guess was an answer, even if not an answer to the question. The oracle said, 'Fellow, you can show it either dead or alive, for each is in your power.' "

The second figure seemed puzzled. "But Schrödinger's cat wasn't either dead or alive, it was both dead and alive." The first figure said, "This is Schrödinger's sparrow. Actually, the bird had to be alive at the moment the man was asking the question, since he could hardly kill it and then resurrect it. But that is part of the point. You see, the man could squeeze the bird to death at the instant of the oracle's answer—if the oracle said the bird was alive—and do nothing to the bird if the oracle said it was dead, just open his hand and show it breathing."

"So what's the story about?"

"What do you think?"

"I'm still working on it. Maybe it's about rivalry in cleverness, about the craftiness of the questioner pitted against the even greater craftiness of the oracle. It's about skepticism being defeated because it isn't clever enough. Not necessarily because it's wrong."

"Yes, and that's where the little Schrödinger effect creeps in. The sparrow is either dead or alive—well, it's alive—but the speed and silence and secrecy with which it can be got to pass from one condition to another make it like the cat in the box. For the oracle, the sparrow is both dead and alive because it can be either within seconds, and because life, for the poor bloody sparrow, has become a mere option, not its normal condition until further notice. There is no right or wrong. It's just game theory."

"It's not easy being trapped in an analogy."

TEN: MEDICINE AND PROBABILITY

For a train of thought is never false.

Joseph Conrad, *Under Western Eyes*

Disputable oracles

Oracle-stories always involve a consultation, a visit to a veiled or mysterious authority. We go to the oracle, it doesn't come to us. We choose to ask its advice, and we get, perhaps, nothing more and nothing less than we deserve. The oracle doesn't batter, ravish, blind, steal into our sleep, perform miracles before our very eyes—to list just a few familiar images of quite different religious experiences. Sometimes it feels as if the consultation of an oracle is not a religious practice at all. This can't be right, since after all there is an encounter, however oblique, mediated, or obscure, with what we take to be a god. But the oracle is certainly the most secular, and most easily secularized, of religious practices.

Conversely, whenever secular practices look like a consultation of an oracle, a whiff of religion creeps into them, however adamantly atheistic or rational the program. At first glance, the most lurid and obvious of such practices in the twentieth century and after would seem to be psychoanalysis, but psychoanalysis, when it is working well, creates something like the "inward oracle" Milton's Christ announced, the one in the heart rather than the one representing an external authority. In fact the most widespread and subtly influential contemporary oracles are given by ordinary medicine. I'm not suggesting that doctors are gods, or (necessarily) behave like gods. Not even that we, in our need and helplessness, believe they are gods. Only that our interpretations of their interpretations frequently make them look very much like oracles in precisely the sense that the ancient world understood the institution. That is, we can't afford not to believe them, and we don't quite know what they mean.

Of course, if we literally and simply believe everything our doctors say, the resemblance to the oracle doesn't arise. Similarly, if we disbelieve everything they say. But how often do we simply believe or disbelieve our doctors? We hear their opinions selectively, choosing the good or bad news according to our temperament. We follow some recommendations and not others—do the exercises, for example, but don't take the pills. The opinion is a text, a modern version of those Delphic hexameters. Behind it is a considerable authority, and a powerful reservoir of prediction. If we didn't believe in medicine at all, we wouldn't be here in the consulting room.

The doctor doesn't choose to speak ambiguously—well, not always. But of course the doctor himself or herself is not the authority, only at this moment its spokesperson and interpreter; and there are other doctors who might say other things, just as in the ancient world there were always other oracles to consult. The ambiguity arises in part because of this possibility of choice, more substantially because doctors themselves frequently lay out alternatives, offering as complete a clinical picture as possible, and most substantially of all because we often need the margin of uncertainty that will appear only if we treat the doctor as an oracle, however oracular or unoracular he or she may be in the instance. I leave aside the ambiguities that arise from the terrified caution of American doctors, daunted by the specter of insurance, but they too, of course, have an effect on the language.

The scene of the doctor as oracle is announced and parodied in a very funny passage in the second volume of Proust's *In Search of Lost Time*. The narrator and the writer Bergotte are discussing medicine and health, and specifically the need for artists and intelligent people to have intelligent doctors, partly in order to avoid being bored by their consultations, and partly because it takes an intelligent doctor to understand the illnesses of the intelligence. "Three quarters of the diseases of intelligent people come from their intelligence," Bergotte says. "They need a doctor who at least recognizes such diseases." The narrator is not convinced. "I doubted very much," he says, "that intelligent people would need a different regime from that of imbeciles," and he has just produced, a moment or so before this sensible statement, a dizzying version of the doctor as oracle:

> That my doctor might be a crashing bore did not bother me; all
> I required of him was that his art, the laws of which were be-
> yond me, should enable him to examine my entrails and utter an
> indisputable oracle on the subject of my health.

Proust's narrator is conflating two ancient practices: that of consulting an oracle and that of divination by the inspection of the innards of sacrificed animals. Of course he doesn't intend to be sacrificed; the doctor is to consult the entrails while the patient is still alive, indeed in order to keep the patient alive. The joke also involves turning the ordinary object of much medicine, the insides of the patient, into a feature of the doctor's hocus-pocus, as if symptoms were not only symptoms but also messages from another world. Instead of consulting the entrails to find out about favorable winds or the wishes of the god, you consult them to find out about . . . entrails. The phrase "indisputable oracle" completes the mockery, which is gentle but capacious, since it includes both the pretensions of medicine to infallibility and the (wildly misplaced) desire of patients for infallible doctors.

We can contrast this comic dream of infallibility with the moment in *The Magic Mountain* where Hans Castorp is pronounced cured but chooses not to believe the diagnosis. Hans first traveled to the Berghof Sanatorium in Switzerland to visit his tubercular cousin Joachim. He was planning to stay for a holiday of three weeks, but is then discovered to have a few "damp spots" on his lungs, and decides to remain. It soon becomes clear that Hans's health, while certainly not good, is probably the least of what is keeping him there—he has fallen in love not only with a fellow patient but with the life of the sanatorium itself, its daily rituals and its apparent exemption from the rushing time of the world, with everything, we might say, which makes the Berghof different from the busy Hamburg where Hans is supposed to be pursuing his industrious career.

The two cousins turn up for their routine examination by the director of the sanatorium, Hofrat Behrens, and Joachim abruptly announces his decision to leave within a week. Behrens has just suggested that another six months might make Joachim fit enough to "conquer Constantinople," but Joachim is adamant. Behrens ironically calls the projected departure a "desertion," but then, after a few questions, takes a kindlier, accepting tone. "Very well, then . . . God be with you. I see you know what you want."

Behrens turns to Hans and asks him if he is leaving too. The implication is that he no longer has a reason to be there—since in any event he never had as good a reason as Joachim. Hans says he wants to yield the decision to the doctor, literally to the doctor's vote. Behrens repeats the word *vote*, and examines Hans, tapping and listening to his chest. The examination is soon over. Behrens says, "You may leave," and Hans is astonished. He stutters, "You mean . . . but how can that be? Am I cured?" Behrens says yes, but

Hans is still trying to deal with the news. "But, Director Behrens. You're not really serious, are you?" Behrens gets angry, or pretends to get angry. "Not serious? What do you mean?" And he makes an allusion to the love interest that he assumes holds Hans in the sanatorium. A few days later Hans sees Behrens again and confirms his decision to stay as long as it takes to effect his complete recovery. Behrens says "Fine" and "No harm done," although he can't resist adding that he always thought Hans had more talent for being a patient than his swashbuckling cousin.

You may leave. Fine. No harm done. A talent for being a patient. These phrases are not difficult or even, in the context, enormously equivocal. But they are oracular. They are the voice of authority, and they speak a kind of truth. Several kinds of truth, perhaps. Behrens no doubt wants to wake Hans out of his passive confusion, where his medical condition allows him not to think about his emotions or what looks like his mild moral stagnation. Hans can stay, of course, he doesn't have to leave. It may even be medically best for him if he stays. But since he's going to stay anyway, indeed is aghast at the idea of leaving, he needs to decide among his reasons for deciding to stay. The reference to Hans's talent for being a patient is an allusion to his distaste for the rigors of ordinary life off the mountain, his affinity with the secluded and the sick. The talent distinguishes him, as all talents distinguish their owners, but it's not an unequivocal distinction. The oracle is far from infallible, but probably right. Everything will depend on the patient.

Yet although Proust is talking about an infallible oracle and Mann is portraying a mischievous doctor, they are manifestly concerned with the same phenomenon. Proust's irony and Mann's attention to his character's particular mode of commentary bring us out in roughly the same place: a desire for authority that also allows a form of disbelief. Or to change the terms slightly: a form of submission that turns out to be a form of freedom, even if that freedom is misused.

Heart murmurs

The cases described by Atul Gawande in his wonderful book *Complications* take us out of oracle territory altogether, but in so doing help us to see more clearly what that territory looks like. And Gawande himself, at one point, also enters that very territory, even if he doesn't stay long. His central question concerns decision making in difficult or dangerous medical cases. "Only a decade ago," Gawande says—he is writing in 1999—the doctors made all the decisions.

> Doctors did not consult patients about their desires and priorities, and routinely withheld information—sometimes crucial information, such as what drugs they were on, what treatment they were being given, and what their diagnosis was. Patients were even forbidden to look at their own medical records. They were regarded as children: too fragile and simpleminded to handle the truth, let alone make decisions.

Then things changed. By the time Gawande went to medical school in the early nineties, future doctors "were taught to see patients as autonomous decision-makers."

> Most doctors, taking seriously the idea that patients should control their own fates, lay out the options and the risks involved. A few even refuse to make recommendations, for fear of improperly influencing patients.

This seems politically impeccable, but as Gawande goes on to show, the medical situation can become very complicated. In the first case he describes the patient doesn't fully understand—can't understand because his mind has blocked out the full horror of understanding—the risks involved in an operation, and so makes a bad choice and finally dies in just the way he had specified he least wanted to. Gawande's most startling and most moving case is that of his own daughter, who stopped breathing when she was eleven days old. She was rushed to the hospital, and various choices needed to be made. Intubation and ventilator or not? "There were risks either way." The child could die if she wasn't intubated, and she could have a lung blowout if she was. "I was the ideal candidate to decide what was best," Gawande says.

> I was the father, so I cared more than any hospital staffer ever could about which risks were taken. And I was a doctor, so I understood the issues involved . . . And yet when a team of doctors came to talk to me about whether to intubate Hunter, I wanted *them* to decide—doctors I had never met before.

Gawande's last case is that of a patient whose life was saved by a doctor who simply and dramatically overruled the patient's wishes. The patient, suffering from a grave postoperation infection, wanted to stay off the breathing machine even if it meant he would die. He persisted in this wish against all professional advice. His wife, present at first, left the room because she couldn't take it anymore. The man lapsed into unconsciousness, and the doctor "went into action," as Gawande says. She "slipped a long, clear plastic breathing tube down into his trachea," took him to the intensive care unit, and put him on a ventilator. Twenty-four hours later the man was able to breath without the machine, and when he could speak, he said, "Thank you."

I think in this case the doctor would have been right even if the man had snarled ungratefully, and hated the medical profession for the rest of his life. His gratitude actually confuses the issue by making it seem as if the dilemma is only apparent or temporary: as if in the long run doctors and patients will always agree. But the dilemma surely is real and constant. Ideally, doctors and patients will collaborate in decisions, and everyone will understand the full extent of the risks and options. But in many actual cases, there can only be conflict. Sometimes the doctor will have to give in; sometimes the doctor will have to insist; at other times the doctor won't have any choice at all. The patient will, these days, almost always have some sort of choice, but one that is seriously constricted by the limits of his or her knowledge.

We are still outside the territory of oracles. Clear and final decisions may have oracles in their history, but the oracle doesn't decide. But then the language that leads to the decision, the whole realm of description, estimate, and intimation, begins to look very familiar in its ambiguities. Gawande describes this realm as one of "strange, almost formulaic conversations." The doctor needs to persuade the patient to have a biopsy, say. The patient doesn't want it, because she's had three biopsies before that showed no malignancy, and of course she has a right to make her own mistake, if this is one. But then the doctor may feel she or he has something like a duty to persuade her otherwise. The good doctor, Gawande says, doesn't "fuss or debate." "The aim isn't to show her how wrong she is. The aim is to win her over." The doctor often just repeats the patient's expression of her worries. Time passes. The patient asks questions. The doctor wonders whether they should consult the radiologist, or the husband. Sometimes the doctor looks disappointed, and waits to see how that works.

This is not just manipulation on the doctor's part, Gawande says; and I'm prepared to believe him, at least in principle. But what's interesting here is how the scene really does begin to look like the consultation of an oracle. The doctor represents, to the best of his or her authority, the advice of the god—the god in this instance being a name for the best medical knowledge of the time. The patient hears the advice, indeed has presented herself or himself at the place where this advice is formally dispensed, and must now decide whether to act on it or not. The patient in a modern hospital doesn't very much resemble an ancient Greek city-state; but the structure of question and response, of mingled authority and freedom, is remarkably consistent over time.

A man in his sixties, my brother-in-law as it happens, is gravely ill, and not in all that good shape generally, apart from his current emergency. The doctor says to the man's wife, "With this degree of infection, it would be difficult even for a twenty-year-old to pull through." The wife says, "We can only wait and see." Later she says, "We can only hope for a miracle." A week or so later the man dies. This exchange, these phrases, represent an indirect and it seems to me touching and genuinely useful collaboration between different idioms and different expectations, to be dismissed only by those who hold that blunt truths are the only kind of truths. The doctor, faithful to a professional caution about the very idea of prediction, cannot say that the man will soon die, although that is almost certainly what he means. The wife's first response presumably means, "I understand I'm not to have much hope, but I can't at this stage give up hope entirely." Her second response allows her to make space for her inward desolation while keeping open a formal, public, and remote possibility, a kind of ritual register of hope. She lives in a Catholic culture, there have been miracles, there is no reason to stop praying because the odds are bad. On the contrary.

Another instance from within my own family, but with a happier ending. My son had a heart murmur from birth, a tiny hole in his heart. It was quickly spotted by doctors, who told us we would need to keep an eye on his condition, but there was nothing to worry about. They were right, mercifully, and the murmur has since disappeared. At one point, when he was about five, we changed country and doctors. The new doctors also spotted the murmur, and also said there was nothing to worry about. A couple of years later a school health visitor picked up the murmur and sent us to a specialist.

The specialist, a charming and intelligent, enormously worldly man, has a medical student with him, and is showing her the ropes. He listens to Tony's heart, says nothing. He asks the medical student to listen. She does so, intently, and the specialist then asks her if she can hear a murmur. She says yes, but it's very faint. More than faint, the specialist says, I couldn't hear anything at all. Do you think you would hear it if you weren't listening for it? The student answers noncommittally, not sure what the game is. I'm not sure what the game is either, except that it's clear that the medical difference between very faint and nonexistent is not important, a question only for philosophers or theologians, so to speak, and I'm very relieved to know this. The specialist tells me there is no heart murmur, all a false alarm.

I thought about this scene a lot afterward—once I was free to be an amateur philosopher or theologian. The interpretative possibilities seemed to me representative of many kinds of occasions, to be met with in quite different contexts. Here is how I see the possibilities, but readers may well see others. First, the specialist really could hear nothing, and simply said so. The murmur, if there had been one, was gone, case closed. The idea of the murmur had provoked the consultation, and the idea carried over into the student's perception—she heard what she was listening for, or thought she did. Second, the specialist heard a murmur, but it was so faint that it didn't matter, and for a variety of reasons—to reassure me, to tease the student a little—he pretended the faint murmur was not a murmur at all. Third, there was a clear murmur, but not an alarming one, or one that needed any action, nothing to be discussed with child and parent at this stage. The specialist and the student could consider later, when Tony and I were no longer there, what they actually heard. Perhaps the specialist had some advice to give her about when to worry patients and when not to, or about the eagerness of local health visitors and general practitioners to hear heart murmurs both when they did and did not exist. I had the impression that although the specialist didn't disbelieve in heart murmurs, he did believe it was usually a rather romantic diagnosis.

I didn't treat the heart specialist as an oracle, or only in an extremely modest way. I took the medical message straight, as meaning no reason for concern, and I chose, as it happened, to believe the second of the options I described above. But the elements of an oracle were there: the consultation, the voice of authority, the need for interpretation, the entailment of a future. However, in order to bring our own oracles—that is, those of the modern, postreligious world, if there is such a place—fully into focus, we need to add a fifth element, largely absent from all instances prior to the twentieth century: that of deep or radical doubt, or sometimes just the offstage presence of deep or radical doubt, the sense that it could set in at any time. The ancients doubted whether they had understood their oracles aright, and even doubted whether the official interpreters had correctly transmitted the message of the god; but they never doubted that the god existed and could be consulted. I need to insist, against a number of current orthodoxies, that doubt, even of the deepest kind, is not a negative form of certainty. What's in question for much of the twentieth century and after is not whether we believe or not—if we knew the answer to that we wouldn't be in doubt, and if we knew we didn't know the answer we would be certain about a lot of things. What's in question, as we learned in our reading of Kafka, is how much we believe and when, and what difference it makes whether the object of our belief exists.

Rational choice

"At the most abstract level," Anthony Grafton writes in *Cardano's Cosmos*, "astrologers ancient and early modern carried out the tasks that twentieth-century society assigns to the economist." A brilliant and detailed (and amusing) parallel follows. Both astrologers and economists try to bring order to chaotic phenomena by means of quantitative models. Both underplay their powers of actual prediction but are willing enough to predict when the price is right. Both are frequently criticized and still found indispensable. And although both generally find that events do not match their predictions, each of them normally receives "as a reward for this confirmation of his art a better job and a higher salary."

The headline of the paragraph in the Business Digest section of the *New York Times* for June 1999 was almost certainly ironic, and bore the faint signature of a witty subeditor: "Oracle Results Beat Expectations." But nothing much in the flagged article showed any sense that the Oracle Corporation might have anything of the oracle about it, or that predictions in its regard might seem a little eerie. "Oracle Posts 31% Increase in Earnings" was the main headline, and the smaller heading read "4th-Quarter Results Exceed Expectations"—maybe the flicker of a grin there. Oracle is in the business of providing software for what is called "enterprise resource planning," and its competitors, according to the *New York Times*, are companies like SAP, Peoplesoft, BAAN, and J. D. Edwards. Are or were: things move fast in the resource planning world. The news story simply and lucidly recounted how Oracle had laid off 325 employees in an attempt to cut costs, and had returned better figures than analysis had predicted. There was nothing very strange in this, and only writers want dead metaphors to be resurrected every minute, but I am interested in the casual assumption that prediction is possible in some areas and risible in others, and in the fact that being wrong does no harm to an analyst, any more than it does to an astrologer.

But surely planning and analysis are part of ongoing life, whether private or public, and there is nothing magical about looking ahead or making previsions. Well, this is where things get a little tricky. François Mitterrand had an astrologer when he was president of France, Nancy Reagan had one when she was in the White House, but the most important of current oracles in the West is surely the chairman of the United States Federal Reserve Bank. Am I saying there is no difference between rational and irrational predictions? On the contrary. There are all kinds of differences. Rational predictions rest on substantial evidence, and economic oracles have enormous impacts, since fears and hopes notoriously alter markets. But once one enters the management of uncertainty, elements of a common logic begin to emerge. Economists too need their amphibologies, and their stories are full of forks in the road.

The old oracles, as we have seen, could be perfectly clear. They said yes, they said no, they said, "Do not dig." Economic advisers frequently do the same. They say buy and sell and "Wait a month or so." But by the same token they sometimes need to be right and wrong, and a word like *futures* tells an interesting story, as does the word *hedging*. A glance at the *Financial Times* on any given day will gather words like *uncertainty, loss, weak markets, embarrassing details, contraction, expansion, boom, caution, fear, suffering*, and at the end of 2002, "The nightmare on Wall Street." Of course these terms all have their up- or downbeat counterparts, but that is what makes this world so risky for analysts. I leave aside the accidental fact that the name of what is the "world's biggest law firm," according to the *Financial Times*, is Clifford Chance.

In the context of such shifts and possibilities, the most fascinating location in economics, and the place where I shall leave this discussion, is the crossroads where rational choice in one sense meets rational choice in another. When in doubt, should you follow cultural tradition and common sense or theory and controlled experiment? If a number of new bidders enter an auction in which you are engaged, should you bid more or bid less? The answer, as Richard H. Thaler shows in his book *The Winner's Curse*, and as publishers are always finding out to their cost, is that you may need to bid more to win the auction, but in so doing may lose the game— that is, have paid much more than the object's or the author's or the company's value, and so never be able to make back anything like what you have spent. One of Thaler's other splendid examples is the empty jar, which we are invited to fill with miscellaneous coins. We are to note down the total value, and to ask people to bid for the jar. "Chances are very high," Thaler says, meaning it's scarcely a matter of chance at all, that "the average bid will be significantly less than the value of the coins," and that "the winning bid will exceed the value of the jar." This is precisely what he means by the winner's curse.

It's not just reasonable, it's a rule of the game, that the highest bidder wins the auction. It also seems reasonable to assume that winning is better than losing, but this turns out not to be true of all games. Conversely, it is reasonable, but counterintuitive, to follow the hard evidence of statistics, where probability, as Von Neumann and Morgenstern suggest, is seen not as "an estimation" but as "frequency in long runs." The very words *reason* and *rational* seem to have alternative meanings—it's rational to trust our own sense of things, and it's rational to trust experts, but often we can't do both. This is true even if we accept, as most economic theories do, the dominance of self-interest, and the exclusion of variables like compulsion, perversity, recklessness, and charity.

In one direction human habit, and in the other the truth of numbers: the very possibility of this fork in the road is what makes game theory so salutary. But of course human beings are more than their habits. In the classic model of the prisoner's dilemma, two criminals are in jail, separated from each other, and are offered the following arrangements:

> if neither of them informs on the other, they both get a reduced
>   sentence of one year for their crime;
> if both of them inform, they get five years;
> if one of them informs but the other doesn't, the informer goes
>   free and the other gets ten years

The question is, which is the best option for a given prisoner? "The assumptions of rationality and self-interest," Thaler says, lead to the prediction that most prisoners will inform, because the option of none or five years is better than the option of one or ten—and also, we may think, because most prisoners in this situation are not full of faith in their fellow men. Math would confirm the psychology, just as Von Neumann and Morgenstern hoped it would when they urged "the truth of a much disputed proposition: That it is possible to describe and discuss mathematically human actions in which the main emphasis lies on the psychological side."

In fact, the model can't tell us anything about real-life cases, because its creatures are too abstract. In order to know what would happen in any individual instance, we would have to learn all we could about the prisoners, their relations with each other and with their friends, their past codes of conduct, their notions of community, their stubbornness, their ideas of loyalty, their sense of honor, their reasoning skills, and their belief (or not) in the deal they were being offered. But of course it is interesting, and a little alarming, to see that the best result (going free) is based on two incommensurate pieces of behavior: your friend keeps quiet while you squeal. If you knew for sure he would keep quiet, you might choose to keep quiet too and settle for the one-year sentence. In the absence of such knowledge, the smart choice is to bet on his squealing, and hope for his silence.

But think of this case, which Von Neumann and Morgenstern also invoke. Seeking to escape the formidable Moriarty, Holmes and Watson take the train at Victoria. When they reach Dover they will board a boat for France. As the train pulls out, Moriarty arrives at the station, moments too late to catch it and them. Watson is relieved, and contented. "As this is an express, and as the boat runs in connection with it, I should think we have shaken him off very effectively." Of course Holmes and we know better, and Holmes takes his usual patronizing tone. "My dear Watson, you evidently did not realize my meaning when I said that this man may be taken as being quite on the same intellectual plane as myself." What he means is that he would not have been "baffled by so slight an obstacle," and neither will Moriarty. Holmes, in Moriarty's place, would have engaged a special train, and that is what Moriarty does. But will the special train catch up? Yes, because the boat-train stops at Canterbury, and the special train won't need to, and there is always some delay at the boat. The options for Holmes and Watson are to get off at Canterbury, taking another route to France, and hope Moriarty's train goes straight through to Dover, or, since Moriarty's mind is as good as Holmes's and he may have foreseen this move, to stay on the train and hope Moriarty stops to look around at Canterbury, allowing them to reach Dover and get away before he arrives. Von Neumann and Morgenstern assign values to all the outcomes and do the math in a very elegant way, concluding that neither Holmes nor Moriarty can get odds of better

than 60 percent but that the choice each makes—Holmes gets off
at Canterbury, Moriarty goes on to Dover—is statistically the best
he could have done. Then follows a truly hilarious footnote, which
leads us, by a long detour, back to Oedipus spinning at the crossroads in Pasolini's film. "The narrative of Conan Doyle—excus-
ably—disregards mixed strategies and states instead the actual
developments. According to these, Sherlock Holmes gets out at the
intermediate station and triumphantly watches Moriarty's special
train going on to Dover. Conan Doyle's solution is the best possible under his limitations . . ." The excusing of Conan Doyle's limitations is delightful. I'm sure he would have given up fiction for the
theory of games if he had thought of it. But would he have been
giving up fiction, and what do we make of that little word *actual*,
which gives a weird finality to the characters and their choice of
stops.

This is "a game at which two may play," Holmes says of his
battle of wits with Moriarty, but what exactly is the game? If Moriarty is as clever as Holmes, shouldn't he foresee that Holmes will
get off at Canterbury? So perhaps Holmes is just that bit cleverer,
after all. Or did Moriarty think perhaps that Holmes would pull a
double bluff: go on to Dover because he imagined Moriarty would
imagine him getting off at Canterbury? This is plainly a version of
the prisoner's dilemma, although it is beginning to sound like the
old Jewish joke that Freud recounts: you're only telling me you're
going to Krakow because you know I'll think you're going to War-
saw, when all the time you're really going to Krakow. But what are
the stakes? Holmes's life, ultimately, since Moriarty does catch up
with him later in the story. But here the moral equivalent of in-
forming or not, or betting on another's doing it, is rating your own
astuteness against another's, and deciding when the bluffing has to
stop. Poe's Dupin discusses a similar calculation at the beginning of
"The Murders in the Rue Morgue." It is as if Oedipus, later to

become such a sleuth, saw a chance to cheat the oracle at the cross-roads, just before Laius arrived, not by closing his eyes and spinning round but by working out the odds.

It's a game at which any number may play, and in ancient Greece or Victorian Britain, as long as there are two roads or the train stops more than once, our choice will lead us to our doom— or away from it. Or to put that in other terms, now familiar to us, I hope, whatever road or stop we choose will have become our doom by the time the story is over. Call it the detective's dilemma.

Clients might be sceptical of a particular
oracle, but never of oracles in general.

Keith Thomas, *Religion and the Decline of Magic*

Turn out the stars

Italo Calvino's collection of folktales contains an intricate little
story from Mantua. It is called "The Peasant Astrologer," and as
Calvino says, it turns astrology to ridicule, "which is rare in folk-
lore." In summary, it goes like this.

The king has lost a precious ring and announces a huge reward
for the astrologer who will help him find it. The peasant Gàmbara
is poor and unable to read or write, but not averse to taking risks.
He thinks, "Would it be so hard to play the astrologer?" and offers
to find the king's missing ring. The king puts Gàmbara in a room
with a large astrology book and various writing instruments. Gàmbara makes a few strange marks on the paper he has been given and
tries to look like an astrologer who knows what he is doing. He
may or may not succeed in this, but he certainly succeeds in scaring
the servants who bring him his meals. They have stolen the ring
and interpret Gàmbara's attempts at looking wise as indications
that he is onto them. He in turn interprets their furtive behavior
correctly and gets them to confess their theft. They give him gold,
asking him not to betray them to the king. He says they are to get

a turkey to swallow the ring and leave the rest to him. Gàmbara tells the king that after much study he has learned where the ring is: a turkey has swallowed it. The turkey is cut open and the ring is discovered. The king heaps riches on Gàmbara and gives a great banquet in his honor.

Is this the end? A tale of superstition foxed by cunning and a bit of luck? There is an epilogue that takes us straight into the world of oracles and amphibologies. Among the many dishes served at the banquet is a plate of crayfish, *gamberi* in Italian, a delicacy unknown in the king's country until this moment. The king, delighted with his new astrologer, asks him to use his powers to divine the name of these things they are eating. Gàmbara, who has never seen or heard of any such creature, mumbles his name to himself in distress. "Ah, Gàmbara, Gàmbara," he says, "you're done for at last." "Bravo," the king says. "You've guessed it, they're called *gamberi*. You're the greatest astrologer in the world."

This is a meeting of names that replays, in the register of sheer extravagant good luck, the verbal gesture we have often seen as a form of trickery of the oracle. Not the Sicily or the Jerusalem you first thought of, the one that comes naturally to mind, but the other one. But still Sicily or Jerusalem—the oracle has not spoken falsely, only craftily. Or not even craftily, merely neutrally. There are more things in the world than there are names for them: the very notion of the pun or mistaken identity arises from this fact. We have just been too eager to think of one instance where there were (at least) two, our Sicily or Jerusalem, the one we wanted the oracle to refer to. With the joke about Gàmbara and the *gamberi*, there is no first and second interpretation, only a kind of linguistic deus ex machina saving the day. But there is a pun, and the sheer surprise of chance's kindly and precise intervention takes us out of the realm of simple ridicule or the mockery of credulity. A man this lucky doesn't need to be an astrologer. In parallel cases—there are many parallel cases, even outside the world of folklore—we don't believe that anything other than chance is at work, but we do believe that chance of this kind is worth watching closely.

It is in a frame of mind similar to this, I suggest, that rational, otherwise unsuperstitious people all over the contemporary world read their horoscopes every day. These are very faint oracles, dimmer than the oracles Kafka's characters grasp at, and a good deal less authoritative than our doctors and economists. I don't want to assimilate oracles to astrology in any wholesale way. Astrology is itself an ancient and fascinating form of knowledge, "one of the oldest disciplines still in widespread use," Anthony Grafton says, the object of many learned studies, and it was a clear alternative to oracle consultation when such consultation was still a widely institutionalized practice. Interestingly, astrology declined as the practice of insurance arose, or better, "insurance, which rested on statistical, rather than celestial, measurements, came into being only in the seventeenth century—and only after astrology and the other occult arts had lost their cultural value." And when astrology is cut loose from any intelligible relation to the stars, when oracles are divorced from the cult of any recognizable god, we have only arrangements of signs, the paragraphs in the newspapers and magazines, the frames on the computer screen, and all the omens we try to elevate into significant otherworldly speech. What is most interesting then is the lingering of the old mentalities, now stripped of former distinctions and happy to mingle their once quite separate logics.

T. W. Adorno, analyzing three months' worth of a daily astrology column in the *Los Angeles Times* (November 1952–February 1953), is surprised at the secularization, the easily socialized nature of the business. People "take astrology for granted, much like psychiatry, symphony concerts or political parties" and "they are hardly interested in the justification of the system." The horoscope writers do not divulge "the mechanics of the astrological system," and no one asks about them. It's true that the old astrologers didn't explain the complicated details of their art to their clients, but no one doubted there was a system, and that the system, a patiently elaborated account of the interconnected workings of the human and stellar worlds, permitted and supported their predictions. People who take astrology seriously today must feel the same. But a mass-produced horoscope is a kind of astrology without stars, or with only paper stars, like paper tigers; an astrology where the stars, far from providing explanations, however unlikely, take the place of the very idea of explanation. The stars lurk behind the print or electronic horoscopes but are never seriously invoked.

Adorno found that the astrology columns he studied scarcely left the realms of popular psychology or advice manuals, and indulged in "the monotonously frequent advice to 'be happy' "— not a vein calculated to appeal to the melancholy theorist. He was amused, though, by the reach of the preoccupations of the columns:

> Obviously an attempt is being made to cater to various layers of demands in the readers, to those more deep-lying ones where the spectacle of the twilight of the gods is hoped for as well as to the level where one wants to be reassured about a raise in one's salary.

Comparing the magazine *Forecast* with the *Los Angeles Times*, Adorno found that readers of both publications were instructed to—I'm summarizing and quoting from the instances he gives—relax, make constructive efforts, not attempt the impossible, exercise caution, keep calm, "get started early," "adapt to present conditions," "know that silence is the best part of valor today," have fun, pitch in, "seek abundance," "be readily cooperative," "placate your opponent," "attend to necessary red tape." There is quite a lot of talk of connections, good friends, confidantes, new acquaintances, "an important person," "a powerful person." Often the columnist seems to know the reader intimately, "on the basis of astrological inspiration," as Adorno says: "Follow up that intuition of yours," "Display that keen mind of yours." The implied life of the readers of the columns can be glimpsed. They are assumed to attend church, entertain, pay their taxes, go in for "amusements, romance, sports," worry about their financial security. Their families sometimes give them headaches, and small conflicts have to be ironed out. My own favorite piece of advice, which Adorno perhaps doesn't read seriously enough, is that given in the *Los Angeles Times* for Scorpio, November 19, 1952: "ridding life of sinister acquaintance makes more assets obtainable." Why am I tempted to read this as meaning "ridding sinister acquaintance of life"? Too many years watching *The Godfather* movies, perhaps.

Adorno was interested in what he called the "fictitious reasonableness" of horoscopes, and he sought to "reveal certain mechanisms which cannot be grasped adequately either in terms of being sensible or in terms of delusions." "It is the pattern of interacting rational and irrational forces in modern mass movements upon which our studies hope to throw some light." Rational and irrational. The horoscope, in Adorno's view, performs a weird circus act, with three identifiable flips. It reflects the real world, with its anxieties and bewilderments; it distorts that world by failing to address real causes; and—neatest of all—in its very distortion it represents the social relations we ordinarily have in a highly developed consumer society. Carroll Righter's column in the *Los Angeles Times* "contains all the elements of reality and somehow catches the actual state of affairs but nevertheless constructs a distorted picture." But then "the discrepancy between the rational and the irrational aspects of the column is expressive of a tension inherent in social reality itself."

So far so good. Adorno is an expert on the modern crises of reason—"irrationality is not necessarily a force operating outside the range of rationality"—but he is desperately afraid of conceding too much to reason's enemies. He repeatedly recognizes the skepticism of horoscope readers. "It should be noted," he says, "that quite a few disciples of astrology accept it with a kind of mental reservation, a certain playfulness which tolerantly acknowledges its basic irrationality and their own aberration." "So many followers of astrology do not seem quite to believe but rather take an indulgent, semi-ironical attitude towards their own conviction." This is shrewd, but something in Adorno's own worries prevents him from acting on this insight.

Many readers will find his otherwise brilliant essay overpsychologized, too prone to talk of the dependency and the weak-mindedness of the readers of the columns, and the columns' manipulation of them. Adorno writes of "psychiatric as well as socio-psychological categories," and, rather unpleasantly, of "the type of people we are concerned with." Surely the objects of study here are reading practices, not types of people. Adorno compares astrology to racism, finds in a devotion to mass horoscopes "the very same traits that play such a conspicuous role in totalitarian social movements," and thinks there is a generalized dependency in modern society that probably "prepares the minds of the people for astrology as well as for totalitarian creeds." Even in the wake of Hitler's rise and fall this seems a bit of a leap from a playful reading of the newspaper.

Where Adorno sees symptoms I want to see intelligible forms of language and logic, and where he finds weakness of mind I want to find a whole set of dispositions, from a desperate belief in the unbelievable to a mild interest in what Paul Auster, in the title of one of his novels, calls the music of chance, with many stations in between. I read horoscopes now because I love the ruses of rhetoric on display in them, the disciplined appearances of saying something when saying nothing much, or perhaps nothing at all. A little laboratory of language. But I remember a time when I read them differently. We had moved from America to England, we were buying a house, and all kinds of things seemed poised to go wrong, from the mortgage to the surveyor's inspection to the price to the purchase. I read the syndicated horoscope column of Patrick Walker every day, and I went to great lengths not to miss it. What was I doing? Did I think Patrick Walker knew something about local banks or buildings or the housing market, or that the stars would tell him? No. I wasn't looking for information, I was looking for signs. Not even that. When the stars said it was a good day for clinching deals I didn't count on it, and when they said a long-drawn-out business was about to come to a conclusion I was not surprised when they were wrong. But there is no doubt that I enjoyed my superstition, and that it helped me put up with the waiting. I didn't feel it was rational, but I didn't feel it interfered with rationality either. I was dabbling in a kind of hoped-for, only half-metaphorical magic. What I looked for in the horoscopes was a reading not of reality or the future but of my luck. Then we bought the house, my superstition turned thoroughly playful again, but I read Patrick Walker until he died, because I was grateful to him, and because of what we had been through together.

But haven't things changed since the 1950s, or since the 1980s, when we were buying the house in England? Not much. Michael Lutin, in *Vanity Fair* in September 2000, was telling his readers to "find a balance" between their "desire for independence" and their "need for companionship," and to "examine some of the forces and undercurrents" that were tugging at them. Of course the new century is not the old one, and *Vanity Fair* is not the *Los Angeles Times*, and still less the *Exeter Express and Echo*. The implied readers are certainly smarter and snappier, not surprised to be told that they "have come to the table with a self-serving agenda," or that they "can't seem to sit still for five minutes," or that they prefer to spend their "quality time on edgy creative endeavors." Nor will they be distressed to be reminded that "eventually, everyone gets to be annoying." They work in offices, these people, and wish they were on holiday, and they have "horrific situations at home." Sex and money are important—perhaps all there is. "Unfortunately, while your integrity is a quality you can someday proudly take to your grave, you can't always take it to the bank." "Remember this: political games are played in every bedroom in the land—not just in Washington, D.C."

This is far more up-front and open than the old stuff, and far more comfortable with the idiom of complaint: "many days of extreme weirdness." But the overall purpose is still to lift the spirits. "See what a good life you actually have," Lutin says in the first months of 2001. "You can finally take a much more positive attitude." "Maintain your inner strength." "You won't go to hell for having an impure thought now and then." "There is always some wisdom in your pessimism." Lutin doesn't mind being rude if it will pick people up. "You are not what you used to be. And what a blessing that is."

"Socially, you're a little off-track at the moment," there is "enormous pressure at work," and "your normally excellent powers of reasoning often fail you at this time"; but when the signs are right, it is easy "to speak from your heart," and it's important not to "alienate every ally you have." Patience is recommended. "Once in a while it's smart to retreat." "You need some focus." "Would you please just slow down long enough to breathe?" "This is the beginning of a quiet, introspective period of your life." Here is a riskier guess, though: "you are still fighting for survival and de-

fending a stupid career that is giving you nothing but heartache."
And again: "the career you thought you wanted so much has disappointed you once too often." And here is a downright threat: "even
your home life is likely to be a wreck until Mars moves forward
later in the summer." But not all is wreckage even here. "There is a
bright spot, however. Venus is in your 8th house, and that means
sex." The function of these darker pronouncements, presumably, is
to make the disappointed feel they are understood and not alone,
and to make all the successful careerists feel delighted that they are
not the ones being spoken about.

The astrological machinery continues to make its mysteriously
sidelined appearance: "the Chiron-Pluto transit in your midheaven
is pounding the living daylights out of you"; "you are experiencing
Saturn's final retrograde in your 12th house"; "the lunation in your
11th house brings it all back now." "Astrologically speaking," Lutin
writes at one point, "one could say that the completion of a fixed
planetary opposition in your 2nd and 8th houses marks the end of
a long and scary fiscal crisis." Isn't he speaking astrologically the
rest of the time? All the time? Well, we are not to take this lingo
too seriously.

Neil Spencer, in the London *Observer*, is also very funny, not
above the well-turned bad joke ("No one enjoys a performance
more than a Leo, especially if you are the star turn") or nicely
placed citation from Woody Allen ("Money is better than poverty,
if only for financial reasons"), but he is entirely serious about
astrology, mainly, I think, because he sees the importance of its
potential for metaphorical if not literal truth. "Its rich poetic
symbolism," he says, "invites us to join with the cosmos to shape
our future." We could accept the symbolism and the shaping without being too sure about the contribution of the cosmos. At the
end of 2000, Spencer announced bad times ("war, terrorism and
uneasy stock markets"—no surprises there) because of the coming

oppositions of Pluto and Saturn (August and November 2001, May 2002), but he did also say, in December 2001, that "no astrologer expected the symbolism of their encounter to be played out in such literal terms as were provided by the attacks of 11 September." Wrong month anyway, a skeptic might say, but that is not quite the point. If Pluto, associated with "power, metamorphosis, death and resurrection," encounters Saturn, "another planet with oppressive associations," why wouldn't we anticipate trouble, and although Spencer didn't foresee the September 11 attacks, he can describe them eloquently in astrological terms: "The dark force of Pluto in Sagittarius, sign of religion and airflight, opposite Saturn, planet of the establishment, in Gemini, sign of the Twins."

When he turns to individuals, Spencer begins to sound a little more like Lutin. "Downsides? Awkward siblings, hostile neighbours, dying cars and dead phones"; "the year's end has the makings of a torrid, dramatic scenario"; "this sector of your chart is concerned with mortgages, bank loans, alimony, inheritances and suchlike"; "given that dominance and submission are not just roles played out in some sordid sex dungeon, try diplomacy"; "work in partnership and stay out of court." He strikes the same upbeat note as Lutin most of the time: "you have emerged from your travails stronger and more focussed"; "the key word here is commitment"; "you are able to morph with the moment"; "you will once more become the formidable and enthusiastic operator feared by your colleagues." But Spencer affirms the metaphorical identities associated with particular star signs much more forcefully. "Aries is about energy and impulse," he says. "The Crab never forgets," and "even astro-sceptics know the Scales is the sign of peace and diplomacy." Saturn is "the reality planet," and I particularly savored this bit of astral surrealism: "And incidentally, since Saturn rules teeth, this is an ideal time to get yours fixed."

Teeth and stars do both exist—it's the relationship that seems problematic to most of us, and as with any reasonably well developed mythology, you do have to wonder now and again. As a Leo, according to Spencer, I was supposed to have struck some old friends, in the latter part of 2002, as being "grand and abrupt, even by your regal standards." I don't think this happened, and I don't have regal standards, of grandness or abruptness or anything else, but then perhaps I'm overcompensating—that interpretation too is well within astrology's brief. For Sagittarius in the same year, because of "the final, scary opposition of Saturn and Pluto," Spencer predicted a major change in a personal relationship. "This can mean either kissing adios to one particular affair, or deepening a bond by waltzing down the aisle to a Mexican brass band." In September 2002, one of the dedicatees of this book, a Sagittarius, was married in Mexico.

It's true that he married another of the dedicatees, an Aries, and that Spencer was vaguer about her prospects. He did say that Jupiter's position after August was "as good as astrological omens get," and he did promise her "the enrichment of your heart's deepest desires." Nothing about Mexico, though, which surely should have been somewhere on the chart. The coincidence is elegant, but that is what it is: a coincidence. We can almost see it happening. Spencer writes "kissing adios" as a variant on the triter "kissing goodbye," and the Mexican brass band marches in on the heels of an idiom. There was, as it happens, no waltz or aisle or band at Chris and Gaby's wedding, only a mariachi trio singing lamentable songs about lost and doomed love. Not ideal auguries, but a repertoire is a repertoire. So all we have is a figure of speech and a country—and the strange feeling that we almost had more, that we had glimpsed the invisible line from the teeth to the stars. After all, Spencer didn't talk about Mexico for any of the other signs, and he could have missed Sagittarius as well as Aries.

If you want to throw a tantrum, Michael Lutin broadly says in one of his 2001 columns, "you can always blame it on astrology." But we don't. We know the fault is not in the stars, we simply entertain ourselves by pretending for a moment that it is. But entertainment tells us things, as well as keeps us amused, and there is a place, I think, where Adorno's gloomy diagnosis and our own ironic lightness of being can be seen to meet. We are often as helpless as Adorno says we are; it does sometimes seem as if the global market and the machinery of government are as inaccessible to us as the motions of the stars. It's not that the horoscope, for all its avuncular advice, can remedy our helplessness, or really tell us what to do—no oracle can do that. But there is a definite thrill in the chance that the words of a stranger will, once in a while, offer an echo or an image of one of our most intimate fears or hopes, as if we had lost it and coincidence had found it. Newspaper horoscopes are far more primitive than the *I Ching*, and far less disinterested than oracles by lots, or the random opening of the pages of Virgil or the Bible. But the principle is the same. The shapeless finds its shape, and somewhere amid the laughter we may be hoping for a glimpse of destiny—not the destiny that binds us but the one that keeps slipping away, the destiny that looks like a terminal loss of control.

Back to Nostradamus

Within days of the attacks of September 11 on New York and Washington, it was widely reported that Nostradamus had predicted them with remarkable precision, including the exact date ("the eleventh day of the ninth month") and a mention of "two metal birds," no doubt a quaint sixteenth-century locution for airplanes. This prophecy, to no one's surprise, turned out to have been made after the event, and so did another one, naming "the city of York," but they were associated with a more interesting bit of fakery. Did Nostradamus write this, or its equivalent in French?

> In the City of God there will be a great thunder,
> Two brothers torn apart by Chaos.
> While the fortress endures,
> the great leader will succumb.

There is a good deal of material much like this in Nostradamus's *Centuries*, first edition 1555, but these particular lines were written by a Canadian student, Neil Marshall, in a 1997 paper illustrating how easily figurative terms can be got to match any number of actual stormy events. The lines were then picked up by an eager interpreter, taken for the real thing, and applied to September 11. A nice reversal, proving that even a fake can be got to tell the truth if the need is great enough. Neil Marshall may have thought he was inventing an example, but what if he was prophesying without knowing it? "Besides," as Borges says in one of his deepest, slyest asides, "who can boast of being a mere imposter?"

Closer inspection reveals that nothing except the word *two* brings the quoted lines anywhere near September 11. But what if someone had predicted the events, accidentally or not, at any time prior to their happening? What if Nostradamus had foreseen them, or we were to find, right now, lines in his work that seemed unmistakably to give us a clue? Like:

> Conjoined here, the open sky hastens,
> Taken, left, mortality not sure,
> Little rain, entry, the sky dries up the earth,
> In fact, death, taken, arrived in evil hour.

Or:

> Portentous deed, horrible and unbelievable,
> The Bold One will rouse the wicked,
> Who afterwards will be supported by the rope,
> And most of them exiled among the fields.

Or:

> The year one thousand ninety-nine seven months,
> A great King of Terror will come from the sky:
> To revive the great King of the Mongols,
> To reign by good fortune before, after March.

Or:

> At forty-five degrees the sky will burn,
> Fire approach the great new city:
> An instant great scattered flame will spring up,
> When one will desire to test the Normans.

The last two quatrains were discussed after the September events, with much talk of who the Normans were and what forty-five degrees meant, less talk of why the third prophecy was two years out.

The question we are asking is slightly different from the one we might raise about the man I mentioned earlier, who dreamed of the September 11 attacks well before the event. In his case we may wonder about the source of his dream, but in practical terms we want to know whether he told anyone about it, and whether anyone could have acted on this information—and whether we are still in the habit of treating dreams as information. If it isn't about the very possibility of prediction, the question is about prevention. But if Nostradamus, or anyone, had foretold the attacks in a readily available text, we would be wondering, I think, about what such foreknowledge could mean rather than what anyone could have done with it. I take it the resource planners at the FBI didn't rush back to their old copies of the *Centuries*, even if thousands of other people did.

But then why fake the prophecy? Just what kind of consolation is to be found in the idea of the foreknown, if we take prevention out of the argument? It would seem that in this case we don't want to know the future but want someone, anyone, to have known our immediate past—we want what used to be the future to have been scripted, however unheeded the script might be. Is this strange? Many sociologists and historians would say not. In moments of deep fright and anxiety—and in many other moments as well—we long for a realm of order, even a horrible order, which will save us not from immediate or local chaos but from the thought of bottomless chaos, chaos without end. To paraphrase Nietzsche and summarize virtually every horror movie, we would rather have a world of purposeful disasters than a world without purpose. This logic is familiar, and must work for some of us much of the time. Why else would the plot of *The Exorcist* seem so persuasive to so many viewers, all attracted, even if only hypothetically, to the notion that a screaming, swearing girl must be possessed by the devil rather than just chaotically growing up? It seems a reckless exchange, though. We are freed of our failure to understand the world by seeing it as structured by evil—we prefer the devil's order to our own disarray. This is fiction and hyperbole, of course, but the pattern of thought remains. I have to say I find the premise of a malign order much more frightening than any disorder I can imagine.

But what if the order is not malign, what if we don't go so far? We are afraid of chaos and we want it to end, even if only potentially, even if only in our imaginations. The exchange is still a bad one, if we pursue it all the way. If Nostradamus had foretold the events of September 11, many of us would not feel consoled, we would feel trapped, strangled by a clutching, age-old hand. There is a certain comfort in fatalism, of course, in the feeling that things could not be otherwise, and sometimes it helps us bear what is unchangeable in our lives. But the comfort comes at a price. If things can't be otherwise, we don't need to understand them, only to suffer them, and historical and contextual explanations of any event become just so many forms of fantasy, ways of passing the irremediable time. The old oracles were wiser than this.

There are several less superstitious versions of the Nostradamus fantasy, and two of them were particularly common in the wake of September 11. One was the claim that nothing like this had ever happened before; the other the claim that plenty of things like this had happened before. Both claims were true in a trivial and obvious sense, untrue in all other ways. The first was effectively a denial of all comparison and comprehension, the second a refusal of the specificity of the event, and in particular of the local and immediate pain and sorrow. And both moves, like the Nostradamus effect, clouded the thought of the hard irregularities of so many ongoing lives.

When Croesus, king of Lydia, was defeated and captured by Cyrus, he managed to have an argument with the god about how he had been treated. The whole story is beautifully told in Herodotus. Croesus, you will remember, had tested a number of oracles by asking them what he was doing on a certain day. Very happy with Delphi's answer, he had showered the temple with inordinately expensive gifts, still shown to tourists in Herodotus' day. Croesus had been told that a great empire would be destroyed if he attacked the Persians; also that he would reign until a mule became king of Persia. After a disastrous campaign, Croesus becomes the prisoner of Cyrus the mule (half-Mede, half-Persian) and as Cyrus' men are busy sacking Sardis, asks his captor what these soldiers are doing. "Plundering and sacking your city and your possessions," Cyrus says with some satisfaction. "It is no city of mine," Croesus says. "What they are sacking and pillaging is yours." Cyrus halts the rampage, and is so delighted with Croesus' advice that he asks him if he can do anything for him—apart from releasing him, of course. Croesus says he would like his chains to be sent to Delphi with the query of whether Greek gods are in the habit of being so ungrateful. Cyrus agrees, and Croesus receives the following reply:

> not even the gods can escape fate;
> the god, in gratitude for the many gifts, had already extended Croe-
>   sus' life and reign three years beyond the term indicated by a
>   previous prophecy;
> Croesus should have asked which empire the oracle had in mind;
> Croesus should have seen that Cyrus was the mule.

We may think the oracle is finessing the points about the empire and the mule, and that if Croesus had asked for details he would only have got another equivocal response. But fate here is plainly a last resort, not a leveling explanation. Fate is what finally happens, what's beyond fixing and beyond discussion. In the meantime, gods and humans can argue and neither of them appeal to predestination, miracle, or historical inevitability—indeed the whole exchange between Croesus and Delphi rests on the assumption that deals can be made, even if this one went badly. Croesus accepts the god's view, no doubt in part because he knows he was wrong about the great empire. Not wrong in not asking further, but wrong, like Macbeth, in taking the oracle to mean just what he wanted it to mean, in asking a question to which he wanted only one answer. We may feel—I do feel—that both men have been swindled by the higher authorities, but they themselves know how deeply their desire got entangled in their acts of interpretation.

Prophecy and terrorism

It's axiomatic in modern liberal societies that a person is innocent until proven guilty. It's also axiomatic, although less frequently asserted, that you can't be a criminal until you have committed a crime, that bad intentions are not enough. This second proposition is certainly contrary to the doctrine of Jesus Christ, who taught that a man who had committed adultery in his heart was as guilty as the man who had done the deed, but applied socially it saves us from the thought police of Orwell's *1984*. Luis Buñuel has a wonderfully dark and funny film about a would-be serial killer who confesses to all the crimes he planned but didn't manage to commit—a woman fell down an elevator shaft before he could strangle her, another committed suicide before he arrived, another died in an accident, and so on. The police inspector listens to the whole story and sends the man home. This film, *The Criminal Life of Archibaldo de la Cruz*, is about helplessness and failure as well as the elusive nature of guilt, about the necessary and sometimes unwanted innocence of the imagination.

But what if Christ was right, even as a political and legal theorist, rather than Orwell? How innocent could a violent imagination be, and how close to completion could a criminal act get and still fall short of a crime? What degrees of planning are criminal, and what are the legitimate forms of crime prevention? Another question for the oracle—and literally so in Steven Spielberg's film *Minority Report*.

The year is 2054, and the Precrime program is up for a vote in Congress. Murder used to be epidemic in Washington but now almost doesn't happen. The program is a triumph, but still there are questions, and an investigation by the Attorney General's office is in progress. How does the program work? By means of precognition. Three gifted seers, two men and a woman called Dot, Dash, and Agatha, and known collectively as the oracle, are immersed in a tank of fluid, wired to an elaborate computer network. As soon as they foresee a crime, a SWAT team is dispatched and the prekiller is arrested. The offender is then frozen and filed away like a human CD in a vast storage system. Where's the problem?

Our hero, Tom Cruise, an ace member of a Precrime police team, doesn't see any problem until his name comes up as that of a killer-to-be. He does distinguish between an intention and a deed but is convinced that the oracle foretells only completed future actions. Things get a little theological around here, but the suggestion is that the oracle really does see the future, which police action revokes or averts, as distinct from seeing a future that may or may not arrive. The oracle doesn't appear to foresee the intervention of the police at all, only what will happen if they don't get there. But can our hero really be a killer? Can the three precogs, as they are also called, be wrong? As Tom Cruise dives deeper into the system and its workings, more and more intricate details emerge. One of the precogs, Agatha, is "more gifted" than the other two. Does this mean she sees more, or sees differently? Apparently the three precogs don't always predict the same future, and then a minority report—hence the title of the film and the Philip K. Dick story it is based on—is electronically filed, although a majority opinion is enough to trigger police action. I won't further summarize the plot, which involves Cruise in all kinds of violent mayhem, to an extent that makes most Bond movies look like exercises in documentary realism, and in a gruesome eye operation he needs in order to disguise his identity from his ex-colleagues and the system that is now hunting him. There is also a long and complicated conspiracy against truth and justice that takes ages to unwind, and that stars Max von Sydow, entirely comfortable in a role of genial malevolence. The real question is precognition, and what freedom it leaves the human agent.

There is a terrific moment in which Cruise arrives at a foretold location, and does in fact commit the killing. But the reasons that got him there, and the person he kills, are not what they seem, and it's clear from his hesitation at the crucial moment that he could have done otherwise. It's not that he can't choose, it's that one of his choices has been foreseen, and that's the one he settles on. It does look as though, like Adam and Eve in paradise, he could assert his freedom only by departing from the preferred script, but even that wouldn't be freedom if he had only the one effective option. In fact, as in a story by Borges, or more pertinently, as in many stories by Philip K. Dick, two roads merge into a single track, and we have to believe that Cruise kills the man both because he decides to and because the killing was correctly predicted. His decision too was part of the precognition; the act is both free and foreknown.

But where does that leave us with Precrime? The movie takes an impeccably liberal tack on the politics of this subject, and of course the cards are stacked by the fact that prekillers are not tried or sentenced, just filed away. If people are innocent until proven guilty, they should certainly have done something before they are dropped in the deep freeze. And no doubt the idea of prosecuting a crime that didn't quite happen was just too dizzying for an already dizzying story. But all the larger speculative questions depend on just what it is that precognition recognizes.

Let's take the case that has occurred in various forms in the past year. You see a person behaving suspiciously, or you're just a suspicious person yourself. You have no evidence except your own sense of the suspect's shiftiness, and the fact that he or she looks to you like an Arab or a terrorist or both. You call the cops, and the man or woman is arrested. The suspect turns out to be completely harmless, your suspicions were merely a sign of your own panic or excessive civic zeal. But what if you had been right? Without evidence, without any basis except your panic, you identified a terrorist carrying a bomb and saved the lives of hundreds of people. It's true that evidence would have been found on the suspect, but it wouldn't have been looked for if you hadn't sounded the alarm. Now you're a hero, and not a crank or a racist.

This is the question raised by the oracle in *Minority Report*, and the film runs through a whole spectrum of answers. The politics are different at either end and in the middle. At one end there is a single time line, and the precogs can see all the way down it: they know a crime will occur and it does. Logically, this possibility would preclude all intervention, and in his story Dick scrupulously spells this reservation out. "If only one time-path existed, precognitive information would be of no importance, since no possibility would exist, in possessing this information, of altering the future." But as a matter of speculative fantasy, we can picture a perfect foreknowledge of what people will do unless they are stopped. If such knowledge existed, and were absolutely certain, its usefulness in crime prevention would indeed be considerable, and counterarguments about civil liberties—the killer hasn't killed anyone yet, although we know he will—begin to look a little frail and abstract. We don't want our man to be deep-sixed, but we are not going to complain about his being arrested.

At the other end of the spectrum there is a picture of several forking paths, and what the precogs are seeing are only possibilities. They are genuine possibilities, not random guesses. All of them could become actual, but only one of them will. Now the civil liberties argument looks indestructible, founded on one of those deeply self-evident truths that Pauline Kael used to berate

Hollywood for trading in. It's wrong to lynch an innocent man, very bad to persecute a guy for being a Communist when he has never been one. How about lynching itself, Kael would ask. All right as long as the man is guilty? Persecution of actual Communists is fine? Certainly we should not arrest a person because crime is among his or her many options, and this is effectively the proposition the film ends up making.

But the middle range is the dangerous territory. Suppose the oracle is not infallible but is very rarely wrong. The time line is not invariably single, but mostly it is, and the precogs see it clearly. We might, just, arrest the wrong person by following their indications, but not often, and a familiar, horrible calculus becomes possible: How many wrong arrests would we put up with to save how many lives? We could, and in my view we should, refuse the whole calculus and insist on the principles and practices of human rights, but in places where terrorism has long been or is becoming a norm, people will want to say that almost any injustice is acceptable if it saves lives. But wouldn't it depend on how systematic the injustice was? And how random the threat?

This argument can and will continue without us—or with us, but in another setting—and I want only to suggest that this oracle, like so many others, has brought us face-to-face, in the most intimate way, not with certainty and not even with our longing for it, but with the appalling attractions and alluring dangers of certainty, its complicated absence and presence in our lives. All things are full of gods, even if the gods keep changing their disguises. The gods appear whenever we think we know more than a human creature ordinarily could, and they disappear again when we turn to ask them what to do.

Off the road

I'm not sure they are the same figures, but I can see them clearly now. They are sitting in a comfortable-looking study, in deep armchairs, firelight glinting on the man's whiskey glass and on a bottle of Evian on the low table. A large sleeping dog gives an excellent impersonation of a rug. The man is in his late sixties, the woman is around thirty. I understand everything they are saying, but only through the same dream-effect: I still have no sense of individual words or national language or particular idiom.

"So we are suggesting," she says, "that we can free ourselves from the idea of destiny by understanding it, by inspecting its machinery, laying out the logic. That destiny is just a story, that oracles are narratives."

"No such luck," he says. "Although it is true that oracles become narratives as soon as we report on the consultation."

"Ah yes," she says, "and when are we going to do that?"

"Later," he says, "when we're less muddled. When we have to. It's also true that all narratives have something of the oracle about them."

"Are you sure?"

"Half-sure. But not all narratives advertise their oracle-moments. Not all narratives are actually about oracles. And destiny is not just a story."

"So what is it?"

"It's destiny. It's what happened to us and couldn't have happened otherwise. It's the way things are. It's all the customs, compulsions, and forces that

really won't let us go. But it isn't destiny until it's over, and there's a big dif-
ference between accepting what's happened and accepting what is going to hap-
pen. It's the difference between historical common sense and fatalism. That's
what we're going to tell them."

"It's what you're going to tell them. I have another idea." The woman takes
a sip of her water, puts the bottle back on the table. "I'm going to say that
understanding the logic of oracles won't liberate us from anything, but that it
doesn't matter."

"Steady on."

"It doesn't matter because we're not imprisoned by the logic of oracles or the
machinery of destiny, we are imprisoned by our fears and hopes. They build the
logic and if we dismantle it they'll build another logic. The logic isn't the point."

"No, but just think. One person, one version of Oedipus or Kafka's K,
realizes that the logic of oracles works only with the consultants' collusion, that
destinies won't become destinies unless you help them along. It needs only one
person to see this and alter his or her life for the whole argument to be worth
making."

"Give me a break. One person gets out, so we shouldn't worry that every-
one else stays in prison? But I wasn't saying that understanding the logic of or-
acles doesn't matter—I was saying that it doesn't matter that we can't free
ourselves that way. Freedom is not the issue."

"You're not going to say understanding is enough in its own right? That's
my line. I was just trying to answer what I thought was your call for practi-
cal results."

There is a silence. The logs in the fire fall in on each other, the man empties his whiskey glass and stares at it, amused but also slightly puzzled. The woman says, "Freedom is not the issue, and understanding is not enough. Nothing is enough. Fears and hopes can't be satisfied and can't be tamed, that's what they are, insatiable."

"You just have to live with them."

"You have to live with yourself. You have to get your fears and hopes to talk, and it's easier to live with yourself if you do that. That's where the oracle helps. It gets your fears and hopes talking. It's not enough, but it's better than silence."

"This is beginning to sound like a conflict of generations. I've always believed fears come true just because we talk about them."

"Yes, and my generation believes that hopes fail for the same reason. We all have our superstitions. But it isn't a question of getting rid of hopes and fears, only of getting along with them. Talking is always dangerous—just not as dangerous as not talking."

The fire flickers, the man throws on another log. Both figures sigh, smile. Their faces say that this particular piece of talking wasn't so dangerous after all, and that it's good to be off the road. Even though the road always begins again tomorrow. The man says, "So what are we going to tell them?"

The woman says, "We'll think of something."

BIBLIOGRAPHY

Achebe, Chinua. *Arrow of God*. New York: Anchor Books, 1989.

———. *Things Fall Apart*. New York: Anchor Books, 1994.

Adelman, Janet. *Suffocating Mothers*. New York and London: Routledge, 1992.

Adorno, Theodor W. *Minima Moralia: Reflections from Damaged Life*. Translated by E.F.N. Jephcott. London: Verso, 1978.

———. *The Stars Down to Earth and Other Essays on the Irrational in Culture*. London and New York: Routledge, 1994.

Aeschylus. *The Oresteia*. Translated by Richmond Lattimore. Chicago: University of Chicago Press, 1960.

———. *Seven Against Thebes*. Translated by David Grene. New York: Washington Square Press, 1968.

———. *The Oresteia*. Translated by Hugh Lloyd-Jones. London: Duckworth, 1993.

———. *The Oresteia*. Translated by Ted Hughes. New York: Farrar, Straus and Giroux, 1999.

Ahl, Friedrich. *Sophocles' Oedipus: Evidence and Self-Conviction*. Ithaca, N.Y.: Cornell University Press, 1991.

Alter, Robert, trans. *The David Story*. With a commentary by the translator. New York and London: W. W. Norton, 1999.

Amandry, Pierre. *La mantique apollinienne*. New York: Arno Press, 1975.

Apollodorus. *The Library*. Translated by J. G. Frazer. Cambridge, Mass.: Loeb Classical Library, 1995.

Atwood, Margaret. *Lady Oracle*. London: Virago, 1982.

Auster, Paul. *The Invention of Solitude*. New York: Penguin, 1988.

———. *The Music of Chance*. New York: Penguin, 1991.

Austin, J. L. *Sense and Sensibilia*. New York: Oxford University Press, 1964.

———. *How to Do Things with Words*. New York: Oxford University Press, 1965.

Barthes, Roland. *Le plaisir du texte*. Paris: Seuil, 1973.

———. *Roland Barthes par Roland Barthes*. Paris: Seuil, 1975.

———. *Leçon*. Paris: Seuil, 1978.

Baynes, Cary F., trans. *The I Ching or Book of Changes*. Richard Wilhelm version. Princeton: Princeton University Press, 1967.

Benjamin, Walter. *Illuminations*. Translated by Harry Zohn. New York: Schocken Books, 1969.

———. *Benjamin über Kafka*. Frankfurt: Suhrkamp, 1992.

Blackburn, Simon. *Think*. Oxford: Oxford University Press, 1999.

Blanchot, Maurice. *De Kafka à Kafka*. Paris: Gallimard, 1981.

Borges, Jorge Luis. *Ficciones*. Translated by Anthony Kerrigan and others. New York: Grove Press, 1962.

Bouché-Leclerq, Auguste. *Histoire de la divination dans l'antiquité*. Paris: Leroux, 1879–1882.

Brooke-Rose, Christine. *Amalgamemnon*. London: Carcanet, 1984.

Brown, Norman O. *Hermes the Thief*. New York: Vintage, 1969.

Browne, Thomas. *Religio Medici and Other Works*. Oxford: Clarendon Press, 1964.

Buñuel, Luis. *The Criminal Life of Archibaldo de la Cruz*. Mexico City: Alianza Cinematográfica, 1955.

———. *The Phantom of Liberty*. Paris: Greenwich Film Production, 1974.

Burkert, Walter. *Oedipus, Oracles, and Meaning*. Toronto: University College Press, 1991.

Calasso, Roberto. *The Marriage of Cadmus and Harmony*. Translated by Tim Parks. New York: Vintage, 1994.

———. *Literature and the Gods*. Translated by Tim Parks. New York: Knopf, 2001.

Calvino, Italo. *Invisible Cities*. Translated by William Weaver. New York and London: Harcourt Brace Jovanovich, 1978.

———. *Italian Folk Tales*. Translated by George Martin. San Diego, New York, London: Harcourt, 1980.

Camesasca, E. *The Complete Paintings of Michelangelo*. New York: H. N. Abrams, 1969.

Cavafy, C. P. *The Essential Cavafy*. Translated by Edmund Keeley and Philip Sherrard. Hopewell, N.J.: Ecco Press, 1995.

Certeau, Michel de. *The Possession at Loudun*. Translated by Michael B. Smith. Chicago and London: University of Chicago Press, 2000.

Cicero. *De Divinatione*. Translated by W. A. Falconer. Cambridge, Mass.: Loeb Classical Library, 1996.

Clark, Stuart. *Thinking with Demons*. New York: Oxford University Press, 1997.

Clubb, Dare. *Oedipus*. Unpublished typescript of play first performed in New York, 1998.

Cocteau, Jean. *La machine infernale*. Paris: Grasset, 1934.

Conan Doyle, Arthur. *Sherlock Holmes: The Complete Novels and Stories*. New York: Bantam, 1986.

Corneille, Pierre. *Théâtre*. Paris: Flammarion, 1898.

Crahay, Roland. *La littérature oraculaire chez Hérodote*. Paris: Les Belles Lettres, 1956.

Danson, Lawrence. *Tragic Alphabet*. New Haven, Conn.: Yale University Press, 1974.

Davreux, Juliette. *La Légende de la prophétesse Cassandre*. Paris: Droz, 1942.

Dayan, Joan. *Haiti, History, and the Gods*. Berkeley, Los Angeles, London: University of California Press, 1998.

Decker, Ronald, Thierry Depaulis, and Michael Dummett. *A Wicked Pack of Cards*. London: St. Martin's Press, 1996.

Delcourt, Marie. *Oedipe, ou la légende du conquérant*. Paris: Les Belles Lettres, 1981.

Deleuze, Gilles, and Félix Guattari. *L'Anti-Oedipe*. Paris: Editions de Minuit, 1972.

Derrida, Jacques. *La carte postale*. Paris: Flammarion, 1980.

———. *D'un ton apocalyptique adopté naguère en philosophie*. Paris: Galilée, 1983.

Detienne, Marcel, and Jean-Pierre Vernant. *Cunning Intelligence*. Translated by Janet Lloyd. Chicago and London: University of Chicago Press, 1991.

Dick, Philip K. *The Man in the High Castle*. New York: Vintage, 1992.

———. *The Minority Report and Other Classic Stories*. New York: Citadel Press, 2002.

———. *Time Out of Joint*. New York: Vintage, 2002.

Dodds, E. R. *The Greeks and the Irrational*. University of California Press, 1974.

Drummond de Andrade, Carlos. *Travelling in the Family*. Translated by Thomas Colchie, Mark Strand, and others. Hopewell, N.J.: Ecco Press, 1986.

Dryden, John. *Dramatic Works*. New York: Gordian Press, 1968.

Dummett, Michael. *Truth and Other Enigmas*. Cambridge, Mass.: Harvard University Press, 1978.

Edgar, David. *The Prisoner's Dilemma*. London: Nick Hern Books, 2001.

Empson, William. *Seven Types of Ambiguity*. New York: New Directions, 1966.

———. *Some Versions of Pastoral*. New York: New Directions, 1974.

Euripides. *Tragedies*. Edited by David Grene and Richmond Lattimore. 3 vols. New York: Modern Library, n.d.

Eusebius of Caesarea. *La Préparation évangélique*. Translated by Odile Zink. Paris: Les Editions du Cerf, 1979.

Evans-Pritchard, E. E. *Nuer Religion*. Oxford: Clarendon Press, 1970.

———. *Witchcraft, Oracles, and Magic Among the Azande*. Oxford: Clarendon Press, 1976.

Felman, Shoshana. *Le Scandale du corps parlant*. Paris: Seuil, 1980.

Fishbane, Michael. *Biblical Interpretation in Ancient Israel*. Oxford: Clarendon Press, 1988.

Flacelière, Robert. *Devins et oracles grecs*. Paris: Presses Universitaires de France, 1961.

Fontenelle, Bernard de. *Histoire des Oracles*. Verviers, Belgium: Editions Gérard, 1973.

Fontenrose, Joseph. *Python*. Berkeley, Calif.: University of California Press, 1959.

———. *The Delphic Oracle*. Berkeley, Calif.: University of California Press, 1978.

———. *Didyma*. Berkeley, Calif.: University of California Press, 1988.

Freud, Sigmund. *The Interpretation of Dreams.* Translated by James Strachey. London: Penguin, 1976.

Gawande, Atul. *Complications: A Surgeon's Notes on an Imperfect Science.* New York: Henry Holt, 2002.

Gibson, William. *Mona Lisa Overdrive.* New York: Bantam Spectra, 1989.

Ginzburg, Carlo. *Ecstasies.* Translated by Raymond Rosenthal. London: Hutchinson, 1990.

————. *The Judge and the Historian.* Translated by Anthony Shugaar. London. Verso, 1999.

Golding, William. *The Double Tongue.* London: Faber and Faber, 1995.

Goldscheider, Ludwig. *Michelangelo: Paintings, Sculpture, Architecture.* London: Phaidon, 1996.

Gould, John. *Herodotus.* London: Weidenfeld and Nicolson, 1989.

Graf, Fritz. *Magic in the Ancient World.* Translated by Franklin Philip. Cambridge, Mass.: Harvard University Press, 1997.

Grafton, Anthony. *Cardano's Cosmos: The Worlds and Works of a Renaissance Astrologer.* Cambridge, Mass., and London: Harvard University Press, 1999.

Graves, Robert. *The Greek Myths.* Harmondsworth, England: Penguin, 1960.

Green, André. *Un Oeil en trop.* Paris: Editions de Minuit, 1969.

Harrison, Jane. *Prolegomena to the Study of Greek Religion.* New York: Meridian Books, 1957.

Hartog, François. *Le miroir d'Hérodote.* Paris: Gallimard, 1980.

Herodotus. *The Histories.* Translated by Aubrey de Sélincourt. London: Penguin, 1972.

————. *The History.* Translated by David Grene. Chicago and London: University of Chicago Press, 1987.

————. *The Persian Wars.* Translated by A. R. Godley. Cambridge, Mass.: Loeb Classical Library, 1997.

Hesiod. *Works and Days, Theogony, and Other Texts.* Translated by Hugh G. Evelyn-White. Cambridge, Mass.: Loeb Classical Library, 2000.

Hofmann, Michael, and James Lasdun, eds. *After Ovid: New Metamorphoses.* New York: Farrar, Straus and Giroux, 1996.

Homeric Hymns. Translated by Hugh G. Evelyn-White. Cambridge, Mass.: Loeb Classical Library, 2000.

Hopkins, Gerard Manley. *Poems.* London, Oxford, New York: Oxford University Press, 1970.

Hopkins, Keith. *A World Full of Gods: Pagans, Jews and Christians in the Roman Empire.* London: Phoenix, 2000.

Hornblower, Simon, and Antony Spawforth, eds. *The Oxford Companion to Classical Civilization.* Oxford and New York: Oxford University Press, 1998.

Hosley, Richard. *Shakespeare's Holinshed*. New York: Putnam, 1968.

How, W. W., and J. Wells. *A Commentary on Herodotus*. Oxford: Oxford University Press, 1989.

Hume, David. *The Natural History of Religion*. Stanford, Calif.: Stanford University Press, 1971.

Huxley, Aldous. *The Devils of Loudun*. London: Chatto and Windus, 1971.

Irwin, William, ed. *The Matrix and Philosophy*. Chicago and La Salle, Ill.: Open Court, 2002.

Jaeger, Werner. *Paideia*. New York: Oxford University Press, 1945.

John, Nicholas, ed. *Opera Guide to Oedipus Rex/The Rake's Progress*. London: John Calder/Riverrun Press, 1991.

Kael, Pauline. *I Lost It at the Movies*. Boston: Little, Brown, 1965.

Kafka, Franz. *The Castle*. Translated by Willa and Edwin Muir. New York: Schocken Books, 1982.

———. *The Trial*. Translated by Willa and Edwin Muir. New York: Schocken Books, 1984.

Knox, Bernard. *Oedipus at Thebes*. New Haven, Conn.: Yale University Press, 1957.

Kurosawa, Akira. *Throne of Blood*. Tokyo: Toho Films, 1957.

———. *Seven Samurai and Other Screenplays*. London: Faber and Faber, 1992.

Leoni, Edgar. *Nostradamus and His Prophecies*. New York: Exposition Press, 1961.

Levi, Primo. *The Periodic Table*. Translated by Raymond Rosenthal. New York: Knopf, 1996.

Lévi-Strauss, Claude. *Anthropologie structurale*. Paris: Plon, 1958.

———. *Le Totémisme aujourd'hui*. Paris: Presses Universitaires de France, 1962.

Lewalski, Barbara. *Milton's Brief Epic*. Providence: Brown University Press, 1966.

Lipsey, Roger. *Have You Been to Delphi?* Albany, N.Y.: State University of New York Press, 2001.

Loewe, Michael, and Carmen Blacker, eds. *Oracles and Divination*. Boulder, Colo.: Shambhala Publications, 1981.

Lucan. *Pharsalia*. Translated by Jane Wilson Joyce. Ithaca, N.Y.: Cornell University Press, 1993.

Lycophron. *Alexandra*. Translated by G. W. Mooney. London: G. Bell, 1921.

Machiavelli, Niccolò. *The Discourses*. Translated by Leslie J. Walker. Harmondsworth, England: Penguin, 1970.

Mann, Thomas. *The Magic Mountain*. Translated by John E. Woods. New York: Vintage, 1996.

Marchal, Roger. *Fontenelle à l'aube des Lumières*. Paris: Honoré Champion, 1997.

Marcus, George E. *Ethnography through Thick and Thin*. Princeton, N.J.: Princeton University Press, 1998.

Mauss, Marcel. *Sociologie et anthropologie*. Paris: Quadrige/Presses Universitaires de France, 1997.

Milton, John. *Poetical Works*. Oxford: Oxford University Press, 1979.

Minois, Georges. *Histoire de l'avenir*. Paris: Fayard, 1996.

Montaigne, Michel de. *Essais*. Paris: Gallimard, 1962.

Morgan, Catherine. *Athletes and Oracles*. Cambridge: Cambridge University Press, 1990.

Morson, Gary Saul. *Narrative and Freedom: The Shadows of Time*. New Haven and London: Yale University Press, 1994.

Muir, Kenneth. *The Sources of Shakespeare's Plays*. London: Methuen, 1957.

Nebesky-Wojkokwitz, René de. *Oracles and Demons of Tibet*. The Hague: Mouton, 1956.

Nehamas, Alexander. *The Art of Living: Socratic Reflections from Plato to Foucault*. Berkeley, Los Angeles, London: University of California Press, 1998.

Niderst, Alain. *Fontenelle*. Paris: Plon, 1991.

Nietzsche, Friedrich. *The Birth of Tragedy* and *The Genealogy of Morals*. Translated by Francis Golffing. Garden City, N.Y.: Doubleday, 1956.

————. *The Portable Nietzsche*. Edited and translated by Walter Kaufman. New York: Penguin, 1976.

Oracula Sibyllina. Translated into German by Alfons Kurfess. Nördlingen: Beck, 1951.

Ovid. *Metamorphoses*. Translated by Rolfe Humphries. Bloomington and London: Indiana University Press, 1967.

Padel, Ruth. *In and Out of the Mind: Greek Images of the Tragic Self*. Princeton, N.J.: Princeton University Press, 1992.

Parke, H. W. *Greek Oracles*. London: Hutchinson, 1967.

————. *The Oracles of Zeus*. Oxford: Blackwell, 1967.

————. *The Oracles of Apollo in Asia Minor*. London: Croom Helm, 1985.

————. *Sibyls and Sibylline Prophecy in Classical Antiquity*. London and New York: Routledge, 1992.

Parke, H. W., and D.E.W. Wormell. *The Delphic Oracle*. Oxford: Blackwell, 1956.

Pasolini, Pier Paolo. *Oedipus Rex*. Rome: Arco Film, 1967.

————. *Oedipus Rex*. Translated by John Matthews. London: Lorrimer Books, 1971.

Patrides, C. A. *Premises and Motifs in Renaissance Thought and Literature*. Princeton, N.J.: Princeton University Press, 1982.

Patterson, Annabel. *Reading Holinshed's Chronicles*. Chicago and London: University of Chicago Press, 1994.

Pausanius. *Description of Greece*. Translated with a commentary by J. G. Frazer. London: Macmillan, 1913.

————. *Guide to Greece*. Translated by Peter Levi. London: Penguin, 1979.

Petronius Arbiter. *Satyricon*. Translated by J. P. Sullivan. Harmondsworth, England: Penguin, 1986.

Pindar. *Odes*. Translated by Richmond Lattimore. Chicago and London: University of Chicago Press, 1978.

Places, Edouard des, ed. *Les Oracles Chaldaïques, avec un choix de commentaires anciens*. Paris: Les Belles Lettres, 1971.

Plato. *The Last Days of Socrates*. Translated by Hugh Tredennick. Harmondsworth, England: Penguin, 1969.

Plutarch. *Moralia*. Vol. V. Translated by Frank Cole Babbitt. Cambridge, Mass.: Loeb Classical Library, 1999.

Potter, David. *Prophets and Emperors*. Cambridge, Mass.: Harvard University Press, 1994.

Proust, Marcel. *In the Shadow of Young Girls in Flower*. Translated by James Grieve. London: Penguin, 2002.

Pucci, Pietro. *Oedipus and the Fabrication of the Father*. Baltimore and London: Johns Hopkins University Press, 1992.

Roberts, Henry C. *The Complete Prophecies of Nostradamus*. New York: Crown Publishers, 1994.

Romm, James. *Herodotus*. New Haven and London: Yale University Press, 1998.

Roper, Lyndal. *Oedipus and the Devil*. London and New York: Routledge, 1994.

Rosen, David, and Andrew Porter, eds. *Verdi's Macbeth*. New York: W. W. Norton, 1984.

Ryle, Gilbert. *Dilemmas*. Cambridge: Cambridge University Press, 1954.

Schérer, Jacques. *Dramaturgies d'Oedipe*. Paris: Presses Universitaires de France, 1987.

Schnackenberg, Gjertrud. *The Throne of Labdacus*. New York: Farrar, Straus and Giroux, 2000.

Scholem, Gershom. *Sabbatai Sevi: The Mystical Messiah*. Princeton, N.J.: Princeton University Press, 1973.

Sciascia, Leonardo. *One Way or Another*. Translated by Sacha Rabinovitch. Manchester, England: Carcanet, 1987.

Segal, Charles. *Sophocles' Tragic World*. Cambridge, Mass.: Harvard University Press, 1995.

Seneca. *Oedipus*. Translated by Ted Hughes. London: Faber and Faber, 1969.

————. *Tragedies*. Translated by Frank Justus Miller. Cambridge, Mass.: Loeb Classical Library, 1998.

Seymour, Charles, ed. *Michelangelo: The Sistine Chapel Ceiling*. New York: Norton, 1972.

Shakespeare, William. *The Winter's Tale*. Edited by Frank Kermode. New York: Signet, 1988.

————. *Macbeth*. Edited by A. R. Braunmuller. Cambridge: Cambridge University Press, 1997.

Smetana, Bedrich. *Macbeth*. Prague: Editio Supraphon, 1989.

Snell, Bruno. *The Discovery of Mind*. New York: Harper, 1960.

Solomon, Maynard. *Mozart: A Life*. New York: HarperCollins, 1995.

Sophocles. *The Three Theban Plays*. Translated by Robert Fagles. New York: Penguin, 1984.

————. *Oedipus Tyrannos, Oedipus at Kolonos, Antigone*. Translated by Timberlake Wertenbaker. London: Faber and Faber, 1992.

————. *Ajax, Electra, Oedipus, Tyrannus*. Translated by Hugh Lloyd-Jones. Cambridge, Mass.: Loeb Classical Library, 1994.

Spielberg, Steven. *Minority Report*. Hollywood, Calif.: Twentieth Century Fox and Dreamworks, 2002.

Strauss, Richard. *Macbeth*. Leipzig: Edition Peters, 1932.

Stravinsky, Igor. *Oedipus Rex*. London: Boosey & Hawkes, 1949.

Taylor, Thomas. *Oracles and Mysteries*. Frome, Somerset, England: Prometheus Trust, 1995.

Thaler, R. H. *The Winner's Curse*. Princeton, N.J.: Princeton University Press, 1994.

Thomas, Keith. *Religion and the Decline of Magic*. Oxford: Oxford University Press, 1997.

Thucydides. *The Landmark Thucydides*. Edited by Robert B. Strassler. New York: Free Press, 1996.

Tolstoy, Leo. *War and Peace*. Translated by Ann Dunnigan. New York: Signet, 1968.

Vasari, Giorgio. *The Lives of the Artists*. Translated by George Bull. London: Penguin, 1987.

Verdi, Giuseppe. *Macbeth*. Milan: Ricordi, 1947.

Vernant, Jean-Pierre. *Mythe et société en Grèce ancienne*. Paris: François Maspéro, 1974.

Vernant, Jean-Pierre, and others, eds. *Divination et rationalité*. Paris: Seuil, 1974.

Veyne, Paul. *Comment écrit-on l'histoire?* Paris: Seuil, 1979.

————. *Les grecs ont-ils cru à leurs mythes?* Paris: Seuil, 1983.

Virgil. *The Aeneid*. Translated by Rolfe Humphries. New York: Scribner's, 1951.

————. *The Aeneid*. Translated by W. F. Jackson Knight. London: Penguin, 1958.

————. *The Aeneid*. Translated by Robert Fitzgerald. New York: Vintage, 1990.

Voltaire. *Théâtre*. Paris: Renouard, 1819.

Von Neumann, John, and Oskar Morgenstern. *Theory of Games and Economic Behavior*. Princeton, N.J.: Princeton University Press, 1980.

Wachowski, Andy and Larry. *The Matrix*. Hollywood, Calif.: Warner Brothers, 1999.

Weaver, William. *Lady Luck*. Garden City, N.Y.: Anchor Books, 1963.

Wheelwright, Philip. *Heraclitus*. New York: Atheneum, 1964.

White, Norman. *Hopkins*. Oxford: Clarendon Press, 1992.

Wilkins, John, and Matthew MacLeod. *Sophocles' Antigone and Oedipus the King: A Commentary*. Bristol, England: Bristol Classical Press, 1987.

Wills, Garry. *Witches and Jesuits*. New York: Oxford University Press, 1995.

Wimsatt, W. K. *The Verbal Icon*. Lexington, Ky.: University of Kentucky Press, 1954.

Wind, Edgar. *The Religious Symbolism of Michelangelo*. Oxford: Oxford University Press, 2000.

Wittgenstein, Ludwig. *The Blue and Brown Books*. Oxford: Blackwell, 1958.

————. *Philosophical Investigations*. Oxford: Blackwell, 1967.

————. *On Certainty*. Oxford: Blackwell, 1993.

Wolf, Christa. *Cassandra*. Translated by Jan van Heurck. New York: Farrar, Straus and Giroux, 1984.

Xenophon. *Conversations of Socrates*. Translated by Hugh Tredennick and Robin Waterfield. London: Penguin, 1990.

Zizek, Slavoj. *Welcome to the Desert of the Real*. London and New York: Verso, 2002.

ACKNOWLEDGMENTS

One of the great pleasures of writing this book was the set of intriguing conversations it got me into, full of anecdotes and arguments. Writing isn't usually like this for me; it's lonelier, more private, less considered, and more intimate with panic and lateness. But there was scarcely anyone I spoke to about oracles who didn't have wonderful things to say, and didn't have a reference or an idea or a story for me. I couldn't use all of this material, but I used a lot of it, and even what I didn't use was lurking in my thoughts. So my warm thanks for all old and continuing talk and for help beyond measure go to Paul Auster, Leonard Barkan, Tom and Marie Barker, Julie Barmazel, Elizabeth Benedict, Sandie Bermann, Sara Blair, Mark Buchan, David Carrasco, Stanley Corngold, Larry Danson, Joan Dayan, Jeff Dolven, Dana Dragunoiu, Caryl Emerson, Elaine Fantham, Denis Feeney, Richard Fenn, John Fleming, Hal Foster, Jonathan Freedman, Alex Gelley, John Glusman, Rebecca Goldstein, Stathis Gourgouris, Tony Grafton, Stephen Holmes, Siri Hustvedt, Daniel Kevles, Irving and Marilyn Lavin, Karen Lawrence, Jacques Lezra, Mark Lilla, Peter Matson, Barry McCrea, Patrick Menget, J. Hillis Miller, Alexander Nehamas, Georgia Nugent, Joyce Carol Oates, Aodaoin O'Floinn, Elaine Pagels, Neni Panourgia, Ricardo Piglia, Starry Schor, Joan Scott, Nigel Smith, Maynard Solomon, Henry Staten, Jenny Uglow, Lawrence Wechsler, Edmund White, Gillian White, Suzanne Wofford, Froma Zeitlin.

I salute, in gratitude, the memory of Chris Brooks and Gareth Roberts.

My thanks too to Princeton University for congenial intellectual surroundings and a year's leave; and to the Institute for Advanced Study for a time of books, shelter, and excellent company.

INDEX

A NOTE ABOUT THE AUTHOR

Michael Wood was born in Lincoln, England, and educated at Cambridge University. He was Research Fellow at St. John's College, Cambridge, and has taught at Columbia University in New York and at Exeter University in England. Currently he is Professor of English and Comparative Literature at Princeton. He has written books on Stendhal, García Márquez, Nabokov, Kafka, and on contemporary fiction in Europe and the Americas. He also writes on film and is the author of *America in the Movies* and a recent monograph on Luis Buñuel's *Belle de Jour*. He is a regular contributor to *The New York Review of Books* and *The London Review of Books*. He would like to believe in oracles, but he can't.